# Afghanistan

# WORLD BIBLIOGRAPHICAL SERIES

General Editors:
Robert G. Neville (Executive Editor)
John J. Horton

Robert A. Myers                      Ian Wallace
Hans H. Wellisch          Ralph Lee Woodward, Jr.

**John J. Horton** is Deputy Librarian of the University of Bradford and currently Chairman of its Academic Board of studies in Social Sciences. He has maintained a longstanding interest in the discipline of area studies and its associated bibliographical problems, with special reference to European Studies. In particular he has published in the field of Icelandic and of Yugoslav studies, including the two relevant volumes in the World Bibliographical Series.

**Robert A. Myers** is Associate Professor of Anthropology in the Division of Social Sciences and Director of Study Abroad Programs at Alfred University, Alfred, New York. He has studied post-colonial island nations of the Caribbean and has spent two years in Nigeria on a Fulbright Lectureship. His interests include international public health, historical anthropology and developing societies. In addition to *Amerindians of the Lesser Antilles: a bibliography* (1981), *A Resource Guide to Dominica, 1493-1986* (1987) and numerous articles, he has compiled the World Bibliographical Series volumes on *Dominica* (1987), *Nigeria* (1989) and *Ghana* (1991).

**Ian Wallace** is Professor of German at the University of Bath. A graduate of Oxford in French and German, he also studied in Tubingen, Heidelberg and Lausanne before taking teaching posts at universities in the USA, Scotland and England. He specializes in contemporary German affairs, especially literature and culture, on which he has published numerous articles and books. In 1979 he founded the journal *GDR Monitor*, which he continues to edit under its new title *German Monitor*.

**Hans H. Wellisch** is Professor emeritus at the College of Library and Information Services, University of Maryland. He was President of the American Society of Indexers and was a member of the International Federation for Documentation. He is the author of numerous articles and several books on indexing and abstracting, and has published *The Conversion of Scripts* and *Indexing and Abstracting: an International Bibliography*. He also contributes frequently to *Journal of the American Society for Information Sciences*, *The Indexer*, and other professional journals.

**Ralph Lee Woodward, Jr.** is Chairman of the Department of History at Tulane University, New Orleans, where he has been Professor of History since 1970. He is the author of *Central America, a Nation Divided*, 2nd ed. (1985), as well as several monographs and more than sixty scholarly articles on modern Latin America. He has also compiled volumes on the World Bibliographical Series on *Belize* (1980), *Nicaragua* (1983), and *El Salvador* 1988). Dr. Woodward edited the Central American section of the *Research Guide to Central America and the Caribbean* (1985) and is currently editor of the Central American history section of the *Hand-book of Latin American Studies*.

VOLUME 135

# Afghanistan

Schuyler Jones

*Compiler*

CLIO PRESS
OXFORD, ENGLAND - SANTA BARBARA, CALIFORNIA
DENVER, COLORADO

British Library Cataloguing in Publication Data

Jones, Schuyler, *1930-* .
Afganistan. - (World Bibliographical Series; 135).
1. Afghanistan - Bibliographies
I. Title II. Series

ISBN 1-85109-140-8


Clio Press Ltd.,
55 St. Thomas' Street,
Oxford OX1 1JG, England.

ABC-CLIO,
130 Cremona Drive,
Santa Barbara,
CA 93117, USA.


Designed by Bernard Crossland.
Typeset using software supplied by Head Software International, Oxted, Surrey, England.
Printed and bound in Great Britain by
Billing and Sons Ltd.,

# THE WORLD BIBLIOGRAPHICAL SERIES

This series, which is principally designed for the English speaker, will eventually cover every country (and many of world's principal regions), each in a separate volume comprising annotated entries on works dealing with its history, geography, economy and politics; and with its people, their culture, customs, religion and social organization. Attention will also be paid to current living conditions - housing, education, newspapers, clothing, etc.- that are all too often ignored in standard bibliographies; and to those particular aspects relevent to individual countries. Each volume seeks to achieve, by use of careful selectivity and critical assessment of the literature, an expression of the country and an appreciation of its nature and national aspirations, to guide the reader towards an understanding of its importance. The keynote of the series is to provide, in a uniform format, an interpretation of each country that will express its culture, its place in the world, and the qualities and background that make it unique.  The views expressed in individual volumes, however, are not necessarily those of the publisher.

## VOLUMES IN THE SERIES

*To the People of Afghanistan*

# Contents

# Contents

# Introduction

"Data on Afghanistan remain sparse and open to question".

*Area Handbook for Afghanistan*

Afghanistan lies in South Central Asia, that is, partly in South Asia and partly in Central Asia, both in themselves rather flexible regions, according to which geographer or historian one consults. In this century up until the Soviet invasion of the country in 1979, few Westerners knew much about it. In the late 1950s when I was living in Kabul, an American AID worker wryly related that, knowing he was going out to teach English in Afghanistan, he had enrolled in two university courses in the USA: one on 'The History of the Middle East' and one on 'The History of South Asia'. He told me that the 'first course covered everything from Israel to Iran and then stopped. The second course started with Pakistan and covered everything eastwards to Burma. In neither course was Afghanistan even mentioned'. One hopes that Afghanistan will now find its proper place in Asian studies courses in Western Universities. As events since 1979 have clearly shown, it is a country that we need to know and understand.

Afghanistan's northern border coincides for the most part with the Amu Darya or Oxus River which also serves to mark the southern boundary of the former Soviet Union. To the west lies Iran and to the south and east is Pakistan. Finally, for a short distance among the Pamirs in her remote north-east corner, Afghanistan joins with China's Xinjiang Province. In the 1950s and 1960s it was the fashion for some Afghan writers to refer to their country as 'The Switzerland of Asia'. Afghanistan and Switzerland have two things in common: they are both land-locked and they are both mountainous; there, however, the comparison ends.

Present-day Afghanistan covers an area of some 260,000 square miles. Its boundaries are a product of political events which took place in the 19th century, which were largely as a result of rivalries between the two superpowers of the day: Britain and Russia. It is to these rivalries that we owe the majority of the 19th-century English-language books and articles

# Introduction

about Afghanistan.

As Russia rolled unchecked across Central Asia towards India, Britain became increasingly nervous and uncomfortably aware of her need to know the lie of the land in those regions that still separated her from her ever-expanding Russian neighbour. As Sir Kerr Fraser-Tytler has pointed out, 'there was in Central Asia no natural or man-made boundary on which the frontiers of Imperial Russia could rest'. Britain had a similar problem, with 'the Empire pushing on in its search for a frontier and finding no halting place, no physical or man-made barrier, on which its outposts could be aligned and behind which its nationals could move in freedom and safety'. Thus began what Kipling called The Great Game - a mixture of exploration and espionage that resulted in the mapping of the more remote regions and which, in recent years, has produced some of the more interesting and readable books on Afghanistan. It also, unfortunately, led to the First Afghan War (1838-42), the Second Afghan War (1878-79), the Third Afghan War (1919), and what some observers are now calling the Fourth Afghan War - the Soviet invasion and occupation of the country (1979-79).

It was Afghanistan's misfortune to lie squarely in the path of two ambitious imperial powers (one writer aptly described her position as a 'grain of wheat between two millstones'). It was their misfortune to think that here was just another disorganized collection of tribes which, like so many others before them, could be overrun, subdued, and fitted more or less neatly into the colonial mosaic.

It is strange that the Soviets, usually credited with being rather clever in matters of this kind, had by 1979 learned so little, either from their own people in Afghanistan or from Britain's disastrous experiences in the country in the last century, that they embarked on a costly, futile, and utterly unsuccessful attempt to take over Afghanistan. As a former American Ambassador to Kabul is reported to have remarked in December, 1979 when learning of the Soviet invasion, 'History has shown that it is easier to march into Afghanistan than it is to march out again'.

Afghanistan's geographical position is such that from earliest times migrations, military or otherwise, gravitated in her direction. Arnold Toynbee described the country as 'the Eastern Roundabout' of the ancient world - a reference to the fact that Afghanistan has been the link between western Asia, India, and Central Asia down through the centuries. In general this has had three main consequences: first she has had a lot of unwelcome visitors such as the armies of Alexander the Great, Genghis Khan, Queen Victoria, and the Soviet Union. Secondly, it has provided her with a rich history and remarkable archaeological treasures. Thirdly, it has given her a culturally diverse population of great ethnic and linguistic complexity. One might add that it has also made her view foreign intervention of any kind with some suspicion.

Afghanistan is situated on a tilted plateau rising from the lowlands of the south-west towards the Pamir Knot in the north-east. It may be divided into three regions: the northern plains which merge into the Central Asian steppes across the Amu Darya, the central highlands, and the south-western plateau. The Hindu Kush range crosses the country for 600 miles from north-east to south-west, its highest peaks reaching 21,000 feet in the east, with mountain passes varying in altitude from 12,000 to 15,000 feet. The lower Koh-i-Baba range runs south of and parallel to the central Hindu Kush, while the Koh-i-Hisar runs northward into the northern plains towards Balkh. To the west the Band-i-Turkestan and the Paropamisus form barriers between Herat and Maimena. South-central Afghanistan from the Pakistan border to the frontiers of Iran is marked by a series of parallel ranges lying in a north-east - south-west direction. Further south still, the south-west plateau, a region of some 50,000 square miles with an average altitude of some 3,000 feet, is characterized by deserts and semi-deserts covered with sandy plains and dunes interspersed with salt flats and expanses of gravel. The northern plains, a region of some 40,000 square miles, belong geographically to Central Asia. They lie at an average altitude of only 2,000 feet above sea level but their fertile loess soils make this one of the country's outstanding agricultural regions. The central highlands, covering an area of some 160,000 square miles, are composed of three main mountain chains descending gradually in altitude to the south-west towards Iran.

The climate of the country as a whole is one of extremes according to season and altitude, but in general it is a semi-arid steppe climate, with an estimated annual average of 11-15 inches of precipitation. Although Afghanistan lies beyond the limits of the monsoon, in the east along the border with Pakistan, its climate is influenced by the monsoon which provides increased cloud cover, higher rainfall, and higher relative humidity that would otherwise prevail. This produces relatively luxuriant vegetation in the mountains north-east of Kandahar all the way up to the crest of the main range of the Hindu Kush. The most striking results of the monsoon influence are to the found in the coniferous forests of Paktia and Nuristan where, in places, the landscape is reminiscent of parts of the European Alps.

Most of Afghanistan's streams and rivers never reach the sea. Of those that do, the Kabul River, the rivers that drain Nuristan, and the Kunar River, all in the eastern part of the country, eventually run together and empty into the Indus. Nearly all the rest of the country's streams and rivers empty into shallow inland desert lakes. The largest drainage area in the south is that of the Helmand basin; in the north it is the Amu Darya. The flow in the country's rivers varies so much from season to season that few stretches of water are suitable for transportation. For the same reason hydro-electric projects are feasible in only a very few localities.

Agriculture is the mainstay of the country's economy. It has been estimated that approximately ninety per cent of the total population is directly engaged in traditional agricultural pursuits, using traditional techniques, with the family as the productive unit and the purpose of production being that of meeting domestic needs. A large proportion of the country's agricultural produce therefore never reaches the market. For many years the main agricultural exports have been fresh and dried fruits to Pakistan and India, while karakul skins and carpets have provided much of the foreign exchange needed to pay for imports.

It has been estimated that only about three per cent of the country's land area is arable. The rest is too dry, too high, or too steep for farming. In the central highlands nearly all the arable land is found in river valley bottoms where it can be irrigated. Winter snowfall is crucial to the following season's agricultural success since melted snow is the main source of water. The main crops cultivated are wheat, barley, maize (corn), rice, sugar beet, and sugar cane, with wheat outranking all other cereals in quantity. Even prior to the Soviet invasion of the country, Afghanistan was not entirely self-sufficient in food. The war and ten years of Soviet occupation have drastically reduced both arable and livestock production, which now probably stand at less than fifty per cent of the 1979 levels. Regaining even an approximation of pre-war food production levels is hampered by the fact that an estimated five million of the country's people are still living outside her boundaries as refugees and that tens of thousands of others are internally displaced. Added to this is the fact that there are still very large numbers of Soviet land-mines and anti-personnel mines scattered over the country.

It was estimated that there were some two million pastoral nomads in the country prior to the Soviet invasion, although their numbers had been reduced by the droughts of the 1970s. In addition there were smaller numbers of trading and harvesting nomads as well as transhumant peoples practising a mixed farming economy. The war and its effects on both people and livestock has largely destroyed pastoral nomadism in the country and a very large number of the rural farming communities, particularly in the eastern part of the country, now hold only a fraction of their former inhabitants.

Manufacturing industries have presumably been hit equally hard by the war. The largest, cotton textiles, was producing more than 55 million metres of cloth annually in the 1960s. The Afghan Textile Company operated three cotton spinning and weaving mills: at Gulbahar, Pul-i-Khumri, and Jabal-us-Siraj, but most of the cotton cloth produced was still being made in private homes and bazaar workshops. Other industries in the country include the production of cement, food processing and preserving (mainly sugar), and tanning. Carpet-making remains largely a cottage industry, except for a few small factories in centres such as Herat, Maimena, Mazar-i-Sherif, and Faizabad.

The geography of Afghanistan has contributed to the isolation of the country in modern times. While road and railway systems were being developed in neighbouring countries, Afghanistan lacked the capital and technological capability to do the same. As a result it was not until the 1960s that all-weather roads were constructed to connect the main cities and, as the 20th century draws to a close, there are still no railways anywhere in Afghanistan. These limitations on communications, together with a lack of capital for investment, have been a hindrance to the development of the economy.

In 550 BC northern Afghanistan, the region known as Bactria, became part of Cyrus the Great's Achaemenid Empire. Just over two centuries later that empire fell before the advances of Alexander the Great and it remained under Greek influence for the next 275 years. The territories south of the Hindu Kush fell to the Indian Mauryan rulers who introduced Buddhism and other aspects of Indian culture. Out of political upheavals in the north was formed the Graeco-Bactrian kingdom and one of its rulers, Demetrius, crossed the Hindu Kush and invaded northern India in the 2nd century BC. Later, under King Menander, a new Indo-Greek Empire came into being and what came to be known as Graeco-Buddhist art flourished.

As Greek influence waned toward the middle of the first century BC, nomadic tribes from Central Asia invaded the land of the Hindu Kush. Out of this emerged the Kushan Dynasty that was to rule the region, including Kashmir and much of northern India, for some 400 years. In Persia the powerful Sassanian Empire expanded eastward into Afghanistan in the 5th century AD, coming into conflict with the Epthalites, a Mongol people who held sway in Central Asia for more than a century. By the 6th century AD the Sassanians controlled most of Afghanistan.

Islam arrived in the 7th century AD, brought by Arab invaders who called the country 'Khorasan' - the name by which it was known for approximately a thousand years. Gradually the inhabitants were converted to the Sunnite branch of Islam, the religion to which most people of Afghanistan adhere to this day.

# Introduction

In the 10th century AD there emerged the Ghaznavid Dynasty, the first great Islamic Empire in the land of the Hindu Kush, which grew to its height under Sultan Mahmud and endured for the best part of two centuries. In addition to being a great military leader Sultan Mahmud also encouraged the arts and founded a university. It is said that at his court there were no less than four hundred resident poets.

The Mongol invasion of Afghanistan under the leadership of Genghis Khan took place in the early part of the 13th century. By 1222 the Mongols, sweeping all before them, had reached the Indus. So successful were these military operations that Genghis Khan's grandson Hulagu ruled over Armenia, Iraq, Iran, and Afghanistan.

The next great monarch to hold power in Afghanistan was Amir Timur or Tamerlane (1336-1404) who built an empire in India. Timur's descendant, Babur (1483-1530) took over the empire in 1504 when he captured Kabul and within twenty years had gone on to found one of the greatest empires in Asian history - that of the Moguls.

For some centuries the Pashtun tribes of the Sulaiman mountains in eastern Afghanistan had harassed all who came their way, showing little respect and no fear at all of Mongols, Turks, or Moguls. Their consistently fierce resistance to all attempts to subjugate them has continued down to the present day and, although they caused great inconvenience to the British Government of India in the 19th and first half of the 20th centuries, they earned the lasting respect of British officers who served on the frontier.

From the 16th to the 18th centuries the land of the Hindu Kush was a battleground between two rival superpowers: Mogul India and Iran. This set a pattern which, with different players, was to be repeated in the 19th and 20th centuries. Throughout much of the 16th to 18th centuries the Safavids controlled Herat and Kandahar, while the Moguls controlled Kabul, Ghazni, and Jalalabad.

The problems faced by the Moguls in regard to Afghanistan were much the same as those confronting the British some 200 years later: in order to protect their political and commercial interests they needed to extend control over the territory between the Indus and the Oxus. This was necessary in order to block the historic invasion routes from Central Asia into India. The problem in doing this was embodied in the fiercely independent tribes who lived between Kabul and the Indus. What the Moguls knew as early as the 16th century and the British found out in the 19th, had to be re-learned by the Soviets in the decade between 1979 and 1989. The cost of the lessons was as usual borne by the people of Afghanistan.

During the long period of Mogul-Safavid rivalry Pashto-speaking pastoralists such as the Abdalis and Ghilzais spread down from the mountains in eastern Afghanistan in search of better grazing lands. In time they succeeded in having one Abdali, Sado Khan, recognized as chief by the Safavid ruler Shah Abbas. Sado's successors eventually became the ruling group, known as the Sadozai, in what is now south-eastern Afghanistan. As Safavid power declined in western and southern Afghanistan the Sadozai and Ghilzais became increasingly influential.

In 1738 one of Iran's greatest monarchs, Nadir Shah (1732-1747) succeeded in capturing Kabul from the Moguls and went on in time-honoured fashion to invade India. A Sadozai chief of the Abdalis named Ahmad Khan Sadozai joined Nadir Shah's service and rose to occupy a high position in his army. When the monarch was assassinated in Iran, Ahmad Khan marched to Kandahar where he was chosen to be leader of the Abdalis and ruler of the Afghans. At a stroke he had acquired the eastern portion of Nadir Shah's empire. Moving eastward at the head of his army he soon added Kashmir and the Punjab to his territories. Kandahar became his capital and he assumed the title *Dur-i-Duran*, 'Pearl of Pearls'. Since that time the Abdali Afghans have been known as 'Durrani' and their founder as Ahmad Shah Durrani. Thus in 1747 was laid the foundations of the country we know as Afghanistan. At the same time the political supremacy of the Pashto-speaking peoples - the Afghans - was also established in a country of great cultural diversity where some thirty other languages are spoken. The domination of the country by Pashto-speaking peoples has now been a source of political discontent for more than two centuries, aggravated by repeated instances of social injustice and the systematic oppression of non-Pashto-speaking peoples, epitomized by the term 'Afghanistan' and the commonly accepted view among foreigners that all the peoples of Afghanistan are 'Afghans'.

Early in the 19th century Britain's increasing nervousness over a possible invasion of India focused first on Napoleon's territorial ambitions and then on Russia's. As the threat from France declined, so the possible threat from Russia appeared to increase. It came to be accepted by some in the British Government of India that the key to the security of the sub-continent was Afghanistan. Once this idea had taken hold Britain felt compelled to take a hand in the political affairs of that country.

Britain's military adventures in Afghanistan are fully and by no means uncritically documented in numerous articles, books and reports, many of which are listed in this bibliography. Suffice to say here that the First Afghan War (1838-42), the Second Afghan War (1878-79), and the Third Afghan War (1919) only served to prove that foreign intervention in the

## Introduction

country is a high-risk low-return activity. The wider history of Afghanistan in the 19th and 20th centuries is also, as this bibliography shows, well-documented in English-language publications, many of them written by those who took part in the events they describe. There is therefore little need to summarize political events in the country from the reign of Abdur Rahman (1880-1901) to that of Nadir Shah (1929-33), important as they are for an understanding of modern Afghanistan.

King Mohammed Zahir Shah (1933-73) who, at the time of this writing lives in exile in Italy, served his country for forty years - considerably longer than any other ruler in the last 200 years except for the renowned Amir Dost Mohammed (1819-39 and 1842-63). Only nineteen years old when he succeeded his father, who had been assassinated by a student for personal rather than political reasons, Zahir Shah pursued his late father's policies, particularly in such areas as social and economic development, tribal pacification, and the maintenance of good diplomatic relations with Iran, India and the Soviet Union. In foreign relations Afghanistan's policy was one of non-alignment. Following the Second World War, India's independence and the emergence of Pakistan, Afghanistan promoted the idea of Pushtun independence - an independent 'Pushtunistan' to be carved out of Pakistan as a homeland for the estimated six-million Pashto-speaking (and therefore 'Afghan') peoples living between the Durand Line (Afghanistan's eastern border) and the Indus. This issue, one legacy of an unsatisfactory boundary demarcated by the British in the closing years of the 19th century, has soured relations between Afghanistan and Pakistan for more than forty years, further fuelled for a time by the aggressive tactics of the King's first cousin, Mohammed Daoud, who kept the issue very much alive, particularly during his years as Prime Minister (1953-63). Although Zahir Shah had occupied the throne since 1933, the real political power during most of his reign had been either in the hands of his uncles, or his cousin Daoud. As Louis Dupree remarked upon the occasion of Daoud's retirement in 1963, 'the patience of King Muhammad Zahir Shah has been phenomenal...'

In March 1963 Prime Minister Daoud resigned. It was, to say the least an unusual political move for someone so popular and influential. Overnight, this made the King the most powerful figure in both the government and the country. In the following year a new constitution was drawn up. Among other things it contained Article 24 which barred members of the royal family from participating in political parties and from holding high government office, specifically that of prime minister, cabinet minister, member of parliament or justice of the supreme court. The constitution also provided for free elections to be held for places in the 216-member Lower House and for two-thirds of the places in the eighty-four-member Upper House, one-third being filled by royal appointment. The change of government and the new constitution raised hopes among intellectuals and students that some kind of 'instant democracy' would come into effect. Student demonstrations orchestrated by Babrak Karmal led to the death of three and the wounding of many when police opened fire in Kabul on October 23rd, 1965, a tragedy witnessed by the writer.

Political and economic problems plagued Mohammed Zahir Shah's decade-long experiment with a constitutional monarchy. In 1970 the country experienced a severe drought which continued in 1971 and 1972. An estimated 500,000 people are said to have died. In 1973, while the king was seeking medical treatment in Europe, Daoud Khan took over the government, declared Afghanistan a republic and named himself President and Prime Minister. Daoud was now sixty-one years old and although still an astute politician, was somewhat out of touch with the mood of the country. There was no improvement in Afghanistan's economic and political situation. Daoud postponed decision-making and dragged his feet over the appointment of a new cabinet. His once sure touch seem to have deserted him. Increasingly, he relied on an 'inner cabinet' of trusted associates. Instead of becoming more liberal, which was what was needed, he became more conservative. The leftists among the educated elite became restive. Members of illegal political parties such as *Khalq* and *Parcham* grew increasingly confident. On April 17th 1978 Mir Akbar, a former officer of the Ministry of the Interior and prominent leftist with whom the writer had been closely (although not politically) associated some twenty years earlier, was murdered. Thousands turned out for his funeral and the government in a panic reaction began arresting leftist leaders. On April 27th while the cabinet met to discuss the situation, a coup which came to be known as the Saur ('April') Revolution, led by Hafizullah Amin, resulted in the murder of President Daoud and some thirteen members of his family.

The Democratic Republic of Afghanistan (DRA) was soon formed, with leaders insisting they were not communists. Nur Mohammed Taraki was chosen President of the Revolutionary Council and Commander of the Armed Forces. The following months saw one political crisis after another. Almost immediately the *Khalq-Parcham* partnership began to fall apart, with the *Khalqis* plotting to remove *Parcham's* leader, Babrak Karmal. Hafizullah Amin was appointed Prime Minister in March 1979. In the meantime unrest spread through much of the countryside and a major uprising occurred in Nuristan. Spontaneous revolts spread throughout the provinces. A serious split developed between Taraki and Amin in the au-

# Introduction

tumn of 1979. Finally, at one meeting between the two, shooting broke out and Taraki was either killed outright or died soon afterwards. On December 24th 1979 the Russians invaded Afghanistan. Hafizullah Amin was among the first to die. A decade of war and brutal occupation was about to begin and soon a flood of refugees clogged the mountain passes leading out of the country.

*The bibliography*

This bibliography has been compiled from books, articles, and reports in the Balfour Library at the Pitt Rivers Museum, Oxford, the Indian Institute Library, Oxford, various collections in Peshawar, the University library in Copenhagen, and private holdings in England, including the compiler's own personal library. As so much of what is available in English has been written by foreign observers over the past 200 years, many of them having but slight acquaintance with their subject, I have made a special effort to include as many English-language works as possible by writers from Afghanistan. As the focus of this bibliography is on English-language sources many works by French, German and Russian scholars have been excluded. Afghanistan has long been a special field of study for Russian and Soviet scholars in all subjects and as a consequence the sheer volume of of Russian-language publications on the country is impressive.

Inevitably perhaps, there is an imbalance in the works listed here. Even the best libraries do not have everything and Afghanistan is still regarded as a rather recondite subject by many librarians; with few requests coming in for books and journals dealing with the area they are reluctant to spend money from hard-pressed budgets to build up collections for which there may be little demand. Thus, while it has been relatively easy to track down works on the history, archaeology, anthropology and languages of Afghanistan, the search for works on banking, finance, the manufacturing industries, the labour force, and the economy has not been equally trouble-free. I hope that those who have made a special study of such subjects in Afghanistan will be indulgent; others I would refer to the other bibliographies listed in the present volume.

Numerous works in this bibliography deal with the North-West Frontier area of what is now Pakistan. This is because the present eastern boundary of Afghanistan - the infamous 'Durand Line' - was drawn on the map only in the closing years of the 19th century and it had then, as it has now, all the disadvantages of a political boundary drawn up by a colonial power to suit 19th-century colonial needs and objectives. Historically, those who ruled in Khorasan and Kabul also ruled in the valley of the Indus. Peshawar, now in Pakistan, was an important Afghan city. For these reasons there are strong cultural connections between Pakistan and Afghanistan, and much of the history of North-West India and, more recently Pakistan, is inseparable from that of the land of Hindu Kush. No apology therefore, is made for the inclusion of some works where the main focus is on the region between the Durand Line and the Indus. There is also an historical and cultural overlap with Iran, though that is much less evident in this bibliography. Particularly in the field of literature, the two countries have much in common. An educated person in Afghanistan would cherish the same literary works in Farsi as his counterpart in Iran. In the same way the very much smaller body of literary works in Pashto would be familiar to educated Afghans on both sides of the Durand Line.

Finally, I would suggest that anyone wanting to a take a general crash course on Afghanistan would do well to concentrate on two books: *Afghanistan* by Louis Dupree (1980) and the most recent available edition of *Area handbook for Afghanistan* compiled under the auspices of the Foreign Area Studies programme at the American University in Washington, DC.

*Acknowledgements*

For very practical assistance at various stages in the preparation of this bibliography I am most grateful to my wife Lis, who tirelessly searched libraries and bookstores in Oxford and London for material. It is also a pleasure to express my gratitude to Sayed Askar Mousavi who went out of his way on numerous occasions to find relevant publications, thus bringing to my attention several important works which I might have otherwise missed. I am also in debt to Leila Jazayery, S. Mossain Razawi, Anthony Hyman, Dr. Robert G. Neville and Milica Djuradjevic for practical suggestions and assistance of all kinds. Vyacheslav Rudnev of the Institute of Ethnology and Anthropology in Moscow gave invaluable help with some Russian sources. However, any blame for the inclusion or exclusion of any publications as well as criticism of any of the remarks made in the annotations should be laid only at the door ot the compiler, he alone being responsible for the contents of this bibliography.

*S.J.*
*Copenhagen*
*July, 1991*

# The Country and Its People

1 **Afghanistan. I: a race of fighters & their highland home.**
Thomas H. Holdich. In: *Peoples of all nations: their life today and the story of their past by our foremost writers of travel, anthropology, & history, illustrated with upwards of 5000 photographs, numerous colour plates, and 150 maps.* Edited by J. A. Hammerton. London: Educational Book Co., [n.d.]. vol. 1, p. 23-42.
An illustrated article which sketches the history of the country and introduces the reader to the land and its peoples.

2 **Afghanistan. II: the story of the gates to India.**
R. W. Frazer. In: *Peoples of all nations: their life today and the story of their past by our foremost writers of travel, anthropology, & history, illustrated with upwards of 5000 photographs, numerous colour plates, and 150 maps.* Edited by J. A. Hammerton. London: Educational Book Co., [n.d.]. vol. 1, p. 43-45. map.
A short historical account of Anglo-Afghan relations during the 19th century is followed by a short section entitled 'Afghanistan: facts and figures', which provides a general introduction to the country.

3 **Afghānistān.**
M. Longworth Dames, H. A. R. Gibb, G. Morgenstierne, R. Ghirshman. In: *The Encyclopaedia of Islam.* Edited by H. A. R. Gibb, J. H. Kramers, E. Lévi-Provençal, J. Schacht. London: Luzac, 1960. vol. 1, p. 221-33. map. bibliog.
An article by various authorities arranged in the following sections: 'Geography', 'Ethnography', 'Languages', 'Religion', and 'History'.

1

4    **Afghan and Pathan, a sketch.**
George B. Scott. London: Mitre, 1929. 188p. map.

A general introductory text for the non-specialist written by the author of *Twenty years on the North West Frontier* (q.v.). A physical description of the country, with historical notes, is followed by a chapter on the North-West Frontier. Then the Hazara district, the Yusufzai, Mohmand, Afridi, and Shinwari tribes are described, as are the districts of Orakzai, Kohat and Bannu. Chapters on the Waziri people and the problems of the Baluchistan border conclude the survey.

5    **Afghanistan.**
Angus Hamilton. London: William Heinemann, 1906. 562p. map. bibliog.

At the time it was written, and for a good many years afterwards, this was the single best source of information available in any language on Afghanistan. The author, a correspondent of *The Pall Mall Gazette* and *The Times of India*, did an exemplary job of background research and has produced an excellent and highly readable reference work that covers just about everything.

6    **Afghanistan.**
Edited by Donald N. Wilber. New Haven, Connecticut: Human Relations Area Files, 1956. 501p. maps. bibliog. (Country Survey Series).

An excellent one-volume compendium of basic information about the country: the politics, economy, geography, history, ethnography, education, culture and religion are all covered. A useful index and bibliography are appended. In 1962 an updated and considerably shorter version of this was published (q.v.), but the 1956 edition is by far the best of the two.

7    **Afghanistan.**
Oskar von Niedermayer, Ernst Diez. Leipzig, Germany: Karl W. Hiersemann, 1924. 313p. maps.

One of the classic books about Afghanistan, this provides a unique photographic record of the country as it was at the time of the First World War. With nearly 250 15 by 20cm sepia photographs of excellent quality, it shows major buildings, streets, markets, and general views of towns and cities as they were in 1915 and 1916. The German text includes chapters on geography, geology, landscape, communications, population, commerce, industry, and the Islamic and Buddhist periods. There are special sections on Herat, Kabul, Balkh, Mazar-i-Sherif, Ghazni, and Qala Bist (Lashkar-i Bazaar).

8    **Afghanistan.**
M. R. Nicod. Innsbruck, Austria: Pinguin, 1985. 144p. maps. bibliog.

Essentially a coffee-table book of glossy colour photographs, this also contains text by various writers on the geographical setting, the peoples of Afghanistan, Islamic architecture, village and town life, religion, and refugees in Pakistan.

2

9    **Afghanistan.**
Joseph Kessel, Roland Michaud. Paris: Hachette, 1970. 60p. map.
Nine pages of text accompany a portfolio of fifty 25 by 30cm colour plates showing
the land and peoples of Afghanistan in colourful and often dramatic style. Many
of these same photographs appear later in other coffee-table books by Roland and
Sabrina Michaud (q.v.).

10    **Afghanistan.**
Paul Bucherer-Dietschi, Christoph Jentsch.    Liestal, Switzerland:
Stiftung Bibliotheca Afghanica, 1986.    492p.    map.    bibliog.
(Schriftenreihe der Stiftung Bibliotheca Afghanica, Band 4).
A social, economic, geographical, and political account of the country in German, in-
cluding sections on agriculture, refugees, political developments (1973-1983), ethnic
groups, and the natural environment.

11    **Afghanistan.**
Roland Michaud, Sabrina Michaud.  London:  Thames & Hudson,
1980. 133p. map.
A collection of 104 colour photographs taken in various parts of Afghanistan mostly,
it seems, in winter to take advantage of dust-free air and good light. A visually
impressive record of the country as it was before the Soviet invasion.

12    **Afghanistan.**
Alain Delapraz, Micheline Delapraz. Neuchâtel, Switzerland: Avanti,
1964. 127p. maps. bibliog.
A general introduction, in French, to the land and its people, with sections on
geography, history, and a summary of the state of the country in the 20th century.
It is lavishly illustrated with colour plates.

13    **Afghanistan.**
Louis Dupree.  Princeton, New Jersey: Princeton University Press,
1980. rev. ed. 778p. maps. bibliog.
A standard reference work since it first appeared in 1973, this remains a useful
introduction to the land, its people, their history, and the main political events in the
country over the past 100 years. There are chapters on 'Ethnic Groups', 'Language',
'Folklore and Folk Music', 'Settlement Patterns', and 'Domesticated Animals', but
the author's main interests are history and politics. The peaceful overthrow of King
Mohammad Zahir Shah in 1973 by Mohammad Daoud is chronicled in an epilogue
in the 1980 edition, as is the Soviet invasion of the country.

14    **Afghanistan: a brief description.**
Kerr Fraser-Tytler. *Journal of the Royal Central Asian Society.* vol. 29,
pts. 3-4. (1942), p. 165-75. map.
A geographical description of the country is followed by a general account of the
people and a glimpse of life in Kabul. The author then takes up the recent political
and economic history of Afghanistan.

3

15 **Afghanistan, a brief survey.**
Jamal-ud-Din Ahmad, Muhammad Abdul Aziz. London: Longmans, Green, 1936. 160p. maps. bibliog.
This book, first published in Kabul in 1934, is, as its title suggests, a general text for the non-specialist - an attempt to introduce the country's history, geography, government, and culture to a wider audience. With numerous illustrations and appendices containing practical information, this is an interesting record of the country as it was in the 1930s.

16 **Afghanistan: ancient land with modern ways.**
Edited by Abdussattar Shalizi. Kabul: Ministry of Planning, Royal Government of Afghanistan, [1960]. 199p. map.
A government publication, consisting mostly of colour and black-and-white photographs, designed to give a favourable impression of the land, its people, and their cultural, technological, and social progress. It provides an interesting photographic record of the country as it was half way through the 20th century. The text is in Pashto and English. The end-paper maps place 'Pashtoonistan', in large letters, from Baluchistan up along the North-West Frontier through Swat and Chitral. 'Pakistan' appears in much smaller letters down toward Lahore and Amritsar.

17 **Afghanistan at a glance.**
Press Department Publications. Kabul: Government Printing House, 1957. 198p.
A general introduction to the geography, climate, flora and fauna, industry and commerce, people, government, travel information, and foreign trade of the country. There are more than 150 sepia-tinted photographs. The book concludes with the text of Daoud's First Five Year Plan speech to the National Assembly.

18 **Afghanistan, crossroad of conquerors.**
Thomas J. Abercrombie. *National Geographic.* vol. 134, no. 3. (Sept. 1968), p. 297-345. map.
A general account of the country and the author's personal experiences, held together by striking photographs which show the land and its people in traditional *National Geographic* style.

19 **Afghanistan, das Land im historischen Spannungsfeld Mittelasiens.**
(Afghanistan, a land in Central Asia's historical zone of tension.)
Max Klimburg. Vienna: Austria-Edition, 1966. 313p. map. bibliog. (Orient-Okzident-Reihe der Österreichischen UNESCO Kommission, Band 4).
An overview of the country, its history, and its people amounting to a German-language equivalent of Donald Wilber's 1962 publication *Afghanistan, its people, its society, its culture* (q.v.).

20    **Afghanistan, das Tor nach Indien.**
(Afghanistan, gateway to India.)
Herbert Tichy. Leipzig, Germany: Wilhelm Goldmann, 1940. 237p.
map. bibliog.
Part travel book and part history, this is a serious study by an Austrian scholar who
travelled round the country by motorcycle in the 1930s. Among other things, the
writer examines the geography and political history of the country.

21    **L'Afghanistan: histoire, description, moeurs et coutumes, folklore,
fouilles.**
(Afghanistan: history, description, manners and customs, folklore, and
archaeological sites.)
René Dollot. Paris: Payot, 1937. 318p. map. bibliog. (Bibliothèque
Géographique).
A general overview of the history, geography, society, and culture of the country,
written by a French diplomat who was posted to Kabul in the early 1930s.

22    **Afghanistan in the 1970s.**
Edited by Louis Dupree, Linette Albert. New York; Washington, DC;
London: Praeger, 1974. 266p. maps. bibliog.
A collection of articles by European scholars on a wide range of subjects including
politics, economics, anthropology, history, education, archaeology, and music.

23    **Afghanistan, its people, its society, its culture.**
Donald N. Wilber, Elizabeth E. Bacon (et al). New Haven, Con-
necticut: Human Relations Area Files, 1962. 320p. maps. bibliog.
(Survey of World Cultures).
An attempt to summarize under various headings a whole range of geographical,
historical, cultural, political, and demographic information relating to Afghanistan.
The scope of the work is such that generalizations are inevitable, but it is a readable
and informative introduction to the country as it was in the 1950s and 1960s.

24    **Afghanistan, land in transition.**
Mary Bradley Watkins. Princeton, New Jersey: D. van Nostrand,
1963. 262p. map. bibliog. (The Asia Library).
Another attempt to introduce the country, its people and their traditions to a wider
audience, this offers the usual blend of history, culture, change, economics, education, and politics. The book is well presented and ably researched.

25    **Afghanistan of the Afghans.**
Ikbal Ali Shah. London: Diamond Press, 1928. 272p.
A general introduction to the land and its people, written in the 1920s, which contains
chapters on folk-life, witchcraft, charms, spells and divination, the supernatural,
popular songs and sayings, folk-tales and legends, religion, and political issues. In
the 1982 reprint by Octagon Press, London, there is no indication that it is a reprint
or that the text was written half a century earlier.

26 **Afghanistan, some new approaches.**
George Grassmuck, Ludwig W. Adamec (et al). Ann Arbor, Michigan: Center for Near Eastern and North African Studies, University of Michigan, 1969. 405p. map. bibliog.
This compilation includes a chapter on the 'Ethnography of Afghanistan' from a Russian text by A. G. Aslanov, a chapter on 'Afghan literature' by D. Wilson, one on 'Political modernization' by L. B. Poullada, 'Modernization & reform' by P. J. Reardon, and 'Afghanistan's relations with Germany' by L. W. Adamec. In addition, there is an historical chronology from 1747-1968 and a specialized bibliography listing publications in Persian, English, French, and German, as well as Soviet publications.

27 **Afghanistan today.**
Edited by Khaidar Mas'ud, Andrei Sakharov, Makhmud Bar'yalai, Leonid Mironov. Moscow: Planeta, 1981. 239p.
Essentially a political coffee-table book, this offers pages and pages of beautiful landscape pictures, clean, modern street scenes, happy workers, well-fed smiling children, and cheerful citizens arm-in-arm with Soviet soldiers in an attempt to drive home the message that all is well in Afghanistan under communist rule. The book is perhaps best described by the fact that it contains no less than thirty-two pictures of Babrak Karmal.

28 **The Afghans.**
Mohammed Ali. Kabul: The Author, 1965. 163p.
This introductory text on the 'The manners and customs of the Afghans' is presented under such headings as 'Love of independence', 'Patriotism', *Pukhtunwali*, 'Hospitality', 'Afghan family system', 'Betrothals and marriages', 'Respect for elders', 'Religious ceremonies', and *Jirga*, to name a few. Literature and folklore are also discussed and the author concludes by offering 100 Afghan-Persian proverbs.

29 **American family in Afghanistan.**
Rebecca Shannon Cresson. *National Geographic Magazine*. vol. 104, no. 3. (1953), p. 417-32. map.
An account of Afghanistan and its people and the experiences of a foreign family living and working as teachers in the capital. The illustrations provide a glimpse of the country as it was in the 1950s.

30 **Area handbook for Afghanistan.**
Harvey H. Smith, Donald W. Bernier (et al). Washington, DC: US Government, 1973. 453p. maps. bibliog. (Area Handbooks).
A comprehensive one-volume reference work on the country and its people, compiled from a wide range of published sources by half a dozen editors. Data is presented in four main sections, each broken down into several chapters. These sections are 'Social', 'Political', 'Economic', and 'National Security'. The various chapters provide useful summaries of geographical, anthropological, and historical information. Agriculture, industry, trade, finance, and foreign relations are dealt with in considerable detail.

31 **A brief presentation on Afghanistan at the summer course.**
A. Rasul Amin. *WUFA, Quarterly Journal of the Writers Union of Free Afghanistan.* vol. 4, no. 2. (1989), p. 81-94.

A general account of the land, its people, and their history by the editor of WUFA, presented at the Summer Course on National Security which was held at the Institute of Political Science at Christian Albrechts University in Kiel in 1989.

32 **Caravans to Tartary.**
Roland Michaud, Sabrina Michaud. London: Thames & Hudson, 1978. 104p. map.

A collection of photographs, mostly in colour, of the Kirghiz peoples of Afghan Turkestan. The authors/photographers made a wintertime journey with the Kirghiz in 1970 to get material for this book, which consists of fourteen pages of text and seventy-six colour illustrations. It successfully captures the immensity and drama of the landscape as well as the dignity of the people.

33 **The Kabul Times Annual.**
Nour M. Rahimi. Kabul: Kabul Times, 1967. 208p. bibliog. (Kabul Times Annuals).

This was the first of a series of volumes designed to provide information in English about the country's history, geography, economy, commerce, education, and culture. It contains concise information about each of the twenty-eight provinces, a 'Who's Who' of prominent citizens, and summarizes foreign relations, agriculture, trade, and the country's climate.

34 **Legende Afghanistan.**
(Legendary Afghanistan.)
Joseph Kessel. Cologne, Germany: M. DuMont Schauberg, 1959. 204p. map.

A book of photographs, with a forty-seven page text in German, showing views in black-and-white and colour of the people, the cities, and the landscape of Afghanistan.

35 **Die materielle Kultur des Kabulgebietes.**
(The material culture of the Kabul region.)
Bruno Markowski. Leipzig, Germany: Asia Major, 1932. 190p. map. bibliog. (Veröffentlichungen des Geographischen Instituts der Albertus-Universität zu Königsberg. Neue Folge, Reihe Ethnographie, Nr. 2.).

A valuable and unique study of the material culture and technology employed in and around Kabul in the 1920s. The geography, climate, settlement patterns, and languages of the area are discussed as a basis for a survey of building materials, building techniques, and house types. Methods of lighting, heating, and decorating domestic dwellings are described. The author also deals with clothing, food, agriculture, shops, markets, trade, currency.

36    A note on Afghanistan.
      Louis Dupree. New York: American Universities Field Staff Reports
      Service, 1960. 32p. maps. bibliog. (South Asia Series, vol. 4, no. 8
      (Afghanistan)).
A general geographical, historical, cultural, and political overview of the country
and its people.

37    Notes sur l'Afghanistan.
      (Notes on Afghanistan.)
      Maurice Fouchet. Paris: Maisonneuve Fèrres, 1931. 228p.
A general account of the land and its people with sections on ancient history and
the politics of King Amanullah's reign. Written by the first French Minister to be
accredited to Afghanistan.

38    The past present: a year in Afghanistan.
      Edward Hunter. London: Hodder & Stoughton, 1959. 352p. map.
An account by an American journalist who spent a year in the country in the 1950s
in order to collect material for a book. There are chapters on *buzkashi*, the status
of women, US aid programmes, and US-Soviet competition for influence in the
country.

39    Post-war developments in Afghanistan.
      H.R.H. Prince Peter of Greece. *Journal of the Royal Central Asian
      Society.* vol. 34, pts. 3-4. (1947), p. 275-86.
A general survey covering historical, economic, and political aspects of the country
is combined with the author's personal observations.

40    Recent progress in Afghanistan.
      Giles Squire. *Journal of the Royal Central Asian Society.* vol. 37, pt.
      1. (1950), p. 6-18.
The author, who went to the country as British Minister and then became Ambassador to the Court of Kabul, spent six years in Afghanistan. Here he gives an
informal account of the country and its people, discussing education, communications, the army, industry, agriculture, and political development.

41    A visit to Afghanistan.
      M. Philips Price. *Journal of the Royal Central Asian Society.* vol. 36,
      pt. 2. (1949), p. 124-34.
A personal account of a 2,000 mile journey through Afghanistan. The author was
the guest of the Prime Minister and had opportunities to meet and talk to other high
government officials. He discusses politics, education, and the economy.

42   Völkerschicksale am Hindukusch: Afghanen, Belutschen, Tadshiken.
     (Destiny of the Hindu Kush Peoples: Afghans, Beluchis, Tadjiks.)
     Burchard Brentjes. Leipzig, Germany: Koehler & Amelang, 1983.
     247p. maps. bibliog.
A cultural history of the country which provides first a geographical description of
the land and then an ethnographical description of the people before going on to
an historical account of ancient Afghanistan. The final section brings the history
forward from the founding of the Mogul Empire to the end of the 19th century.
Richly illustrated with photographs and drawings.

**Afghanistan.**
*See* item no. 44.

**A new guide to Afghanistan.**
*See* item no. 89.

**Resa till Afghanistan.** Journey to Afghanistan.
*See* item no. 167.

**A review of the political situation in Central Asia.**
*See* item no. 275.

**Afghanistan.**
*See* item no. 894.

**Afghanistan in pictures.**
*See* item no. 895.

**The land and people of Afghanistan.**
*See* item no. 898.

**The story of Afghanistan.**
*See* item no. 899.

# Geography and Geology

## Geography

43 **Afghanische Studien.**
Edited by René König, Ludolph Fischer. Meisenheim am Glan, Germany: Anton Hain, [various dates].

A series of monographs by several scholars issued at irregular intervals throughout the 1970s on a wide range of subjects such as forestry, agriculture, cultural geography, nationalism, communications and development, academic elites, and nomads, to name but a few.

44 **Afghanistan.**
Patricia Kingsbury, Robert C. Kingsbury. New York: Nelson Doubleday, 1965. 64p. maps. (Around the World).

A short illustrated account of Afghanistan, covering geographical, historical, social, and commercial aspects, prepared 'with the co-operation of the American Geographical Society'.

45 **Afghanistan and the Soviet Union: collision and transformation.**
Edited by Milan Hauner, Robert L. Canfield. Boulder, Colorado: Westview, 1989. 219p. maps. bibliog.

This book is one result of an interdisciplinary conference on 'Foreign Policy Research' held in Washington, DC in 1986 and it arises from the panel which discussed 'Central Asia in a Wider Context'. Afghanistan's position as part of 'Greater Central Asia' is considered in the light of changes in the Soviet Union - not just political changes, but the spread of modern transportation and communication facilities, the search for exploitable resources, and the growing influence of Islamic values as a means of expressing local and regional interests.

46   **Afghanistan, eine landeskundliche Studie auf Grund des vorhandenen Materials und eigener Beobachtung.**
(Afghanistan, a geographical study based on available materials and personal research.)
Emil Trinkler. Gotha, Germany: Justus Perthes, 1928. 83p. maps. bibliog. (Petermanns Mitteilungen, Ergänzungsheft, Nr. 196).
A geographical study of the mountain systems and plateaux of South Central Asia with a detailed description of the mountain ranges of Afghanistan is followed by an outline of the geology of the country, its climate, water resources, flora and fauna, and relief. The peoples of Afghanistan, their settlements, and trade routes are also described. Numerous photographs and maps are included, as well as a good bibliography.

47   **Afghanistan from the geographical point of view.**
Sayed Qasim Reshtia. *Afghanistan.* vol. 2, no. 1. (1947), p. 13-18.
A general geographical description of the country which deals systematically with the various mountain ranges, valleys, and basins.

48   **Afghanistan's mountains.**
Mohammed Ali. *Afghanistan.* vol. 8, no. 1. (1953), p. 46-52.
A geographical description of the mountain ranges, routes, and passes of the country.

49   **Badakhshan Province and northeastern Afghanistan.**
Edited by Ludwig W. Adamec. Graz, Austria: Akademische Druck- u. Verlagsanstalt, 1972. 257p. maps. (Historical and Political Gazetteer of Afghanistan, Vol. I.).
The first of six volumes of a revised and updated British gazetteer which lists, locates, and describes cities, towns, villages, and geographical features (rivers, valleys, mountains, etc.) throughout the region. In addition to the alphabetical listings there is a nineteen-page glossary of terms, a twenty-four-page index of entries, and a sixty-five-page map section.

50   **Band-i-Amir.**
W. R. Hay. *The Geographical Journal.* vol. 87, no. 4. (1936), p. 348-50.
A brief descriptive account of the lakes which lie at an altitude of nearly 10,000 feet above sea level some forty-five miles to the west of Bamiyan. The local myths regarding Hazrat Ali, in whose honour a shrine has been built at Band-i-Haibat, are told.

51   **Farah and southwestern Afghanistan.**
Edited by Ludwig W. Adamec. Graz, Austria: Akademische Druck- u. Verlagsanstalt, 1973. 466p. maps. bibliog. (Historical and Political Gazetteer of Afghanistan, Vol. 2).
As is the case with each volume in the series, this provides an alphabetical listing of place names, including both towns and geographical features, a glossary of terms,

an index of entries, and an eighty-one page map section. In addition, this volume also contains three reports written by British medical and veterinary officers who worked in Seistan in 1903-05.

52    A geographical introduction to Herat Province.
James Matthai. Kabul: Kabul University Press, 1966. 69p. map.

A study, based on fieldwork, of the vegetation, soils, climate, agriculture, industry, and communications of the country's westernmost province. About half of the report is given over to the case study of a typical farm with information on taxes, farm labour, crops, and changing agricultural practices. Climate statistics are provided for fifteen of the country's largest towns and cities.

53    A geographical introduction to the history of Central Asia.
K. de B. Codrington. *The Geographical Journal.* vol. 104, nos. 1-2. (1944), p. 27-40. maps.

This authoritative paper appeared in two parts; the second was published in the same volume of *The Geographical Journal*, but appeared in nos. 3-4, p. 73-91. The article provides useful historical background to an understanding of the ancient history and archaeology of the country, and the influence of geography on the region's history.

54    La géographie de l'Afghanistan.
(The geography of Afghanistan.)
J. Humlum. Copenhagen: Gyldendal, 1959. 421p. maps. bibliog.

A description of the physical geography, relief, rivers, climate, and vegetation is followed by an account of ethnic and economic factors with sections on population, towns, natural regions, crops, irrigation projects, nomadism, industry, communications, and foreign trade. A special section deals with subterranean irrigation channels (*karez*) and another looks at the country's position as a buffer state between the Soviet Union and South Asia. It is profusely illustrated with maps, diagrams, drawings, and photographs.

55    The geography and politics of Afghanistan.
R. Gopalakrishnan. New Delhi: Concept, 1982. 280p. maps. bibliog.

This analyses the politico-geographical viability of Afghanistan as a developing landlocked state, and identifies the basic geographical infrastructure of the nation-state by drawing upon the fields of geography, history, economics, and political systems. An interesting study in political geography.

56    A great north road.
Kerr Fraser-Tytler. *Journal of the Royal Central Asian Society.* vol. 29, pt. 2. (1942), p. 129-35. map.

A geographical and historical description of the old road from Kabul to Mazar-i-Sherif, Balkh, and Andkhui, and the efforts of Amanullah to make a motor road through the Hindu Kush - a project completed by Nadir Shah in 1933 and subsequently improved and used by the Soviets to invade the country.

57    **Herat and northwestern Afghanistan.**
      Edited by Ludwig W. Adamec. Graz, Austria: Akademische Druck-u.
      Verlagsanstalt, 1975. 574p. maps. bibliog. (Historical and Political
      Gazetteer of Afghanistan, Vol. 3).
Together with other volumes in the series (q.v.), this is a useful reference work
for anyone carrying out research on the history, geography, or archaeology of the
region. The alphabetical listing of place names is followed by a glossary of terms,
index of entries, and a fifty-three page map section.

58    **In Persia and Afghanistan with the Citroën trans-Asiatic expedition.**
      Joseph Hackin. *The Geographical Journal.* vol. 83, no. 5. (1934), p.
      353-363. map.
A French archaeologist, who accompanied the expedition from Beirut to Gilgit, describes the journey across southern Afghanistan from the Persian border to Peshawar
via Herat, Farah, Kandahar, and Kabul.

59    **India's North-West Frontier.**
      William Barton. London: John Murray, 1939. 308p. maps.
A general description, geographical and political, of the Afghan borderland and
an account of the consequent problem of the North-West Frontier, which divides
the Pathans of Afghanistan from those of Pakistan, as well as dividing present-day
Afghanistan from a large tract of land extending to the Indus River which formed
part of her historical territory. A discussion of this boundary invariably traces the
history of relations between Afghanistan and Britain.

60    **A journey in Afghanistan and on the North-West Frontier.**
      Arnold Toynbee. *Journal of the Royal Central Asian Society.* vol. 49,
      pts. 3-4. (1962), p. 277-88.
The famous historian's informal account of a journey made in 1960 in which he
examines, among other things, the political rôle of the royal family, the spread of
formal education, and relations between Afghanistan and Pakistan.

61    **Kabul and south-eastern Afghanistan.**
      Edited by Ludwig W. Adamec. Graz, Austria: Akademische Druck-u.
      Verlagsanstalt, 1985. 926p. maps. bibliog. (Historical and Political
      Gazetteer of Afghanistan, Vol. 6).
The last volume in the series, this covers the provinces of Kabul, Parwan, Maidan,
Logar, Ghazni, Paktia, Nangrahar, Bamian, Kunar, and Kapisa. As in the other
volumes, historical, geographical, and cultural names and places are listed and described.

62    **Kafiristan: Versuch einer Landeskunde auf Grund einer Reise im Jahre 1928.**
(Kafiristan: an attempt at a general study of the country based on an expedition in 1928.)
Martin Voigt. Breslau, Germany: Ferdinand Hirt, 1933. 141p. maps. bibliog. (Geographischen Wochenschrift, Beiheft 2).
A study in the human geography of the little-known Nuristan region, with sections on the people, their languages, their economy, the environment, geology, climate, hydrology, and flora and fauna. Numerous maps, photographs, and line drawings make this report of early field research particularly interesting. German text.

63    **Kandahar and south-central Afghanistan.**
Edited by Ludwig W. Adamec. Graz, Austria: Akademische Druck-u. Verlagsanstalt, 1980. 722p. maps. bibliog. (Historical and Political Gazetteer of Afghanistan, Vol. 5).
Covers the provinces of Kandahar, Oruzgan, and Zabul in south-central Afghanistan, listing and describing all settlements, named geographical features, and historical sites in alphabetical order. Taken together with the maps, it forms an invaluable research aid for anyone working on the region. An appendix, not listed in the table of contents, contains a sixty-eight page essay on the Durrani tribes for which neither date nor author is given.

64    **The Khaibar Pass as the invaders' road for India.**
Annette S. Beveridge. *Journal of the Central Asian Society.* vol. 13, pt. 3; vol. 13, pt. 4. (1926), p. 250-58; p. 368-74.
An examination of early texts to provide an historical and geographical account of the importance of the Khyber in the history of Afghanistan and India.

65    **The Kohistan of Eastern Province, Afghanistan.**
D. R. Crone. *Journal of the Royal Central Asian Society.* vol. 23, pt. 2. (1936), p. 468-72. map. bibliog.
The author seeks to define the region by rejecting both 'Kafiristan' and 'Nuristan' in favour of 'Kohistan of the Eastern Province'. He discusses the physical geography and history of the area and speculates on the origins of its inhabitants.

66    **Making a map of Afghanistan.**
Fairchild Aerial Surveys. *Afghanistan.* vol. 15, no. 3. (1960), p. 1-6.
A description of the air photography project, begun in 1957, which the Fairchild Company, under contract to the Government of Afghanistan, undertook in order to prepare photo-mosaics and 1:250,000 scale maps of the country. The aircraft used for this task were B-17s.

67    **Mazar-i-Sharif and north-central Afghanistan.**
       Edited by Ludwig W. Adamec. Graz, Austria: Akademische Druck-u.
       Verlagsanstalt, 1979. 738p. maps. bibliog. (Historical and Political
       Gazetteer of Afghanistan, Vol. 4).
As its title indicates, this volume is a geographical and historical reference work on
the region formerly known as Afghan Turkestan. The alphabetical listing of place
names and tribal names is followed, as in the other volumes in this series (q.v.), by
a glossary of terms, an index of entries, and a forty-five page map section.

68    **National atlas of Afghanistan: a call for contribution.**
       John F. Shroder. *Afghanistan Journal.* vol. 2, no. 3. (1975), p.
       108-11.
This is a proposal for the preparation of a national atlas for Afghanistan. It includes
a description of the scope, format, and content of the work, ending with a call for
contributions from relevant specialists.

69    **Nelles map of Afghanistan.**
       Munich: Nelles Verlag, [n.d.].
A colour folding map, scale 1:1,500,000, which shows relief, major and minor roads,
and the towns and villages which one would expect, given the scale of the map.
There is also a town plan of Kabul with some main sites picked out in red.

70    **Observations concerning Andkhoy water.**
       Abdul Wahab Khan. *Afghanistan.* vol. 5, no. 2; no. 3. (1950), p.
       36-46; p. 18-24.
A geographical description of a region in the north of Afghanistan focusing primarily
on its water resources and the use made of these by local inhabitants.

71    **The Panjsher.**
       Ahmad Ali Kohzad. *Afghanistan.* vol. 3, no. 4. (1948), p. 17-29.
A description of the Panjsher Valley north of Kabul, its roads, villages, rivers, and
other attractions. The passes leading out of the region are named and described and
an account of the inhabitants is given. A bright future for the valley is predicted in
terms of touring and sight-seeing.

72    **The Pathan borderland.**
       James W. Spain. The Hague: Mouton, 1963. 293p. map. bibliog.
       (Near and Middle East Studies, Columbia University).
A geographical, historical, and cultural study of the Pashto-speaking peoples whose
territory was split down the middle by the 'Durand Line' in 1893, leaving half in
eastern Afghanistan and half in what are now the tribal territories of Pakistan.

73  **Remote sensing of Afghanistan.**
John F. Shroder, Cathleen M. DiMarzio, Dennis E. Bussom, David Braslau. *Afghanistan Journal.* vol. 5, no. 4. (1978), p. 123-28. maps. bibliog.
A discussion of the advantages of data-gathering using satellite imaging sensors (return-beam vidicon cameras, and multi-spectral scanner subsystems) to obtain images which can be analysed for data on cultural features, vegetation, topographic information, and land use.

74  **A short history of the Helmand Valley.**
Mohammed Ali. *Afghanistan.* vol. 10, no. 1. (1955), p. 34-43.
A geographical description and historical account of one of the country's largest river systems.

75  **Some notes on a recent journey in Afghanistan.**
Christopher Sykes. *The Geographical Journal.* vol. 84, no. 4. (1934), p. 327-36. map.
Description of a 930-mile car journey across northern Afghanistan from the Iranian frontier to Kabul via Herat, Maimena, Mazar-i-Sherif, and Bamiyan, illustrated with five photographs by Robert Byron.

76  **Some problems of Central Asian exploration.**
Evert Barger. *The Geographical Journal.* vol. 103, nos. 1-2. (1944), p. 1-18. map.
An historical and geographical review of the impact of nomads on the settled peoples of those lands lying between the Indus and the Oxus, with particular reference to the first five centuries AD.

77  **The upper basin of the Kabul River.**
Clements Robert Markham. *Proceedings of the Royal Geographical Society.* vol. 1 (new series). (1879), p. 110-20.
The geography of the southern watershed of the Hindu Kush is described and this then serves to introduce a history of the exploration of eastern Afghanistan, with particular reference to routes and passes. There are numerous references to the works of Mogul and other early historians and geographers.

# Geology

78  **Earthquakes in Afghanistan.**
Edward Stenz. *Afghanistan.* vol. 1, no. 1. (1946), p. 41-50.
An historical account of the principal earthquakes recorded in Afghanistan from the early 16th century onwards is followed by a discussion of the geological zone in which the country lies.

79    Fossils of north-east Afghanistan.
      A. von Schouppé, P. D. W. Barnard, C. Rossi Rouchetti, A. Berizzi
      Quarto di Palo, I. Premoli Silva. Leiden, The Netherlands: E. J. Brill,
      1970. 323p. maps. bibliog. (Italian Expeditions to the Karakorum
      (K2) and Hindu Kush).
Presents further results of the 1961 expedition (q.v.) comprising reports on Carboniferous fossils, Triassic fossils, Jurassic fossils, and Cretaceous and Paleogene fossils.

80    Geology of central Badakhshan (north-east Afghanistan) and surrounding countries, III geology-petrology.
      Leiden, The Netherlands: E. J. Brill, 1975. 628p. maps. bibliog.
      (Italian Expeditions to the Karakorum (K2) and Hindu Kush).
This contains results of the Italian 1961 expedition to the Karakorum and Hindu Kush with sections on stratigraphy, metamorphic formations, plutonic rocks, tectonics, and the Pleistocene. There are also micropalaeontological notes on Cretaceous-Eocene sections taken and an appendix on megafossils. Most of the other volumes deal with the geology of northern Pakistan, but see A. von Schouppé, et al, *Fossils of north-east Afghanistan* (q.v.) in that same series.

81    The history of lapis lazuli in Afghanistan.
      A. Nasiri. *Afghanistan.* vol. 17, no. 4; vol. 18, no. 1; no. 2. (1962),
      p. 48-56; p. 51-56; p. 23-28.
An historical, geographical, geological, and economic study of the mineral and its exploitation. The names and locations of the principal mines are given.

82    Into northern Afghanistan.
      L. F. Rosset. *Afghanistan.* vol. 2, no. 4. (1947), p. 22-51.
A personal account of travel through a landscape that is described in geographical/geological terms. The author provides a detailed description of the coal mines at Doab.

83    Notes on the Wakhan formation of the Great Afghan Pamir and the eastern Hindu Kush.
      M. F. Buchroithner, H. Kolmer. *Afghanistan Journal.* vol. 6, no. 2.
      (1979), p. 54-61. maps. bibliog.
The mineralogical analysis of shales and hornfelses from the Wakhan formation, together with stratigraphic and paleoecological data, suggests that during the Lower Triassic the area was covered by a warm shallow sea.

84    Precious stones in Afghanistan: the diamond.
      L. F. Rosset. *Afghanistan.* vol. 2, no. 1. (1947), p. 19-38.
A geological discussion of the formations where diamonds occur is followed by a run-down of the characteristic features of the diamond, a mineralogical description, points to look for in identifying stones, classification of stones according to value, and the technicalities of diamond cutting.

Notes on Afghanistan and part of Baluchistan, geographical, ethnographical, and historical, extracted from the writings of little known Afghán and Tájzík historians, geographers, and genealogists; the histories of ...
*See* item no. 580.

# Tourism and Guide Books

**85    Afghanistan.**
Masatoshi Konishi. London: Ward Lock, 1969. 146p. map. (This Beautiful World).
An informal guide to the country aimed at a popular audience. Most of the book is taken up with colour photographs.

**86    Afghanistan.**
Marie-Claude Villenaud, Georges Villenaud. Paris: Éditions Vilo, 1969. 264p. maps. (Les Guides Modernes Fodor).
A general guidebook for travellers, this offers practical information about travel arrangements, the rules and regulations which Customs officials seem to live by, currency, languages and religion, climate, hotels, and various facilities for visitors. It goes on to give a sketch of the country's history, economy, and a description of the food one is likely to encounter before offering a series of suggested itineraries for visiting the main cities and sights.

**87    Herat, a pictorial guide.**
Nancy Hatch Wolfe. Kabul: Afghan Tourist Organization, 1966. 79p.
A brief guide to the city of Herat, containing a chronological summary of the city's history from 800 BC to 1930 AD, descriptions of the main buildings and places of interest, and forty-two black-and-white photographs.

**88    Here and there in Afghanistan.**
Prita K. Shalizi. Kabul: Ministry of Education, [n.d.]. 105p. map.
A travel book, written by the Indian wife of an Afghan government official, in which she describes the main cities and principal archaeological sites in the country, interspersing her personal observations with historical information.

89    **A new guide to Afghanistan.**
Mohammed Ali. Kabul: Mohammed Ali, 1958. 301p. map. bibliog.
The first edition of this pioneering guide book appeared in 1938. It offers an interesting and comprehensive overview of the country in a number of sections including geography, the people, language and literature, history, visitor information, and tour itineraries. Also included are a useful bibliography and some appendices containing additional practical information on the Afghan calendar, banking and currency, weights and measures, etc.

# Travel and Exploration

## The Early Period

90    **The golden road to Samarkand.**
      Wilfrid Blunt. London: Hamish Hamilton, 1973. 280p. maps. bibliog.
As the author explains, in this book he has 'chosen a number of men associated with that rather ill-defined territory that we call Central Asia - conquerors, travellers, merchants, patrons, priests, pilgrims and archaeologists - and written essays about them...' To this the publisher has added a very large number of black-and-white and colour illustrations. Afghanistan's rulers and travellers figure prominently.

91    **The great Chinese travelers.**
      Edited by Jeannette Mirsky. New York: Random House, 1964. 309p. maps.
Among other selections, this contains an account of the Chinese pilgrim Huang-tsang's (Hiuen-Tsiang) journey across China to Afghanistan in the 7th century AD. From Samarkand he went to Bactria, visited Balkh and then proceeded to Kunduz. He then went to Bamiyan, crossed the Hindu Kush in a blizzard, and made his way down to the Kabul River, following it to Nangarhar where he visited numerous sacred Buddhist sites in the area near present-day Jalalabad before continuing to Gandhara.

92    **The life of Hiuen-Tsiang.**
      Hwui Li. London: Kegan Paul, 1911. 218p.
A biography of one of the greatest Asian travellers. The Buddhist pilgrim Hiuen-Tsiang crossed Afghanistan in the 7th century AD in the course of a sixteen-year journey from China to find Buddhist texts and relics.  When he finally returned

home, he brought with him from India 657 volumes of sacred books, seventy-four of which he translated into Chinese, and 150 relics of Buddha packed on the backs of twenty horses.

# 19th Century

93 **An account of the Kingdom of Caubul, and its dependencies, in Persia, Tartary, and India; comprising a view of the Afghaun nation, and a history of the Dooraunee monarchy.**
Mountstuart Elphinstone. London: Richard Bentley, 1839. 2 vols. map.
The third edition of this famous book, first published in 1815, appeared in 1839, corrected and revised. It describes the author's 1808-09 mission to the Court (then at Peshawar) of Shah Shuja-ul-Mulk, King of 'Caubul', and gives a geographical description of Afghanistan as well as an account of its people.

94 **Among the wild tribes of the Afghan frontier.**
T. L. Pennell. London: Seeley, 1909. 318p. map.
A chronicle of events and tales written by a medical missionary who, at the time of writing, had spent sixteen years on the North-West Frontier of India. Many of his tales, like his patients, came from Afghanistan across the border.

95 **At the court of the Amir, a narrative.**
John Alfred Gray. London: Richard Bentley, 1895. 523p.
A personal narrative of travels in Afghanistan and of the life of an English medical doctor living in Kabul while in the service of the Amir Abdur Rahman. Arriving in 1889, Dr. Gray apparently did not keep a diary, but later used his letters home in preparing this book. This provides interesting descriptions of Kabul and Court life in the closing years of the 19th century.

96 **Beyond Bokhara, the life of William Moorcroft, Asian explorer and pioneer veterinary surgeon, 1767-1825.**
Garry J. Alder. London: Century, 1985. 417p. maps. bibliog.
The biography of one of the foremost of early British Central Asian explorers. Moorcroft (1767-1825) travelled widely in Afghanistan during 1823-25 with George Trebeck and is buried at Balkh.

97 **Bokhara Burnes.**
James Lunt. London: Faber & Faber, 1969. 220p. maps. bibliog. (Great Travellers).
A biography of Sir Alexander Burnes (1805-41), an officer with the East India Company who travelled widely in Central Asia from 1830 until his death in Kabul

eleven years later. Burnes was the author of *Travels into Bokhara* (1834) and *Cabool* (q.v.).

98  **Cabool, being a personal narrative of a journey to, and residence in that city, in the years 1836, 7, and 8.**
   Alexander Burnes. London: John Murray, 1842. 398p.
One of the best known of the 19th-century books about Afghanistan, this describes the author's 1836-1838 journeys as head of a mission to examine the commercial potential of the River Indus and 'the countries beyond it'. While in Kabul, Burnes collected a good deal of geographical and ethnographical information about the surrounding country and its inhabitants. His mission ended in Peshawar in 1838 on the eve of the First Afghan War. As political agent he returned to Kabul where he was murdered on November 2nd, 1841, shortly before the disastrous retreat of the British Army from Afghanistan.

99  **Caravan journeys and wanderings in Persia, Afghanistan, Turkistan, and Beloochistan; with historical notices of the countries lying between Russia and India.**
   J. P. Ferrier. London: John Murray, 1857. 534p. map.
The author set out from Baghdad in disguise in 1845 with the intention of travelling overland to Lahore. His account of the journey stands among the best and most interesting of 19th-century records of travel across Afghanistan. As he was a keen observer, the descriptive passages relating to people and places are a valuable record of the time. The book was reprinted by Oxford University Press (Karachi) in 1976.

100  **Central Asia: personal narrative of General Josiah Harlan, 1823-1841.**
   Edited by Frank E. Ross. London: Luzac, 1939. 155p. map.
Josiah Harlan ranks among the early and most extraordinary of all European travellers in Afghanistan. Born in Pennsylvania in 1799, he travelled to India in 1823, served the East India Company for three years, befriended Shuja-ul-Mulk, and went to Afghanistan as a spy at the court of Dost Mohammad. Back in the Punjab he served Ranjit Singh, becoming governor of three provinces. Later, turning against the Sikh ruler, Harlan returned to Kabul and became a General in Dost Mohammad's army, which he led in battle, defeating the Sikhs at Jamrud. In 1838 he raised the Stars and Stripes in a lofty pass of the Hindu Kush while leading his troops to Kunduz. Returning to America in 1841 he lived to lead men into battle again, serving as Colonel of a cavalry regiment in the Army of the Potomac during the Civil War. He died in San Francisco in 1871.

101  **Charles Masson of Afghanistan: explorer, archaeologist, numismatist, and intelligence agent.**
   Gordon Whitteridge. Warminster, England: Aris & Phillips, 1986. 181p. bibliog.
A biography of Afghanistan's most famous explorer and, indeed, of one of the most celebrated European travellers in Asia. Charles Masson, whose real name was James Lewis, was born in London in 1800. He sailed for Bengal in 1822 and spent the next twenty years travelling, often under extremely difficult conditions, in India,

the Punjab, Afghanistan, and Baluchistan. His published accounts of his work and travels in this part of the world remain the best, as far as Afghanistan is concerned, to come out of the 19th century.

102  **European adventurers of northern India, 1785-1849.**
     C. Grey, edited by H. L. O. Garrett. Lahore: Punjab Government, 1929. 401p. bibliog.

The authors draw mainly upon official Punjab government records to produce this fascinating account of the lives and times of some remarkable men in the 18th and 19th century history of South and Central Asia. Chapters 10 to 13 deal mainly with early European travellers in Afghanistan; among them Charles Masson, Josiah Harlan, and Alexander Gardner.

103  **L'exploration du Kafiristan par les Européens.**
     (The exploration of Kafiristan by Europeans. )
     Robert Fazy.  *Asiatische Studien, Zeitschrift der schweizerischen Gesellschaft für Asienkunde.* vol. 1, no. 2. (1953), p. 1-25.

A brief but excellent survey of early accounts and early travellers in the Kafiristan (Nuristan) region.

104  **The Gilgit game: the explorers of the western Himalayas, 1865-1895.**
     John Keay. London: John Murray, 1979. 277p. maps. bibliog.

Although mostly about what is today known as northern Pakistan, many of the principal characters in this absorbing narrative were much involved in trans-frontier exploration and intrigue; some of them were given the task of establishing Afghanistan's boundaries. The Great Game is recounted in style.

105  **The Gilgit mission, 1885-86.**
     William S. A. Lockhart, R. G. Woodthorpe. London: Eyre & Spottiswoode, 1889. 448p. maps.

A secret government report on the geography of the Hindu Kush region prepared with a view to providing information about Chitral, Kafiristan and its people, routes and passes, the natural resources, and 'other matters of interest'. The result is a remarkable volume of detailed geographical and ethnographical information with numerous maps and photographs which contains an account of the first confirmed European penetration into Kafiristan (Nuristan).

106  **The great game: on secret service in high Asia.**
     Peter Hopkirk. London: John Murray, 1990. 562p. maps. bibliog.

Afghanistan lies in the centre of the stage on which the century-long Great Game was played out. The names of those who took part are inscribed in the 19th century history of the country. The story, in which exploration, politics, and adventure is mixed in roughly equal proportions, is told here.

107 **Index to Sir George Scott Robertson's The Kafirs of the Hindu Kush.**
Lennart Edelberg, Lis Gramstrup. Moesgaard, Denmark: Jutland Archaeological Society, 1971. 59p. map.
Scholars interested in the cultures of the Hindu Kush and Karakorum regions of Central Asia will find this index to Robertson's classic study (q.v.) extremely useful. As regards place names, the large folding map included with it is the most accurate ever made of the Nuristan (Kafiristan) region.

108 **Journal of a political mission to Afghanistan in 1857, under Major (now Colonel) Lumsden; with an account of the country and its people.**
Henry Walter Bellew. London: Smith, Elder & Co., 1862. 480p.
An account of the British Mission to Kandahar in 1857-58 written by the expedition's medical officer. Part history, part anthropology, part report, and part travel book, this is a lively and informative work in the Victorian mould.

109 **Journals of travels in Assam, Burma, Bootan, Affghanistan and the neighbouring countries.**
William Griffith. Calcutta: Bishop's College, 1847. 529p.
This journal, by a well-known Victorian botanist, describes extensive travels in Afghanistan in the years 1839-41. Travelling from Quetta to Kandahar and then on to Ghazni and Kabul, he made his way to Jalalabad and then up the Kunar Valley to Chaga Sarai. From there he went to Katar in Tregam, thereby becoming the first European known to have reached the borders of Kafiristan (now Nuristan). A keen and reliable observer, his descriptive account of eastern Afghanistan is particularly valuable. The book was reprinted in 1971 in Taiwan by Ch'eng Wen.

110 **Journey to the north of India, overland from England, through Russia, Persia, and Affghaunistaun.**
Arthur Conolly. London: Richard Bentley, 1834. 2 vols. map.
Setting out from London in August, 1829, the author reached the western border of Afghanistan in September, 1830. His journey across the country is described in chapter 19 of volume one and chapters 1 to 9 of volume two. Conolly offers an interesting essay on the feasibility of a Russian invasion of India through Afghanistan in volume two (p. 299-339).

111 **A journey to the source of the River Oxus.**
John Wood. London: John Murray, 1872. 280p. maps.
Beginning with chapter ten the book describes the author's travels across Afghanistan in 1837-38, in search of the source of the Oxus. One of the classic books of Central Asian travel, this also contains Sir Henry Yule's essay on 'The geography of the valley of the Oxus'.

## 112 The Kafirs of the Hindu Kush.

George Scott Robertson. London: Lawrence & Bullen, 1896. 658p. map.

An excellent example of pioneering fieldwork carried out by a British medical doctor in 1889-1891 in unexplored Kafiristan. As an anthropological monograph it has few 19th-century equals and it remains to this day the most important study of the peoples of the region now known as Nuristan. Serious readers will find Lennart Edelberg's index to the volume (q.v.) invaluable. The book was reprinted by Oxford University Press, Karachi in 1974.

## 113 Leaves from an Afghan scrapbook.

Ernest Thornton, Annie Thornton. London: John Murray, 1910. 225p.

Ernest Thornton, in the employ of Amir Abdur Rahman in 1892-93, and Amir Habibullah in 1902-1908, lived and worked in Kabul, setting up a tannery and boot factory in the days when heavy machinery was pulled from Peshawar to the Afghan capital by elephants.

## 114 Lives of Indian officers illustrative of the history of the civil and military service of India: Henry Martyn, Sir Charles Metcalf, Sir Alexander Burnes, Captain Conolly, Major Pottinger.

John William Kaye. London: Strahan, 1869. 494p. (Lives of Indian Officers).

Informative biographical accounts of three of the most famous English officer-explorers of Afghanistan: Alexander Burnes, Arthur Conolly, and Eldred Pottinger.

## 115 Memoir of William Watts McNair, late of 'Connaught House,' Mussooree, of the Indian Survey Department, the first European explorer of Kafiristan.

J. E. Howard. London: D. J. Keymer, 1889. 83p.

This is an interesting account of the professional life and travels of a member of the Indian Survey Department, made more interesting by the controversy surrounding McNair's claim to have entered the Bashgal Valley of eastern Kafiristan. There is no doubt about his travels through Swat and Chitral, but on the evidence he himself presents it seems doubtful if he ever set foot in the Bashgal Valley or any other part of Kafiristan. The secret records of the India Office Library in London reveal that both Sir George Robertson and Sir William Lockhart also disputed his claim. See McNair's article 'A visit to Kafiristan' (q.v.).

## 116 The mission to Kandahar with appendices and supplementary report of the expedition into upper Meeráwzye and Koorrum in 1856.

H. B. Lumsden. Calcutta: C. B. Lewis, 1860. 282p. maps.

A report on political and military leaders in Afghanistan, together with information on the army, its officers, their policies, rules and regulations, arms and equipment, administration, and government. The appendices, of which there are ten, provide details of various routes, accounts of tribes and clans, field sports, trade and traders, Kafiristan and its people, and notes on the flora of the country. This is a remarkable intelligence report, even by the high standards of the British Raj, and an impressive example of early documentation on the Great Game.

117  **Narrative of various journeys in Balochistan, Afghanistan, the Panjab, and Kalât, during a residence in those countries to which is added an account of the insurrection at Kalât and a memoir on eastern Balochistan.**
Charles Masson. London: Richard Bentley, 1844. 4 vols. map.

In the 19th century a remarkable band of resourceful travellers and explorers made their way into Afghanistan, none of whom was more remarkable or mysterious than Charles Masson. Thought by some to be an American, it was revealed decades after his death that he was English, his real name was James Lewis, and that he was a deserter from the Bengal Artillery. From 1826, he travelled some fifteen years in Afghanistan and neighbouring regions and this account is among the most interesting and valuable records ever written. Sir Thomas Holdich, writing in *The gates of India* (q.v.), remarked that 'the most amazing feature of Masson's tales of travel is that in all essential features we knew little more about the country of the Afghans after the last war with Afghanistan than he could have told us before the first'. A large collection of Masson's drawings and unpublished papers are to be found in the India Office Library and Records Office, 197 Blackfriars Road, London SE1 8NG.

118  **Ney Elias, explorer and envoy extraordinary in high Asia.**
Gerald Morgan. London: George Allen & Unwin, 1971. 294p. map. bibliog.

A biography of the noted Victorian explorer Ney Elias (1844-97) who went to China at the age of 22, crossed the Gobi Desert from the Great Wall of China to Novgorod, joined the Indian Foreign Office, and travelled widely in South and Central Asia between 1877 and 1889. He also explored the Pamirs, the Oxus, Badakshan, and Balkh, adding much to the geographical knowledge of northern Afghanistan.

119  **Northern Afghanistan, or letters from the Afghan Boundary Commission.**
C. E. Yate. Edinburgh; London: William Blackwood, 1888. 430p. maps.

Personal experiences of an officer who was with the British Commission in western and northern Afghanistan in 1885-87. He describes Herat and the country lying between it and Balkh, Mazar-i-Sherif, and Tashkurghan, as well as the road from the North to Kabul. It is written in the best style and tradition of the British officer serving in the field.

120  **The Pamirs and the source of the Oxus.**
George Nathaniel Curzon. *The Geographical Journal.* vol. 8. (1896), p. 15-54, 97-119, 239-64.

An account of Central Asian exploration with a summary of earlier travels and travellers in the region. This is an authoritative work by the eminent Victorian traveller, politician, and diplomat who became Viceroy of India.

121 **A peep into Toorkisthan.**
Captain Rollo Burslem. London: Pelham Richardson, 1846. 240p. map.

A narrative of a journey made during 'a few weeks snatched from a soldier's life in Affghanistan...' in the year 1840. The author, although travelling through country to the north and west of Kabul which few Europeans had then seen, modestly refers to his journey as a 'ramble' and gives a good deal of valuable geographical and ethnographical information.

122 **A person from England and other travellers.**
Fitzroy Maclean. London: Jonathan Cape, 1958. 384p. map. bibliog.

A masterly account of some of the leading figures in the European exploration of Central Asia. Although mainly concerned with the geographical regions north of the Hindu Kush, the events described are part of the larger history of 19th-century Afghanistan - particularly Anglo-Russian rivalries in Central Asia.

123 **A personal narrative of a visit to Ghuzni, Kabul, and Afghanistan, and of a residence at the Court of Dost Mohamed: with notices of Runjit Sing, Khiva, and the Russian expedition.**
Godfrey Thomas Vigne. London: Whittaker, 1840. 479p. map.

G. T. Vigne was among the early European travellers in Afghanistan, being a contemporary of the legendary Charles Masson. In this book he describes the country he travelled through and the people he met in eastern Afghanistan.

124 **Report of 'the Mirza's' exploration from Caubul to Kashgar.**
Thomas George Montgomerie. *Journal of the Royal Geographical Society.* vol. 41. (1871), p. 132-93.

In the 19th century officers of the Survey of India frequently employed trained 'natives' to explore the regions beyond the frontiers of India. These men travelled in disguise, took great risks, and occasionally failed to return. The Mirza contributed much to the geographical knowledge of eastern Afghanistan between the First and the Second Afghan Wars.

125 **A ride to Khiva: travels and adventures in Central Asia.**
Fred Burnaby. London: Cassell Petter & Galpin, 1878. 487p. maps.

Essentially a book of travels, this contains a description of Russian expansion in Central Asia and routes in Afghanistan drawn up by various Russian officers. The author also quotes Russian writers who have their own 'Forward Policies'.

126 **The road to Kabul, an anthology.**
Edited by Gerald de Gaury, H. V. F. Winstone. London; Melbourne: Quartet, 1981. 235p. maps.

The editors have searched through accounts of Central Asian travel and picked out an array of European writings to produce this collection. Everything is here from Marco Polo to Francis Younghusband and from Mogul Emperors to Rudyard Kipling. Half a dozen of the twenty-eight selections are about Afghanistan.

127 **A scetch on Kaffiristan & the Kafirs.**
Alexander Gardner, introduced by Schuyler Jones. *Afghanistan Journal.* vol. 4, no. 2. (1977), p. 47-53.
Transcript of an original handwritten manuscript dated 'Cashmear 20th Octr / 69' which is held in the Centre of South Asian Studies, University of Cambridge. It appears, however, to be a document which reveals more about the author than about the subject it addresses.

128 **Soldier and traveller, memoirs of Alexander Gardner, Colonel of artillery in the service of Maharaja Ranjit Singh.**
Alexander Gardner, edited by Major Hugh Pearse. Edinburgh; London: William Blackwood, 1898. 359p.
The life of an adventurer whose origins are obscure and some of whose adventures are suspect. Although Gardner claimed to have travelled widely in Afghanistan and particularly in Kafiristan in the 1820s, there is nothing to support this except his own journals and these do not inspire confidence. See his paper *A scetch on Kaffiristan & the Kafirs* (q.v.) and C. Grey and H. L. O. Garrett's *European adventurers of northern India, 1785-1849* (q.v.).

129 **Tales of travel.**
George Nathanial Curzon. New York: George H. Doran, 1923. 405p.
Chapter two contains a description of Amir Abdur Rahman, his personality, and his career, based on personal observations made when the author was the Amir's guest in 1894. Another essay in chapter nine offers practical suggestions, now perhaps somewhat dated, regarding the matter of appropriate dress for anyone invited to meet a head of state in Asia.

130 **Through the unknown Pamirs: the second Danish Pamirs expedition, 1898-1899.**
Ole Olufsen. London: William Heineman, 1904. 229p. maps.
An account by the famous Danish explorer of his expedition along the frontiers of northern and northeastern Afghanistan in the last years of the 19th century.

131 **Travels in the Himalayan provinces of Hindustan and the Panjab; in Ladakh and Kashmir; in Peshawar, Kabul, Kunduz, and Bokhara [in the years] 1819-1825.**
William Moorcroft, George Trebeck. London: John Murray, 1841. 2 vols.
The personal narrative of this early journey through Afghanistan is found in volume two, part four, chapters one to four. Moorcroft, a veterinary surgeon, died at Andkhui and was buried at Balkh in 1825. His writings provide an interesting glimpse of Afghanistan as it was in the early years of the 19th century.

132 **Travels into Bokhara; containing the narrative of a voyage on the Indus from the sea to Lahore...and an account of a journey from India to Cabool, Tartary, and Persia, performed by order of the supreme government of India, in the years 1831, 32, and 33.**

Alexander Burnes. London: John Murray, 1835. 3 vols. map.

The information on Afghanistan is contained in volumes two and three, beginning with the author's arrival in Peshawar in 1832, then under the rule of Kabul. From the Afghan capital the traveller continued across the Hindu Kush to Kunduz and on to Balkh and Bokhara. Volume three contains a chapter on the Hindu Kush, an historical account of Afghanistan during the first quarter of the 19th century, its political organization, and its trade and commerce. Burnes was an enterprising traveller, keen observer, and able writer.

133 **Travels with the Afghan boundary commission.**

A. C. Yate. Edinburgh; London: William Blackwood, 1887. 481p. maps.

The author was a member of the 1884-85 commission which was set up to demarcate part of the boundaries between Persia and Afghanistan, and Russia and Afghanistan. The book describes his travels and experiences in the field from Quetta through Baluchistan to the Helmand River and then north to Herat and the Russian frontier.

134 **Under the absolute Amir.**

Frank A. Martin. London: Harper, 1907. 330p.

A personal account of eight years spent in Afghanistan in an era when it took a week to travel from Peshawar to Kabul if the going was good. Martin provides an interesting picture of the country and the people as viewed through the eyes of an English engineer during the last days of Abdur Rahman's reign and the first years of Habibullah's reign.

135 **A visit to Kafiristan.**

W. W. McNair. *Proceedings of the Royal Geographical Society.* vol. 6 (new series). (1884), p. 1-18.

The suspicion that McNair never actually reached Kafiristan is not dispelled by reading this account. It remains a minor geographical curiosity and is perhaps explained by the fact that, for much of the 19th century, Kafiristan was regarded by Europeans as the last unexplored region of Central Asia. Many aspired to the honour and recognition that would go to the man responsible for its unveiling.

136 **When men and mountains meet: explorers of the western Himalayas, 1820-1875.**

John Keay. London: John Murray, 1977. 277p. maps. bibliog.

A fascinating account of the men who explored the Hindu Kush, the Karakorams, and the Pamirs, their adventures, and the political rivalry between Britain and Russia that lay behind it all. Here are gathered the great travellers and explorers of Afghanistan: Charles Masson, William Moorcroft, Joseph Wolff, Godfrey Vigne, Alexander Burnes, John Wood, and the enigmatic Alexander Gardner. The book provides a valuable background to understanding Britain's interests in Afghanistan and why she persisted in sending her armies into that country for over seventy years.

# 20th Century

### 137 Nuristan: lost world of the Hindu Kush.
Schuyler Jones. In: *Mountain people.* Edited by Michael Tobias. Norman, Oklahoma; London: University of Oklahoma, 1986. 219p. maps. bibliog.

A short general illustrated article on the land of Nuristan and its people written for a popular audience.

### 138 Adventures in Afghanistan.
Louis Palmer. London: Octagon, 1990. 239p. map.

The reader is left wondering if this is fact or fiction. The author's abstract, impressionistic style, together with his view that a full stop normally marks the end of a paragraph, and the difficulties of finding anything either interesting or real in what he has to say, makes this almost unreadable.

### 139 Afghan interlude.
Oliver Rudston de Baer. London: Chatto & Windus, 1957. 223p. maps.

A light-hearted account of an overland expedition made in 1955 by a number of Cambridge University students, during which the members drove out to Afghanistan, toured various parts of the country, and drove back to England, all in one summer.

### 140 Afghan journey.
Ben James. London: Jonathan Cape, 1935. 285p. map.

An account of a journey through the country undertaken in the early 1930s which is described in such a manner as to leave the reader to sort out which passages recount first-hand experiences, which have been picked up from written accounts, and which were made up on the spot. It is not up to the publisher's usual standards. The endpaper maps are curious in the extreme, but the quality of the black-and-white illustrations is unusually good.

### 141 Afghan quest, the story of the Abinger Afghanistan expedition of 1960.
Joyce Dunsheath, Eleanor Baillie. London; Toronto: George G. Harrap, 1961. 236p. map.

The authors present an account of this mountaineering expedition in which they make their way up the Panjshir Valley, subsequently reaching the top of the Anjuman Pass for a view of the Pamirs.

31

142 **Afghanistan, cockpit in high Asia.**
Peter King. London: Geoffrey Bles, 1966. 224p. map.
An undistinguished travel book interesting mainly for a chapter on 'Nuristan, the home of the Aryans' in which a wholly fictional journey to Nuristan is presented as fact. Among numerous other curiosities we are told that Chaga Sarai in the Kunar Valley lies at an altitude of 12,000 feet (twice the altitude of Kabul) and that villagers in Kamdesh were 'working with stone knives and axes of great keenness'. The author then claims to have travelled on horseback and foot from Kamdesh to Bamiyan via Panjshir - a journey which, if undertaken, would have made a book in itself, but which he passes over in three paragraphs. Louis Dupree described it as 'the worst book about Afghanistan I ever read'.

143 **Afghanistan: en norsk leges reise i Hindu-Kusj-landet.**
(Afghanistan: a Norwegian doctor's journey in the land of the Hindu Kush.)
Leiv Kreyberg. Oslo: J. W. Cappelen, 1951. 165p. map. bibliog.
A personal account of travels in the country shortly after the end of the Second World War. In addition to the usual tours, Kreyberg visits hospitals, clinics, and the medical faculty, discusses the reforms of King Amanullah, and provides a chapter on ancient coins and the light they throw on Afghanistan's history.

144 **Afghanistan, land of the high flags.**
Rosanne Klass. London: Adventurers Club, 1966. 224p. map.
Personal experiences of an American woman who went to the country in 1951 and stayed some two years to teach English.

145 **After you, Marco Polo.**
Jean Bowie Shor. New York; Toronto; London: McGraw-Hill, 1955. 294p. map.
During the course of this journey the author crossed northern Afghanistan from Herat to Maimena, Mazar-i-Sherif and Faizabad, going as far as the end of the Wakhan corridor, with a side trip to Kabul. Photographs and articles by the same author from this journey appeared in the *National Geographic Magazine* (q.v.).

146 **Along the Koh-i-Baba and Hari-Rud.**
Ahmad Ali Kohzad. *Afghanistan*. vol. 6, nos. 1 & 2; vol. 7, no. 1. (1951; 1952), p. 1-16; p. 1-21; p. 50-55.
An historian's diary of a journey from Kabul to Herat via Bamiyan and the Hazarajat in the 1950s. At the time it had just become feasible to make this journey by car.

147 **An American engineer in Afghanistan.**
A. C. Jewett. Minneapolis, Minnesota: University of Minnesota, 1948. 335p.
First-hand account of life in Afghanistan, written by a man who lived there from 1911 to 1919, working on the installation of a hydro-electric plant for Kabul.

148 **Between Oxus and Jumna.**
Arnold J. Toynbee. London: Oxford University Press, 1961. 211p. map.
The author's account of his six-month journey in 1960 through India, Pakistan, and Afghanistan. It is a superior but very readable book of travels.

149 **Beyond Khyber Pass.**
Lowell Thomas. London: Hutchinson, [n.d.]. 223p.
An account of a car journey from Peshawar to Kabul, made in about 1924 by the American journalist, traveller, and author, Lowell Thomas.

150 **Bold horsemen of the steppes: Afghanistan's Turkomans hold fast to traditions of their nomadic forefathers, who once terrorized Central Asia.**
Sabrina Michaud, Roland Michaud. *National Geographic Magazine.* vol. 144, no. 5. (1973), p. 634-69. map.
Like many *National Geographic* articles, this is a fine photo-essay held together by a few pages of undistinguished text. It describes the Turkmen people of northern Afghanistan, with an emphasis on horses and horsemanship.

151 **The cruel way.**
Ella K. Maillart. London; Toronto: William Heinemann, 1947. 217p. map. bibliog.
The record of a 1939 journey by motor car from Geneva to India by this well-known traveller of Asian byways. The title does not refer so much to the road as to the relationship between the writer and her travelling companion. Maillart ably sketches a vision, now vanished, of Afghanistan as it was on the eve of the Second World War.

152 **Danziger's travels: beyond forbidden frontiers.**
Nick Danziger. London: Paladin, 1988. 426p. maps.
Part of this travel book (p. 123-81) records the author's personal experiences in Afghanistan. There is much about the author's experiences, but little about the country. His journey with the *Mujahideen* took him from Herat to Quetta, by-passing Kandahar. There are no photographs to record this part of the journey as in some areas he was not allowed to take pictures and in others his camera was lost.

153 **Desert, marsh, and mountain: the world of a nomad.**
Wilfred Thesiger. London: Collins, 1979. 304p. maps.
Part of this book (p. 224-65) is concerned with the author's travels during the 1950s and 1960s in the Hazarajat in central Afghanistan and Nuristan in the north-eastern part of the country. There are two maps and numerous black-and-white photographs.

### 154  The Hazaras of central Afghanistan.
Wilfred Thesiger. *The Geographical Journal.* vol. 71, no. 3. (1955), p. 312-19. map.

The author travelled through the Hazarajat in 1954 and collected 211 specimens of plants which are now in the British Museum of Natural History. The article describes the Hazaras, their modes of livelihood, their settlements, and the environment they inhabit.

### 155  In the footsteps of Alexander the Great.
Helen Schreider, Frank Schreider. *National Geographic Magazine.* vol. 133, no. 1. (1968), p. 1-65.

An illustrated article by an American couple who make an overland journey across South Asia to Afghanistan in a Land Rover called Bucephalus.

### 156  A journey through Afghanistan: a memorial.
David Chaffetz. Chicago; London: University of Chicago, 1981. 258p.

A travel book written by a young American to celebrate a journey in western, north-western, and northern Afghanistan made shortly before the Soviet invasion. The purpose of the journey was to meet nomads, but the bulk of the narrative is about the writer's journeys by bus, lorry, and on horseback.

### 157  A journey to Nuristan.
Wilfred Thesiger. *The Geographical Journal.* vol. 123. (1957), p. 457-64. map. bibliog.

In 1956 the author travelled up the Panjshir Valley, crossed the Chamar pass, and entered the western borderlands of Nuristan. After visiting Kulam he descended the Alingar River to Jalalabad. His illustrated article provides geographical and ethnographic information.

### 158  Land des Lichtes, deutsche Rundfahrt zu unbekannten Völkern im Hindukusch.
(Land of light, a German expedition to an unknown people in the Hindu Kush.)
Albert Herrlich. Munich, Germany: Knorr & Hirth, 1938. 180p. maps.

An informal account of the 1935 German Hindu Kush Expedition to Chitral and Afghanistan, this deals mainly with the journey through Nuristan (hence the title). Even after half a century, it remains one of the very few book-length accounts of the region. The official account of the expedition was edited by Arnold Scheibe and published in 1937 under the title *Deutsche im Hindukusch, Bericht der deutschen Hindukusch-Expedition 1935 der deutschen Forschungsgemeinschaft* (q.v.).

159 **The light garden of the angel king: journeys in Afghanistan.**
Peter Levi. London: Collins, 1972. 287p. map.
An entertaining and erudite book of travel, very much what one might expect from
the man who was later elected Oxford Professor of Poetry. The journey was made
in 1969 in the company of Bruce Chatwin and a good many out-of-the-way places
were visited, including Nuristan.

160 **Mandana Baschi, Reisen und Erlebnisse eines deutschen Arztes in
Afghanistan.**
(Mandana Baschi [May you never be tired!]: life and travels of a
German doctor in Afghanistan.)
F. Börnstein-Bosta. Berlin: Reimar Hobbing, 1925. 176p. map.
The doctor set out in 1923, travelling to Moscow and then by boat down the Volga
and on to the Aral Sea from where he made his way, mostly by horseback, to Herat.
He reached Kabul only three months after setting out and remained in the country
until June 1924. The narrative is mainly concerned with personal experiences and
adventures.

161 **The minaret of Djam, an excursion in Afghanistan.**
Freya Stark. London: John Murray, 1970. 99p. map. bibliog.
A travel diary of journeys made in the late 1960s, partly with the object of visiting
the 12th-century Ghorid minaret in western Afghanistan which gives the book its
title.

162 **The narrow smile: a journey back to the North-West Frontier.**
Peter Mayne. London: John Murray, 1955. 264p. maps.
A light-hearted and somewhat self-conscious travel book, this records the personal
experiences of an Englishman who returns, in the immediate post-independence
years, to the scenes of his RAF days to wander in remote valleys along the Afghan
border, making a side trip to visit Kabul.

163 **North from Kabul.**
Andrew Wilson. London: George Allen & Unwin, 1961. 190p. map.
An account of an overland journey in 1959 from Iran through Afghanistan in which
irony. humour, and modest adventures are mixed in roughly equal quantities.

164 **Notes of a journey.**
A. Hashmat. *Afghanistan.* vol. 3, no. 4. (1948), p. 30-43.
Diary of an Afghan who travelled in Nuristan and Badakhshan with Knud Paludan
and Lennart Edelberg during part of the Third Danish Central Asian Expedition
which took place during 1947-49.

165 **The people of the Khyber: the Pathans of Pakistan.**
James W. Spain. New York: Frederick A. Praeger, 1963. 190p. map.
As the definition of an 'Afghan' is one whose mother tongue is Pashto, this book
is relevant, though it is mainly about Afghans who live on the Pakistan side of the

Durand Line. In what is first and foremost a book of travels, the author writes of his journey to Kabul in chapter 16.

166  **A Persian spring.**
Wilfrid Blunt. London: James Barrie, 1957. 252p. map.
A cultured, witty travel book in the grand manner designed to entertain and inform the armchair traveller; this is a poor man's *Road to Oxiana* (q.v.). Chapters eight to ten concern the author's visit to Herat in western Afghanistan.

167  **Resa till Afghanistan.**
(Journey to Afghanistan.)
Paul Mohn. Stockholm: P. A. Norstedt & Söners, 1930. 364p.
A first-class, serious travel book, written by a well-informed and perceptive traveller who also represented Sweden at the Court in Kabul. The book provides an unusually clear and accurate picture of the country as it was in the 1920s.

168  **The road to Oxiana.**
Robert Byron. London: John Lehmann, 1937. 292p. map.
Parts three and five of this justly famous travel book contain an account of the author's visits to Afghanistan in 1933 and 1934. Byron's sharp eye misses little and he wields an able pen to bring to the reader both his personal experiences and the glories of Islamic architecture.

169  **A short walk in the Hindu Kush.**
Eric Newby. London: Secker & Warburg, 1958. 246p. map.
This is a justly famous light-hearted account of travel and adventure in the wilderness by an escapee from the London rag trade who proves that an unlikely background, an implausible project, a sharp eye, keen wit, and able pen can combine to produce an enduring travel book.

170  **The tent pegs of heaven: a journey through Afghanistan.**
Lucie Street. London: Travel Book Club, 1967. 189p. map.
Personal experiences of an English woman who travelled in northern and eastern Afghanistan from Kabul to Bamiyan and from the Amu Darya River to Jalalabad.

171  **Three women of Herat.**
Veronica Doubleday. London: Jonathan Cape, 1988. 225p. maps.
Life in Herat in the 1970s as seen by an English musicologist who lived and worked there with her husband John Baily. The book's remarkable strength is that it provides an account of the world of women behind the compound walls and the veil  an aspect of life in Afghanistan that few foreigners see, and fewer still come to understand.

172  **Through the heart of Afghanistan.**
Emil Trinkler. London: Faber & Gwyer, 1928. 246p. map.
The author, a geographer, travelled across Russia to reach the Afghan border south of Merv in August 1923. He then made his way to Herat and on across Afghanistan

to Kabul, travelling through the centre of the country on horseback. He spent the winter there, investigating coal and iron deposits, observed an eclipse of the moon, and proceeded on to India in March of 1924. This account consists of Trinkler's personal experiences and geographical observations.

### 173  A tour through Afghanistan.
J. C. French. *Journal of the Royal Central Asian Society.* vol. 20, pt. 1. (1933), p. 27-45. map.

An account of the author's experiences, with historical and geographical asides, encountered in the course of a journey by car across Afghanistan from Jalalabad to Herat and from Kandahar to Bamiyan.

### 174  A trip to the Oxus.
H.R.H. Prince Peter of Greece. *Journal of the Royal Central Asian Society.* vol. 34, pt. 1. (1947), p. 51-55. maps.

An informal account of a journey by road from Mazar-i-Sherif to the Oxus (Amu Darya) at a point opposite Termez, a journey which few foreigners have been allowed to make in this century.

### 175  Under a sickle moon; a journey through Afghanistan.
Peregrine Hodson. London: Sphere, 1986. 226p. maps.

A narrative account of a journey made in 1984 through eastern Afghanistan during the Soviet occupation.

### 176  Wakhan: or how to vary a route.
H. W. Tilman. *Journal of the Royal Central Asian Society.* vol. 35, pts. 3-4. (1948), p. 249-54. maps.

A British mountaineer travels from Kashgar to Chitral via the Wakhan Corridor.

### 177  We took the highroad in Afghanistan.
Jean B. Shor, Franc Shor. *National Geographic Magazine.* vol. 98, no. 5. (1950), p. 673-706. map.

An account of the travels and adventures experienced by an American couple who went to the Wakhan Corridor by road from Kabul and made their way up toward the Chinese frontier on foot and horseback.

### 178  West from the Khyber Pass.
William O. Douglas, Mercedes H. Douglas. *National Geographic Magazine.* vol. 114, no. 1. (1958), p. 1-44. map.

A member of the US Supreme Court drives across Afghanistan via the north *en route* from Peshawar to Baghdad by car.

**In Persia and Afghanistan with the Citroën trans-Asiatic expedition.**
*See* item no. 58.

**Travel and Exploration.** 20th Century

**Some notes on a recent journey in Afghanistan.**
*See* item no. 75.

**The upper basin of the Kabul River.**
*See* item no. 77.

**The gates of India, being an historical narrative.**
*See* item no. 262.

**From Herat to Kabul.**
*See* item no. 922.

# Flora and Fauna

179 **Botanical literature of Afghanistan.**
S.-W. Breckle, W. Frey, I. C. Hedge. *Notes from the Royal Botanic Garden Edinburgh.* vol. 29. (1969), p. 357-71. bibliog.
A valuable bibliographic survey of publications relating to phanerogams (flowering plants), cryptogams (non-flowering plants), and the vegetation of Afghanistan in general. Although mainly concerned with indigenous plants, it also contains references to cultivated plants and the geography, climate, and ecology of the country. A supplement to this work appeared in *Notes from the Royal Botanic Garden Edinburgh*, vol. 33, no. 3 (1975), containing a significant number of additions to the original survey.

180 **Flora Iranica: Flora des Iranischen Hochlandes und der umrahmenden Gebirge, Persien, Afghanistan, Teile von West-Pakistan, Nord-Iraq, Azerbaidjan, Turkmenistan.**
(Flora Iranica: Flora of the Iranian uplands and the surrounding mountains [in] Persia, Afghanistan, parts of west Pakistan, northern Iraq, Azerbaijan, and Turkmenistan.)
Karl Heinz Rechinger. Graz, Austria: Akademische Druck-u. Verlagsanstalt, 1963-. (Flora Iranica).
A comprehensive description and classification of all species of plants gathered in the region by many botanists over several decades. The first fascicule, on Araceae, was published in December, 1963. The most recent, on Pontederiaceae, was issued in May, 1990. By the spring of 1990 nearly 170 fascicules had been published under the general editorship of Karl Heinz Rechinger of Vienna. Much of the text in each issue is in Latin, though with supplementary descriptions in German. For each plant type the exact find sites, together with altitude, known distribution, and other details are given. The issues vary in length from four pages to 600 pages and are illustrated with line drawings and photographs.

## Flora and Fauna

181 **On the birds of Afghanistan.**
Knud Paludan. Copenhagen: C. A. Reitzel, 1959. 333p. maps. bibliog. (Videnskabelige Meddelelser fra Dansk Naturhistorisk Forening i København, vol. 122).

The author, an ornithologist and a member of the Third Danish Expedition to Central Asia, travelled widely in Afghanistan in 1947-1949, collecting and observing birds in all parts of the country. The text provides detailed descriptions of the routes followed, the relief, vegetation, and other conditions found. He recorded 389 species, each of which is described here.

182 **Soma, divine mushroom of immortality.**
R. Gordon Wasson. New York: Harcourt Brace Jovanovich, 1968. 381p. maps.

One of the mysteries encountered by all who study the ancient history of Central Asia is the identity of the sacred plant *Soma* which is mentioned in the *Rig Veda*. The author presents convincing evidence to show that it was the hallucinogenic mushroom Amanita muscaria (Fly agaric) which is known to have been used up until recent times in shamanistic rites in Siberia. In his search for evidence, Wasson travelled, among other places, into remote areas of Afghanistan, and his enquiry ranges across the fields of archaeology, linguistics, ethnobotany, folklore, and plant ecology. A highly readable and fascinating book.

# Archaeology

183  **Evidence of a fire cult at Tapa Sardâr, Ghazni (Afghanistan).**
Maurizio Taddei. In: *South Asian Archaeology, 1981.* Edited by Bridget Allchin. Cambridge, England: Cambridge University, 1984. p. 263-70. map. bibliog.

A consideration of possible fire altars at Gandharan sites in eastern Afghanistan derived from archaeological field research at Ghazni. The author concludes that 'shrine 87' at Tapa Sardâr (itself a Buddhist sanctuary) may 'be the only possible fire altar found in Afghanistan besides that of Surkh Kotal'.

184  **Gandharan imagery at Tapa Sardâr.**
Giovanni Verardi. In: *South Asian Archaeology, 1981.* Edited by Bridget Allchin. Cambridge, England: Cambridge University Press, 1984. p. 257-62. bibliog.

It is the author's view, based on an examination of finds from the partially excavated site, that the Buddhist world had during the Kusâna period reached a strong cultural unity in Gandhara and Central Asia: 'there are no significant differences between what was made north of the Hindu Kush and what was made south of it'.

185  **Afghanistan's importance from the viewpoint of the history and archaeology of Central Asia.**
A. H. Habibi. *Afghanistan.* vol. 20, no. 4. (1968), p. 1-19.

A general account of the country's history, drawn from archaeological remains and historical documents. It is divided into two periods: prehistoric and historical.

186  **An ancient Hindu temple in eastern Afghanistan.**
J. E. van Lohuizen-de Leeuw. *Oriental Art.* vol. 5, no. 2 (new series). (1959), p. 3-11.

A discussion, based on Lennart Edelberg's findings, of the sculptured stone blocks which lie in the Muslim cemetery above Chaga Sarai in the Kunar Valley of eastern Afghanistan. The author concludes that the stones indicate the former existence at that spot, not of a Buddhist stupa as Edelberg suggested (q.v.), but of a Hindu temple 'belonging to the middle phase of the medieval architecture of North-West India of about the 8th or the 9th century' AD.

### 187 The archaeological exploration of Afghanistan: results achieved and prospects for the future.
Daniel Schlumberger. *Afghanistan*. vol. 2, no. 4. (1947), p. 1-21.
A general geographical and historical survey of the pre-Islamic archaeology of Afghanistan, by the Director of DAFA (Délégation Archéologique Française en Afghanistan).

### 188 Archaeological gazetteer of Afghanistan.
Warwick Ball. Paris: Editions Recherche sur les Civilisations, 1982. 2 vols. maps. bibliog.
An indispensable reference work on the archaeological sites of the country. Each site is listed in alphabetical order and the exact location is given, together with information as to who carried out the fieldwork and when. There is a bibliography of sources and an atlas which includes both location maps and site plans.

### 189 Archaeological research.
Walter A. Fairservis. *Afghanistan*. vol. 6, no. 4. (1950), p. 31-34.
A summary report on the work of the First Afghan Expedition of the American Museum of Natural History in the Helmand Valley (1950).

### 190 Archaeology in Afghanistan.
Mohammed Nabi Kohzad. *Afghanistan*. vol. 11, no. 4. (1956), p. 1-8.
A brief overview of the principal archaeological sites in the country, a survey of archaeological research carried out, and short notes on the Kabul Museum.

### 191 Archaeology in Afghanistan.
A. A. Motamedi. *Afghanistan*. vol. 20, no. 3. (1967), p. 28-34.
A survey of archaeological research in the country, with a brief history of the various archaeological missions and a description of the main sites found and excavated.

### 192 Archaeology in Soviet Central Asia.
Grégoire Frumkin. Leiden, Netherlands: E. J. Brill, 1970. 217p. maps. bibliog. (Handbuch der Orientalistik, Siebente Abteilung, III Band, 1 Abschnitt).
As many of the present cultures of Central Asia are represented both north and south of the Amu Darya River it is scarcely surprising that archaeological finds from much earlier periods are found across the whole of south Central Asia, regardless of present-day political frontiers. This book, therefore, despite its title, is of importance for any scholar interested in the archaeology of Afghanistan. A forty-page annotated bibliography makes the volume particularly useful.

193 **The archaeology of Afghanistan from earliest times to the Timurid period.**
Edited by F. R. Allchin, Norman Hammond. London; New York: Academic, 1978. 471p. maps. bibliog.
A lavishly illustrated work which begins with a geographical account of the country and goes on to examine the palaeolithic period, the later prehistoric periods, the early historic period (Achaemenids and Greeks), the pre-Muslim period, Islam and the Mongol invasion, and the period from the Mongols to the Moguls. Previous archaeological work in the country is summarized, sites are described and discussed, and principal finds are shown.

194 **Archeology and metallurgical technology in prehistoric Afghanistan, India, and Pakistan.**
C. C. Lamberg-Karlovsky. *American Anthropologist.* vol. 69. (1967), p. 145-62. map. bibliog.
As a wide range of copper and bronze objects appear in the earliest levels of Indus Valley sites and as these are 'far beyond an experimental stage' the author suggests that the technology has been brought to the area from the west. In Afghanistan the site of Mundigak has produced the earliest known metal in this area, suggesting a date of ca. 3,100 BC 'for the inception of a metallurgy in Afghanistan'.

195 **Ariana Antiqua: a descriptive account of the antiques and coins of Afghanistan, with a memoir on the buildings called topes, by C. Masson, Esq.**
H. H. Wilson. London: The Honourable Court of Directors of the East India Company, 1841. 452p. map.
An historical, numismatic, and archaeological survey of the early periods relating to Afghanistan with notices of Ariana (the name of a region roughly corresponding to present-day Afghanistan and synonymous with Ancient Afghanistan), the Kings of Bactria, the Buddhist period, the Indo-Parthians, the Indo-Scythians, the Sassanians, and the Hindus. Much of the material evidence on which Wilson's study is based was obtained by Charles Masson (*pseud. for* James Lewis) during the many years he spent in Afghanistan. Masson's own annotated copy of this book is in the Indian Institute Library, Oxford.

196 **Bamian, Führer zu den buddhistischen Hohlenklöstern und Klossalstatuen.**
(Bamiyan, a guide to the Buddhist cave-monastaries and the great statues.)
Joseph Hackin, Ria Hackin. Paris: Les Éditions d'Art et d'Histoire, 1939. 68p. map. (Publication de la Délégation Archéologique Française en Afghanistan).
An historical and archaeological guide to one of the most famous Buddhist sites in Central Asia, with photographs, plans, and drawings. The text is in German.

Archaeology

197  **Bamiyan, Afghanistan: study of cultural heritage.**
Abdul Wasay Najimi. Peshawar, Pakistan: UNOCA, Peshawar, June 1990. 52p. maps. (Mission Reports).
A survey of the famous Buddhist monuments of Bamiyan together with a detailed report on their condition in the spring of 1990 after a decade of war, and proposals and recommendations for their immediate preservation and reconstruction needs. Written by an architect and town planner, this report also includes information and recommendations about other sites in east Afghanistan.

198  **Bamiyan: symbol of Indo-Afghan cultural unity.**
Mohammed Ali. *Afghanistan.* vol. 16, no. 2. (1961), p. 1-7.
A description of one of the largest and most famous Buddhist sites in Central Asia with references to Buddhism in India. The author seeks to show that both Afghanistan and India have a common historical and cultural background.

199  **Beyond the Oxus: archaeology, art and architecture of Central Asia.**
Edgar Knobloch. London: Ernest Benn, 1972. 256p. maps. bibliog.
Geographically speaking, the centre of gravity of this book lies north of the Oxus, but the subjects with which it deals are all closely related to, if not actually part of, the art, archaeology, and architecture of Afghanistan. Chapter eleven deals with the main sites south of the Oxus.

200  **The Buddhist monastery of Fonduqistan.**
Joseph Hackin. *Afghanistan.* vol. 5, no. 2. (1950), p. 19-35.
An illustrated account of the archaeological work carried out at a Buddhist site 117 kilometres north-west of Kabul in the district of Ghorband. This is a posthumous publication as the author and his wife died in 1941 while carrying out a wartime mission to occupied France.

201  **A Chinese handle-bearing mirror from northern Afghanistan.**
William Trousdale. *Afghanistan.* vol. 19, no. 4. (1964), p. 27-38.
An illustrated article describing a bronze Chinese mirror from the Kunduz area, the first-known example to be found in Afghanistan. Its similarity to one in the Hermitage Museum in Leningrad, said to have been found in Kirghiz SSR, is noted. It is suggested that the Kunduz mirror may date from the 11th or early 12th centuries AD.

202  **A dash through the heart of Afghanistan, being [a] personal narrative of an archaeological tour with the Indian Cultural Mission.**
M. A. Shakur. Peshawar, Pakistan: The Author, 1947. 126p. maps.
An account of the author's month-long tour of Afghanistan in 1947 with Mortimer Wheeler and others as a member of the Government of India's Cultural Mission. They visited Kabul, Bamiyan, Kunduz, Mazar-i-Sherif, Balkh, Ghazni, and Kandahar.

203 **The excavation of the Afghan archaeological mission in Kapisa: a preliminary report on the first period.**
Shahibye Mustamandi, Mari Mustamandi. *Afghanistan.* vol. 20, no. 4. (1968), p. 67-79.
An illustrated report of excavations at a Buddhist site north of Kabul which revealed the base of a stupa 14 metres square. Gold coins found on the site are Kushan. Relief carvings, statues, and other artefacts were also found. The authors speculate that the site may have been part of the summer capital of the Kushan kings.

204 **Excavations at Kandahar, 1974, first interim report.**
David Whitehouse. *Afghan Studies.* vol. 1. (1978), p. 9-39. maps. bibliog.
The British Institute of Kabul, established in 1973, began a preliminary survey and excavation of the site of 'Old Kandahar' (Shar-i-Kuna) to the west of the modern city. This report, illustrated with maps, drawings, and photographs, describes progress during the first phase.

205 **Excavations at Kandahar, 1975, second interim report.**
Anthony McNicoll. *Afghan Studies.* vol. 1. (1978), p. 41-66. map. bibliog.
This second report provides an account of the 1975 season of excavations and is illustrated with photographs, drawings, plans, and sections.

206 **Excavations at 'the city and the famous fortress of Kandahar, the foremost place in all of Asia'.**
S. W. Helms. *Afghan Studies.* vol. 3-4. (1982), p. 1-24. maps. bibliog.
An illustrated historical/archaeological account of the Old City of Kandahar and a description of the excavations carried out there over six seasons.

207 **Excavations of the Kamar rock shelter: a preliminary report.**
Carelton S. Coon, Henry W. Coulter. *Afghanistan.* vol. 10, no. 1. (1955), p. 12-16.
Archaeological research at a prehistoric site eight miles north of Haïbak on the road between Pul-i-Khumri and Tashkurghan, with a description of the site and of the finds unearthed.

208 **Exploration of ancient sites in northern Afghanistan.**
Evert Barger. *The Geographical Journal.* vol. 93, no. 5. (1939), p. 377-98.
The account of a 1938 survey in which the author travelled some 2,000 miles to record archaeological sites.

Archaeology

209 **Fragments d'un stûpa dans la vallée du Kunar en Afghanistan.**
(Fragments of a stupa in the Kunar Valley, Afghanistan.)
Lennart Edelberg. *Arts Asiatiques.* tome 4, fasc. 3. (1957), p. 199-
207. map. (Annales du Musée Guimet et du Musée Cernuschi).
Description of some ancient ruins on the heights to the north of Chaga Sarai at the
confluence of the Kunar and the Pech rivers in eastern Afghanistan. The author
concluded that the ruins were of a Buddhist stupa, but see J. E. van Lohuizen-de
Leeuw's article 'An ancient Hindu temple in eastern Afghanistan' (q.v.).

210 **Geomorphic history of the Mundigak Valley.**
Rodman E. Snead. *Afghanistan Journal.* vol. 5, no. 2. (1978), p.
59-69. maps. bibliog.
A geographical description of the valley twenty miles north-west of Kandahar where
the 4,500-year-old tepe (mound) of Mundigak is located. The author was with the
team of archaeologists that examined the site in 1972.

211 **The golden hoard of Bactria from the Tillya-tepe excavations in northern Afghanistan.**
Victor Sarianidi. Leningrad; New York: Aurora Art, 1985. 259p.
An account of excavations carried out by Soviet archaeologists in 1978-79 in the
Shibarghan area, in the course of which nearly twenty thousand gold artefacts were
found in six 2,000-year-old graves. This richly illustrated book offers an interesting
non-technical narrative account of the two successful seasons, 166 superb colour
plates, and a detailed catalogue with black-and-white illustrations of all the finds at
the back. The artefacts are Graeco-Bactrian, Graeco-Roman, local Bactrian, Scytho-
Sarmatian, and eastern Iranian or Old Bactrian in style and origin.

212 **The Hephthalite inscriptions of Uruzgan.**
A. D. H. Bivar. *Afghanistan.* vol. 8, no. 4. (1953), p. 1-4.
Description and translation of two rock inscriptions in Hephthalite Greek found near
the village of Uruzgan, 150 miles northwest of Kandahar.

213 **International meeting on the coordination of Kushan studies and archaeological research in Central Asia, Kabul Afghanistan, May 12-18,
1970.**
Edited by Mohammed Kazem Ahang. *Afghanistan.* vol. 23, no. 1.
(1970), p. 62-69.
This meeting, set up by the UNESCO project on the Study of the Civilizations of
the Peoples of Central Asia, attracted a number of specialists from Europe, Asia,
and America. Discussions were held and decisions made regarding the preservation of historic sites and monuments, the publication of the results of archaeological
research, and ways of improving communications between scholars in order to coordinate research.

214 **Introduction to the excavation at Ghazni: summary report of the Italian Archaeological Mission in Afghanistan.**
Alessio Bombaci. *Afghanistan.* vol. 14, no. 4. (1959), p. 1-23.
An account of archaeological research in the ancient trade centre of Ghazni and a description of the ruins and artefacts unearthed is set against an historical background which traces the development of the city from its pre-Islamic beginnings to its greatest period under the Ghaznavids in the 10-12th centuries AD.

215 **Italian mission activities in Samangan area.**
Puglisi. *Afghanistan.* vol. 17, no. 4. (1962), p. 26-31.
Description of preliminary archaeological excavations carried out in 1962 at the prehistoric site of Hazar Sum by the head of the Italian Archaeological Mission.

216 **The Khosh Tapa-Fullol hoard.**
K. R. Maxwell-Hyslop. *Afghan Studies.* vol. 3-4. (1982), p. 25-37. map. bibliog.
This is an illustrated description of the Kabul Museum's hoard of five gold and seven silver vessels which may have come from the Baghlan area. The author concludes that these artefacts may date from the Neo-Sumerian period with 'c. 2110-2003 B.C. [being] perhaps the most probable'.

217 **Marenjan hill.**
Ahmad Ali Kohzad. *Afghanistan.* vol. 4, no. 4. (1949), p. 24-26.
Description of the Chamen-Hozoori Pool hoard of silver Greek coins from the 5th-6th centuries BC, found near Kabul. This, together with Buddhist ruins found on the hill, indicate that the site was important in pre-Islamic times.

218 **Mémoires de la Délégation Archaéologique Française en Afghanistan.**
(Reports of the French Archaeological Delegation to Afghanistan.)
Paris: Délégation Archaéologique Française en Afghanistan (DAFA), 1942-. (Mémoires de la Délégation Archaéologique Française en Afghanistan).
The first volume in this series appeared in 1942. The most recent (vol. 31) appeared in 1987. These works comprise a full and detailed account of the archaeological work carried out in the country by a succession of French archaeological teams working in Bamiyan, Khair Khaneh, Shotorak, Begram, Mundigak, Lashkar-i Bazaar, Ai Khanum, Gandhara, and Surkh Kotal. In addition, some of the volumes in the series are devoted to cataloguing and describing the finds which include coins and jewellery etc. The series provides a valuable record of Afghanistan's past.

219 **The most ancient temple in Bamyan.**
Ahmed Ali Kohzad. *Afghanistan.* vol. 8, no. 2. (1953), p. 12-17.
Archaeological investigations indicate that the oldest Buddhist temple in Bamiyan dates from the first century AD. The finds resulting from excavations of the site (known as 'Cave G'), most notably the fine wall paintings in bright colours, are described.

Archaeology

220  **The Nau-Bahar of Balkh.**
P. E. Caspani. *Afghanistan.* vol. 2, no. 1. (1947), p. 39-43.
A description of that part of the ancient city of Balkh known as Nau Bahar and
of the notable ruins found in it, namely Tope-i-Rustam and Takht-i-Rustam. The
author considers that the latter building may not have been Buddhist, but rather a
Zoroastrian fire temple.

221  **New Palaeolithic localities near Dasht-i-Nawur.**
Louis Dupree. *Afghanistan Journal.* vol. 2, no. 3. (1975), p. 105-07.
A brief illustrated account of some Lower and Middle Palaeolithic surface finds
(flakes, cores, cleavers, side scrapers, and bifacially worked tools) picked up in
eastern Afghanistan.

222  **Nokonzok's well.**
Ilya Gershevitch. *Afghan Studies.* vol. 2. (1979), p. 55-73. map.
Describes the archaeological and linguistic detective work applied to a 2nd cen-
tury AD Greek-letter inscription in Bactrian found by the French Archaeological
Delegation in Afghanistan at Surkh Kotal in 1957.

223  **Note on the historical results deducible from recent discoveries in
Afghanistan.**
H. T. Prinsep. London: Wm. H. Allen, 1844. 124p.
A descriptive account and historical analysis derived from the study of a collection of
ancient Bactrian coins and associated notes assembled by James Prinsep, here edited
and written up by his brother. In it he pays tribute to the work in Afghanistan of
Charles Masson (James Lewis) who identified ancient sites and collected thousands
of coins which are now in the British Museum.

224  **Old Kandahar excavations 1976: preliminary report.**
S. W. Helms. *Afghan Studies.* vol. 2. (1979), p. 2-8. maps. bibliog.
An account of the 1976 season of excavations, illustrated with plans and sections,
in which work was carried out on the stupa and vihara which may date from the 4th
century AD, the citadel which is thought to date from the 1st millennium BC, the
fortifications which may date from the 15th century AD, and the town, thought to
span the period from the Iron Age to 1738 AD.

225  **On Alexander's track to the Indus: personal narrative of explorations
on the North-West Frontier of India.**
Sir Aurel Stein. London: Macmillan, 1929. 182p. maps.
As the author deals with the Graeco-Buddhist period, this account, although treating
the North-West Frontier and especially Swat, is relevant for those interested in the
early history and archaeology of eastern Afghanistan.

226 **On the fringe of the Indus civilisation.**
*Afghanistan.* vol. 8, no. 1. (1953), p. 43-52.
An account as reported by the *Manchester Guardian* of preliminary archaeological investigations carried out at Mundigak which revealed evidence of Neolithic and Bronze Age settlements.

227 **Palamedes at Bağlan.**
P. M. Fraser. *Afghan Studies.* vol. 3-4. (1982), p. 77-78.
Discussion of a Tocharian inscription and a Greek inscription found at the temple and fortress site of Surkh Kotal.

228 **Pre-historic Afghanistan: a source book.**
V. C. Srivastava. Allahabad, India: Indological Publications, 1982. 234p. maps. bibliog.
An archaeological survey which examines published accounts with a view to re-constructing the modes of livelihood of the prehistoric inhabitants of the country. The author, a lecturer in archaeology at Kabul University, sketches the climatic and environmental setting and then traces the development of archaeological research in the country, shows the results of that research, and finally attempts a reconstruction of the cultures represented in the archaeological record.

229 **Pre-Islamic coins in Herat Museum.**
D. W. MacDowall, M. Ibrahim. *Afghan Studies.* vol. 2. (1979), p. 44-53. bibliog.
An illustrated catalogue of coins as described in the title. The coins examined by the authors fall into the following catagories: Greek, Indo-Greek, Saka and Yue-chi, Indo-Scythian and Indo-Parthian, Kushan, Later Kushan, Kushan-Sassanian, Sassanian, Mediaeval, and Roman.

230 **Pre-Islamic coins in Kandahar museum.**
D. W. MacDowall, M. Ibrahim. *Afghan Studies.* vol. 1. (1978), p. 67-77. bibliog.
A description and catalogue of the ancient coins assembled in the Kandahar collections.

231 **Pre-Islamic fortifications, habitation, and religious monuments in the Kunar Valley.**
Klaus Fischer. *Afghanistan.* vol. 15, no. 3. (1960), p. 7-10. bibliog.
A brief description of unexcavated archaeological sites in eastern Afghanistan as an indication of where future fieldwork might be undertaken.

232 **The prehistoric period of Afghanistan.**
Louis Dupree. *Afghanistan.* vol. 20, no. 3. (1967), p. 8-27. map.
The first archaeological survey of the country expressly set up to identify prehistoric sites was in 1949. This paper gives an overview of the progress made from that date to 1966.

233 **Preliminary field report on excavations at Shamshir Ghar, Koh-i-Duzd, and Deh Morasi Ghundai (south-west Afghanistan).**
Louis Dupree. *Afghanistan.* vol. 6, nos. 2; 3. (1951), p. 22-31; p. 30-35. map.
This is, in the author's words, 'a very, very preliminary report' and it is written in the informal, not to say off-hand style, which characterizes most of his later writings. Future archaeological investigators are referred to as 'visiting firemen' and one cave site which yielded no artefacts is first described as a 'dud in the desert' and then as 'the damned thing'.

234 **Preliminary notes on some ancient remains at Qunduz.**
Klaus Fischer. *Afghanistan.* vol. 16, no. 1. (1961), p. 12-26. map. bibliog.
An historical and archaeological survey of the Kunduz region, with illustrations of the landscape and archaeological finds.

235 **A preliminary report on the excavation of Tapa-i Shotur in Hadda.**
Shahiby Mustamandi. *Afghanistan.* vol. 21, no. 1. (1968), p. 58-69.
The Director of the Afghan Archaeological Mission describes, with illustrations, the results gleaned from three seasons' (1965-67) work at the Buddhist site near Jalalabad. Among other things a rare bronze head of Buddha was found. Also uncovered were a large number of shrines, temples, and statues.

236 **Project for an archaeological gazetteer of Afghanistan.**
Warwick Ball. *Afghan Studies.* vol. 3-4. (1982), p. 89-93. bibliog.
An outline of the project, with a discussion of existing gazetteers and catalogues, and specimen entries to illustrate the manner in which the data is to be handled. The completed work, published in two volumes, appeared in Paris in 1982 (q.v.).

237 **Recent researches in ancient Seistan.**
Klaus Fischer. *Afghanistan.* vol. 16, no. 2. (1961), p. 30-39. bibliog.
An account of the archaeological survey work carried out by a German expedition in 1960.

238 **Results of an archaeological survey for stone age sites in north Afghanistan.**
Louis Dupree. *Afghanistan.* vol. 18, no. 2. (1963), p. 1-15. map.
In the course of the survey a collection of surface finds was made (stone tools and potsherds). It is the flint tools, mostly flakes, scrapers, and cores, which are described here.

239 The ruins of Surkh Kotal: French archaeologists discover ancient temple in Afghanistan.
Gabrielle Bertrand. *Afghanistan.* vol. 13, no. 1. (1958), p. 7-9.
A brief description of archaeological excavations and the results obtained at the Surkh Kotal site in the 1950s.

240 Shamshir Ghar, an historic cave site in Kandahar Province, Afghanistan.
Louis Dupree. *Afghanistan.* vol. 13, no. 2. (1958), p. 27-32.
A description of the results of archaeological excavations which revealed occupation levels from the 3rd-4th centuries AD (late Kushan), the 5th-9th centuries AD (Kushano-Sassanian), and early Islamic periods (9th-13th centuries AD).

241 Some impressions of Swat and Afghanistan.
W. V. Emanuel. *Journal of the Royal Central Asian Society.* vol. 26, pt. 2. (1939), p. 195-213. map.
An informal account of an archaeological expedition, under the leadership of Evert Barger, which set out in 1938 to locate Graeco-Buddhist sites in Northern Afghanistan.

242 The son of Aristonax at Kandahar.
P. M. Fraser. *Afghan Studies.* vol. 2. (1979), p. 9-21.
An attempt to reconstruct a Greek inscription consisting of two elegiac couplets on a statue base found in a late Hellenistic horizon during the 1979 excavations at Old Kandahar.

243 South Asian archaeology, papers from the first international conference of South Asian archaeologists held in the University of Cambridge.
Edited by Norman Hammond. London: Duckworth, 1973. 308p. maps. bibliog.
A collection of twenty-one papers on a range of archaeological topics, some of which deal with sites and periods in Afghanistan, such as Klaus Fischer's report on field surveys carried out in the Seistan (q.v.), George Dales' paper on radiocarbon chronologies, and Maurizio Taddei's work on a site in Ghazni (q.v.). Other papers in the volume deal with sites and research along Afghanistan's eastern frontier.

244 The stupa and monastery at Guldarra: report on the British Institute's preservation programme.
G. K. Rao, R. Pinder-Wilson, W. Ball. *South Asian Studies.* vol. 1. (1985), p. 79-88. map. bibliog.
An account of archaeological preservation work carried out at Guldarra during three seasons from 1977 to 1979.

245 **Summary of the history of archaeological research in Afghanistan.**
J. C. Courtois. *Afghanistan.* vol. 16, no. 2. (1961), p. 18-29. map.
Archaeological research in the country is traced from the time of Charles Masson
down to the 1960s and includes the work of the French teams beginning in 1922,
as well as the Italians, the Americans, and the Germans.

246 **Surkh Kotal: a late Hellenistic temple in Bactria.**
Daniel Schlumberger. *Afghanistan.* vol. 9, no. 2. (1954), p. 41-47.
The Director of DAFA (Délégation Archéologique Française en Afghanistan) describes the finding of the Graeco-Iranian temple of Surkh Kotal in 1951 and gives
the results of the first season's work there (1952).

247 **Survey of archaeology and architecture in Afghanistan: part 1, the
south-Ghazni, Kandahar and Sistan.**
Edgar Knobloch. *Afghanistan Journal.* vol. 8, no. 1. (1981), p. 3-20.
maps. bibliog.
A record of the sites and buildings in the southern part of the country. The report
is well-illustrated with line drawings, plans, and photographs.

248 **Time off to dig: archaeology and adventure in remote Afghanistan.**
Sylvia Matheson. London: Odhams, 1961. 286p.
The author worked at the archaeological site at Mundigak in south-eastern
Afghanistan for a season in 1955 and returned for another in 1957. This is a
combination of travel book and an informal account of archaeologists at work.

249 **The tour of the archaeological mission of the American Museum of
Natural History in Afghan Seistan.**
A. K. *Afghanistan.* vol. 5, no. 1. (1950), p. 29-32.
An announcement of the expedition's arrival and its aims, together with a summary
of the mission's report of its first season's work.

250 **Two Azes hoards from Afghanistan.**
David W. MacDowall. *South Asian Studies.* vol. 1. (1985), p. 51-55.
bibliog.
Description of thirty-five copper coins (from a hoard of 'some 600' found in an
earthenware vase near Khost in 1978) from the reign of Azes II (1st century AD),
plus descriptions of eighteen coins from a similar hoard discovered in Gardez in the
1960s.

251 **The universal value of archaeological researches in Afghanistan dur-
ing forty years.**
Afghan Delegation, Asian Historical Congress, New Delhi.
*Afghanistan.* vol. 17, no. 1. (1962), p. 45-52. bibliog.
An overview of archaeological research in the country which singles out three main
sites: Mundigak, Surkh Kotal, and Ghazni.

**Merve Rud.**
*See* item no. 293.

**Kabul Museum stone inscription of the year 83.**
*See* item no. 644.

**Ancient arts of Central Asia.**
*See* item no. 911.

**Art of the Bronze Age: southeastern Iran, western Central Asia, and the Indus Valley.**
*See* item no. 914.

**Buddhism in Afghanistan and Central Asia.**
*See* item no. 915.

**Arms of the Arian heroes in Avesta period.**
*See* item no. 947.

# History

## General

252 **Afghanistan, a study of political developments in Central Asia.**

Kerr Fraser-Tytler. London: Oxford University Press, 1950. 330p. maps. bibliog.

Although the viewpoint is undeniably British, the author is not uncritical, and provides here quite possibly the best single volume of history available on Afghanistan. Written by a British officer and diplomat, the account is at its best when describing Russian expansion in Asia and the finer points of the Great Game.

253 **Afghanistan, an historical sketch.**

Mohammed Ali. Kabul: Historical Society of Afghanistan, [n.d.]. 30p. (Historical Society of Afghanistan, no. 46).

This covers successive periods from the advent of Islam to the reign of Mohammad Zahir Shah.

254 **Afghanistan and the Central Asian question.**

Fred H. Fisher. London: James Clarke, 1878. 264p. map. bibliog.

A general survey of the country, its climate and products, people, languages, literature, and antiquities, is followed by an historical summary from ancient times down through the First Afghan War. The concluding chapter examines the policies of Lord Northbrook and Lord Lytton towards Afghanistan and offers scathing remarks about Britain's dealings with Sher Ali. These remarks turned out to be prophetic as the book was published on the eve of the Second Afghan War.

## 255 Afghanistan as a meeting-place in history.
Arnold Toynbee. *Afghanistan.* vol. 15, no. 2. (1960), P. 51-59.
The noted historian describes the country as the 'Eastern Roundabout' of the ancient world (the 'Western Roundabout' being Syria), his point being that Afghanistan has been the connecting link between Western Asia, India, and Central Asia down through the centuries. He develops this point in an historical summary of cultural epochs in the country's history.

## 256 Afghanistan from Darius to Amanullah.
George MacMunn. London: G. Bell, 1929. 359p. map. bibliog.
A competent and readable history, written from the viewpoint of a British army officer, of the 'Land of the Afghans' from early times down to the end of Amanullah's reign in 1929.

## 257 Afghanistan, highway of conquest.
Arnold Fletcher. Ithaca, New York: Cornell University Press, 1965. 325p. bibliog.
A history of the country from ancient times to the Cold War, with emphasis on the 19th century, but also tracing the main political events of the first half of the 20th century.

## 258 Afghanistan: its history, and our dealings with it.
Philip F. Walker. London: Griffith, Farran, Okeden, & Welsh, 1885. 2 vols. map.
A history written by a British officer who served in the Second Afghan War. The author's viewpoint, in keeping with the times, was that Russian expansion in Asia must be stopped and that 'the blunders committed by Mr. Gladstone's Government' must be put right.

## 259 Aryana, ancient Afghanistan.
Rahman Pazhwak. Hove, England: Key Press, [n.d.]. 144p.
A short history prepared by the Afghan poet, writer, and diplomat who became President of the 21st General Assembly of the UN. The book divides Afghan history into the pre-Muslim era and the Islamic period and traces the main political and cultural trends of each. The final section is on modern Afghanistan. Although no date is indicated, the book was probably published in about 1950.

## 260 A brief political history of Afghanistan.
Abdul Ghani. Lahore: Najaf, 1989. 956p.
Part one traces the earliest history of the region from pre-Islamic times down to Shah Shuja and Shah Mahmud. Part two deals with the Mohammadzai period from Amir Dost Mohammad to Amir Habibullah. Part three covers the period from Amanullah to Muhammad Zahir Shah.

261 **A cultural history of Afghanistan.**
Mohammed Ali. Kabul: The Author, 1964. 255p.

An interesting and authoritative work by the Professor of History at Kabul University, this traces the development of the peoples of south Central Asia from earliest times to the coming of Islam and down through the ruling dynasties to the founding of the modern state. With engaging frankness the author states that one of his aims has been to make the book pleasant reading and that, conscious of his shortcomings, he has attempted to provide a guide for others in the hope of provoking further studies.

262 **The gates of India, being an historical narrative.**
Thomas Hungerford Holdich. London: Macmillan, 1910. 555p. maps.

The early history of the country is traced from the days of Greek and Persian empires down through Alexander to Chinese and Arab travellers and on to the era of European exploration. The accomplishments of Masson, Wood, Moorcroft, Burnes, Vigne, Broadfoot, and Ferrier are recounted in style.

263 **The heart of Asia: a history of Russian Turkestan and the Central Asian Khanates from the earliest times.**
Francis Henry Skrine, Edward Denison Ross. London: Methuen, 1899. 444p. maps.

As the boundary between Afghanistan and Russia is political and not cultural, this provides an excellent historical background to any study of our subject. Part two of the book traces the nature and extent of Russian expansion in Central Asia. The authors do not regard the capture of India as part of the Russian dream.

264 **A history of Afghanistan.**
Percy Sykes. London: Macmillan, 1940. 2 vols. map. bibliog.

This is probably the best history of the country available in English, and possibly in any other language. It is well written and has been ably researched by an officer with many years of experience in South and Central Asia, including Afghanistan.

265 **History of Afghanistan, from the earliest period to the outbreak of the war of 1878.**
George Bruce Malleson. London: W. H. Allen, 1878. 456p. map.

A major work and for several decades the best available in English, this is well organized and clearly written. The sources are identified with a meticulous accuracy not always found in the works of Victorian authors.

266 **History of the Afghans.**
J. P. Ferrier. London: John Murray, 1858. 491p. map.

A history of the people and the country from earliest times to the middle of the 19th century, written by a French general who served in the Persian army. The main part of the text is devoted to the period from 1700-1850.

267 **History of the Afghans, translated from the Persian of Neamet Ullah by Bernhard Dorn.**

Neamet Ullah, translated by Bernhard Dorn. London: Oriental Translation Committee, 1829. 241p.

This is divided into two main parts, each with an introduction, and the translator provides seventy-two pages of annotations at the end. The work traces Afghan history from Adam to the 16th century AD. Book three contains the lives of sixty-eight sheikhs and an account of numerous tribes. Neamet Ullah was attached to the Court of the Mogul Emperor Jehangir from about 1609 AD. The translator provides a list of thirty manuscripts (in Persian, Pushtu, Arabic) which he consulted.

268 **Islam and resistance in Afghanistan.**

Olivier Roy. Cambridge, England; London: Cambridge University Press, 1986. 253p. bibliog. (Cambridge Middle East Library).

This work examines the rôle of Islam in the political history of Afghanistan, with special attention to fundamentalist movements of the 16th to 19th centuries. The author also provides a history of the main political leaders and tribal movements of the past before examining the political history of the 1978-84 period of resistance to various governments following the death of President Daoud and the subsequent Soviet invasion. A useful account which, among other things, helps to sort out the various resistance groups.

269 **The kingdom of Afghanistan, a historical sketch.**

George Passman Tate. Bombay: Times of India, 1911. 224p. maps. bibliog.

In preparing this work the author consulted not only the standard English-language histories of the day, but also a substantial number of Persian texts. He provides a general geographical outline and an ethnic description of the country and then traces its history, particularly its relations with India and Persia, through the Mogul period and on to the end of the 19th century.

270 **Lords of the Khyber: the story of the North-West Frontier.**

André Singer. London: Faber & Faber, 1984. 234p. map. bibliog.

This draws historical parallels between Britain's experiences in Afghanistan and those of Russia while, at the same time, tracing the political history of the region from the 17th century through the momentous events of the 19th century. A postscript shows how Russia, like Britain, became 'enmeshed in the quagmire of Afghan politics'.

271 **North-West Frontier: people and events, 1839-1947.**

Arthur Swinson. London: Hutchinson, 1967. 354p. maps. bibliog.

As it is not possible to write about the history of the North-West Frontier without at the same time exploring the 19th-century relations between Britain and the peoples living between the Indus and the Oxus, this is as much as anything else a political and military history of Afghanistan from Victoria's reign to the end of the Raj.

272 **Pak-Afghan common destiny.**
Mohammad Haidar. *WUFA, Quarterly Journal of the Writers Union of Free Afghanistan.* vol. 1, no. 3. (1986), p. 47-51.
The author draws on historical precedent to show how the mountains and passes to the north-west of the subcontinent have been used by invaders to change the history of South Asia. He concludes that the peoples on either side of the Hindu Kush have a common past and should recognize that they have a future in common.

273 **The Pathans, 550 B.C. - A.D. 1957.**
Olaf Caroe. London: Macmillan, 1958. 521p. maps. bibliog.
A history of the Pashto-speaking peoples of Afghanistan and Pakistan written by a British officer who 'had the fortune to spend half a lifetime among Pathans'. Both well-written and well-researched, this occupies a prominent place among the main works on the subject.

274 **The political organization of the Kam Kafirs: a preliminary analysis.**
Schuyler Jones. Copenhagen: Royal Danish Academy of Science and Letters, 1967. 61p. maps. bibliog.
Using George Scott Robertson's 19th century account, *The Kafirs of the Hindu Kush* (q.v.) of the peoples who inhabited the Bashgal Valley of eastern Kafiristan (present-day Nuristan), the author extracts and organizes data with a view to understanding the political organization of these communities in the pre-Muslim era.

275 **A review of the political situation in Central Asia.**
Abdul Ghani. [no publisher], 1921. 297p.
An examination of government departments and policies concerned with revenue, transport, army, administration, and customs tariffs among others, is sandwiched in between accounts of the reigns of Abdur Rahman, Habibullah, and Amanullah, and discussions of the Russian advance across Asia, and the rise of Bolshevism. The author, writing in 1920 with startling accuracy, predicts that Russia will 'readily help Afghanistan with money and material'. He forsees great power rivalry between Russia and America, and considers that Bolshevism will run its course in Russia and 'will ultimately fail', producing a 'Soviet Democracy'.

276 **The role of Afghanistan in the civilization of Islam.**
M. Ghubar. *Afghanistan.* vol. 1, no. 1. (1946), p. 26-32.
The title should perhaps read 'The rôle of Afghanistan in Islamic civilization', as this is a brief account of the spread of Islam and the contributions made by key 'Afghans' to its history. The author's definition of Afghanistan is very broad, as is his definition of 'Afghan'.

277 **A short history of India and of the frontier states of Afghanistan, Nipal, and Burma.**
J. Talboys Wheeler. London: Macmillan, 1894. 744p. maps.
This concise history contains five chapters on the Mogul Empire and two on Central Asia, Afghanistan, and the First Afghan War.

278   **The survival of Afghanistan: 1747-1979, a diplomatic history with an analytic and reflective approach.**
N. D. Ahmad. Lahore: Institute of Islamic Culture, 1990. 345p. bibliog.
The author examines recent events in Afghanistan against an historical background, examining both the external and internal factors which contribute to the country's survival as a sovereign nation. The work concludes with an analysis of the nature of Russian imperialism.

# The Early Empires (500 B.C. - A.D. 650)

279   **Afghanistan between east and west: second century B.C. to 1222 A.D..**
Louis Dupree. *Journal of the Royal Central Asian Society.* vol. 43, pt. 1. (1956), p. 52-60. map. bibliog.
The article is divided into the following sections: 'The early movements out of Central Asia', 'The rise and fall of the Kushans', 'The Kushano-Sassanian period of small independent states', 'The Gupta Wars', 'The Epthalite Huns', and 'From the Islamic to the Mongol invasion'.

280   **Aryana, or Ancient Afghanistan.**
Mohammad Ali. Kabul: Historical Society of Afghanistan, 1957. 117. (Historical Society of Afghanistan, Special Issue No. 47).
This book divides what is known about pre-Islamic Khorasan or Aryana (the term 'Afghanistan' is very recent) into the generally accepted periods which have been identified by historians and archaeologists: pre-Aryan, Achaemenid, Greek, Graeco-Bactrian, Saka, Mauryan Dynasty, the Parthians, the Kushans, the Ephthalites or Hephthalites, the Turks, and the Kushano-Hephthalite Dynasties.

281   **Bactria, the history of a forgotten empire.**
H. G. Rawlinson. London: Probsthain, 1912. 175p. maps. bibliog. (Probsthain's Oriental Series, vol. VI).
A history of the eastern portion of the Persian Empire which, following the Macedonian invasion, became an independent Greek kingdom and included Sogdiana, most of modern Afghanistan, and the Punjab.

282   **Cultural relations between Afghanistan and India.**
Ahmed Ali Kohzad. *Afghanistan.* vol. 1, no. 2. (1946), p. 12-30.
A paper presented to a conference held in Calcutta to mark the 200th anniversary of the birth of Sir William Jones (1746-94), widely considered to be the founder of modern linguistics. The author, an historian, traces early historical and cultural connections between Afghanistan and the sub-continent. For more about Jones,

see *The life and mind of Oriental Jones: Sir William Jones, the father of modern linguistics* by Garland Cannon.

283  **The cultural, social and intellectual state of the people of Afghanistan in the era just before the advent of Islam.**
A. H. Habibi. *Afghanistan.* vol. 20, no. 3. (1967), p. 1-7.
An account which draws upon the historical and archaeological records relating to 'greater Khorasan' in pre-Islamic times. It looks at the achievements of the Buddhists of Gandhara, the Zoroastrians, and the Graeco-Bactrians.

284  **The culture sequence of Bactria.**
F. R. Allchin. *Afghanistan.* vol. 15, no. 1. (1960), p. 1-20.
An account of ancient Bactria based on archaeological finds and historical documents in an attempt to sort events into a meaningful cultural sequence.

285  **Darius I's foundation charters from Susa and the eastern Achaemenid Empire.**
David Fleming. *Afghan Studies.* vol. 3-4. (1982), p. 81-87. maps. bibliog.
Discussion of the boundaries of two eastern Achaemenid provinces: Bactria and Sogdia, in the light of an Old Persian text which mentions the importation to Susa of semiprecious stones including turquoise and lapis lazuli.

286  **The development of Graeco-Bactrian culture.**
Mohammed Ali. *Afghanistan.* vol. 19, no. 3. (1963), p. 1-11.
Two centuries of Greek rule between the Indus and the Oxus is examined in the light of the writings of ancient historians and archaeological discoveries. (This issue of the journal was misnumbered as vol. 19, no. 3, but actually follows on from vol. 18, no. 2.)

287  **Early contacts between China and Afghanistan and the origin of the 'Silk Route'.**
P. E. Caspani. *Afghanistan.* vol. 1, no. 3. (1946), p. 30-35.
A work which draws heavily on W. W. Tarn's *The Greeks in Bactria and India* (q.v.) (Cambridge University Press, 1951), for its historical information.

288  **The early empires of Central Asia: a study of the Scythians and the Huns and the part they played in world history, with special reference to the Chinese sources.**
William Montgomery McGovern. Chapel Hill, North Carolina: University of North Carolina, 1939. 529p. maps. bibliog.
A standard work on the history of Central Asia, this provides a highly relevant basis for any study of the earlier periods relating to Afghanistan, particularly 'Book one: the Aryan background', which deals with Turkistan and Bactria.

## 289 The first horsemen.
Frank Trippett, Ruth Tringham. New York: Time-Life Books, 1974. 160p. map. bibliog. (The Emergence of Man).
This is a brief account of ancient Central Asian history, particularly of the rôle of horses in the development of early empires. The book is written in a popular style and is well illustrated with drawings and colour plates showing archaeological artefacts in bronze and gold, and archival photographs depicting the Turkoman and Kirghiz peoples of northern Afghanistan. Geographically, the book covers a vast area from China and Mongolia to the southern USSR and south to the Hindu Kush. It thus serves as a useful introduction to the peoples and events that shaped the history of the plains of northern Afghanistan.

## 290 Geography of Bactria in Greek sources.
Sami Said Ahmed. *Afghanistan.* vol. 20, no. 4. (1968), p. 27-39.
As the title suggests, this examines the Bactrian region with reference to Herodotus, Arrian, Polybius, Strabo, and other ancient writers.

## 291 The Greeks in Bactria and India.
W. W. Tarn. Cambridge, England: Cambridge University Press, 1938. 539p.
A much acclaimed and widely quoted work representing decades of research, this treats the early history of kings and battles in Central Asia and Afghanistan. An indispensable work for any serious study of this particular time and place.

## 292 The Invasion of India by Alexander the Great as described by Arrian, Q. Curtius, Diodoros, Plutarch, and Justin, being translations of such portions of the works of these and other classical authors as describe Alexander's campaigns in Afghanistan, the Panjab, Sindh, Gedrosia and Karmania, with an introduction containing a life of Alexander..
J. W. M'Crindle. Westminster, England: Archibald Constable, 1893. 432p. map. bibliog. (Ancient India as Described by the Classical Writers).
Presents historical accounts of Alexander's marches (330-327 BC) across the country that was later to be called Afghanistan.

## 293 Merve Rud.
Mia Hussein. *Afghanistan.* vol. 9, no. 3; no. 4. (1954), p. 8-17; p. 19-25.
An historical account of an ancient city in the north-west of the country and a discussion of its exact location in the light of early records and archaeological evidence.

294 **Sir Aurel Stein's identification of Aornos.**
D. L. R. Lorimer. *Journal of the Central Asian Society.* (1926), p. 259-65.
A brief account of Alexander's campaigns in eastern Afghanistan and north-west India with a view to solving both geographical and historical problems.

# The Rise of Islam (A.D. 650-1218)

295 **The early Islamic history of Ghur.**
C. E. Bosworth. *Afghanistan.* vol. 17, no. 3; no. 4. (1962), p. 46-56; p. 14-25.
An account of the religious and cultural development of the independent kingdom of Ghor, 'one of the least known regions of the eastern Islamic world', by one of Britain's leading historians of South-Central Asia.

296 **The Ghaznavids, their empire in Afghanistan and eastern Iran, 994-1040.**
Clifford Edmund Bosworth. Edinburgh: Edinburgh University Press, 1963. 331p. maps. bibliog. (History, Philosophy and Economics, vol. 17).
A history of the Muslim peoples who in the 11th century ruled over a great empire in southern Asia from western Persia to the Ganges. Their dynastic centre was at Ghazni in eastern Afghanistan and their rapid expansion took place under the leadership of the renowned Sultan Mahmud.

297 **The Later Ghaznavids: splendor and decay. The dynasty in Afghanistan and northern India, 1040-1186.**
Clifford Edmund Bosworth. Edinburgh: Edinburgh University Press, 1977. 196p. map. bibliog.
This sequel to the author's earlier work *The Ghaznavids, their empire in Afghanistan and eastern Iran 994-1040* (q.v.), carries the history of the Turco-Iranian dynasty forward to the 12th century AD.

298 **The life and times of Sultan Mahmud of Ghazna.**
Muhammad Nazim. Cambridge, England: Cambridge University Press, 1931. 271p.
A 'kings and battles' history based mainly on primary sources providing a very readable account of events in 11th-century Afghanistan.

299 **Punjwai.**
Abdul Raouf Benava. *Afghanistan.* vol. 8, no. 3. (1953), p. 23-26.
Brief historical sketch of a suburb of Old Kandahar, some of the legends about it, and some of its famous sons.

300 **The role of Afghanistan (Khurasan) in the movement of people and ideas in the early medieval ages.**
Afghan Delegation, Asian Historical Congress, New Delhi. *Afghanistan.* vol. 17, no. 1; no. 2. (1962), p. 25-44; p. 18-39. bibliog.
Early historical accounts and archaeological research are used to show the country's rôle and influence in Asian affairs.

301 **The Shahis of Afghanistan and the Punjab.**
D. B. Pandey. Delhi: Historical Research, 1973. 287p. bibliog. (Indo-Afghan Studies, III).
This deals with the historical geography of the North-West Frontier of India during early mediaeval times. A geographical description of the region is followed by evidence gleaned from manuscripts, inscriptions, and coins which throw light on the Shahis from the 5th to the 10th centuries AD.

302 **Sultan Mahmud of Ghaznin.**
Mohammad Habib. New Delhi: S. Chaud, 1951. 128p. bibliog.
The life and times of the king who created the Ghaznavid Empire and ruled the lands between the Oxus and the Indus during the last part of the 10th and the first quarter of the 11th century AD. At its height his realm stretched from Persia into the heart of India, but his capital remained at Ghazni and it was there that he died in 1030.

303 **Turkestan down to the Mongol invasion.**
W. Barthold. London: Luzac, 1928. 513p. map. bibliog. (E. J. W. Gibb Memorial Series).
Translated from the original Russian and revised and amplified by the author in the light of new evidence, this remains one of the most enduring accounts of Central Asian history available in English. The bibliography and chronological summary of events alone are worth the price of admission. The gentle, but devastating critique of some of H. G. Raverty's manuscript translations is a bonus.

# The Mongols and Timurids (A.D. 1218-1506)

### 304 The effect of the culture of Herat on Asia.
A. H. Habibi. *Afghanistan.* vol. 21, no. 1. (1968), p. 1-7.
This looks at Herat's place in history in the light of the kingdoms and empires which flourished in Khorasan and the circumstances which eventually made the city a centre of learning and culture.

### 305 The Mongol empire, its rise and legacy.
Michael Prawdin. London: George Allen & Unwin, 1940. 581p. map. bibliog.
One of the more enduring histories of the Mongol Empire, this traces the life and times of Temuchin, who later became famous as Chinghiz Khan. An interesting and highly readable account of the land between the Oxus and the Indus as it was in the 12th and 13th centuries.

# The Mogul Empire (A.D. 1504 - 1747)

### 306 The Afghans versus the Mughals.
Mohammed Ali. *Afghanistan.* vol. 11, no. 1. (1956), p. 9-14.
An historical look at the military difficulties the Moguls had in attempting to deal with the Afghans in the 16th and 17th centuries AD.

### 307 History of the Afghans in India, A.D. 1545-1631, with especial reference to their relations with the Mughals.
Muhammad Abdur Rahim. Karachi: Pakistan Publishing House, 1961. 326p. map.
This relates the history of the Afghans in India from the death of Sher Shah (1549) to the death of Khan Jehan Lodi (1631) with a view to restoring the Afghan presence to its proper place in the history of Muslim rule on the subcontinent. Key figures are illuminated and their place in Mogul history is noted.

### 308 A history of the Moghuls of Central Asia, being the Tarikh-i-Rashidi of Mirza Muhammad Haidar, Dughlát.
Ney Elias, E. Denison Ross. London: Sampson Low, Marston, 1898. 535p. map.
The history of that branch of the Mogul Khans who separated from the main group of Chaghatai (the ruling dynasty in Transoxiana) in about 1321 AD. It was originally written in Persian in 1541-42 and 1544-47, when the author was Regent of Kashmir.

As a boy he had accompanied his relative, the Mogul Emperor Babur, on numerous campaigns in Central Asia, many of them in what is today Afghanistan

309 **Memoirs of Zehir-ed-Din Muhammed Baber, Emperor of Hindustan, written by himself in the Jaghatai Turki, with notes and a geographical and historical introduction; together with a map of the countries between the Oxus and Jaxartes, and a memoir regarding its construction.**
Zehir-ed-Din Muhammed Baber, translated by J. Leyden, W. Erskine.
London: Longman, Rees, Orme, Brown, & Green, 1826. 432p. map.
These justly famous memoirs tell the life story of the founder of the Mogul dynasty. Born in 1483, Babur was descended from Timur-i-Leng and Chingiz Khan. For some twenty years his home was in Kabul and his memoirs describe the city and the country as it was in the late 15th and early 16th century. Babur invaded India in 1526, laying the foundations of the Mogul Empire. He died in 1530.

310 **Niamatullah's history of the Afghans.**
Nirodbhusan Roy. Santiniketan, India: Bidyut Ranjan Basu, 1958. 211p.
Translated from the Persian *Makhzan-i-Afghani* which was written by Niamatullah Khan of Samana, a librarian and chronicler at the court of the Emperor Jahangir (1569-1627), this deals with the history of Afghans during the 15th and 16th centuries.

311 **The Padishah Bābur, 1483-1530, his passage at Kabul.**
L. F. Rosset. *Afghanistan*. vol. 1, no. 3. (1946), p. 36-46.
A description of Babur's garden and grave on a hillside in Kabul is followed by a brief account of the Great Mogul's life and character.

312 **Sifat-Nāma-Yi Darvīs Muhammad Hān-i Ġāzī: Cronaca di una crociata musulmana contro i Kafiri di Laġmān nell'anno 1582. Manoscritto persiana-kābulī edito e tradotto, con introduzione e indici dei nomi, da Gianroberto Scarcia.**
(A tribute to darvish Muhammad Khan-e Ghazi: chronicle of a Muslim crusade against the Kafirs of Laghman in the year 1582; a Kabuli-Persian manuscript published in translation with an introduction and an index of [personal, tribal, and geographical] names.)
Edited by Gianroberto Scarcia. Rome: Istituto Italiano per il Medio ed Estremo Oriente, 1965. 368p. maps. (Serie Orientale Roma, no. XXXII).
This contains both the Persian text and the Italian translation of the 16th-century Persian account by Muhammad Khan-e-Ghazi which describes an early Muslim attempt to invade western Kafiristan. The original manuscript was written by Ghazi Muhammad Sālim in 990 AH (1582 AD). The manuscript in the Kabul Museum from which the Italian translation was made was re-written 290 years later by Muhammad Rahim, a descendent of Darvish Muhammad Khan-e Ghazi. Although some pages

at the beginning and end of the Persian manuscript are missing, it tells of the wars waged in 'sixty-six' valleys of Lamghān (Laghman), against the Kafirs and gives some ethnographic information about these 'infidels'. The author's style might be described as a mixture of traditional epic and literary Sufi.

### 313  The walls of Kabul.
P. E. Caspani. *Afghanistan.* vol. 1, no. 2. (1946), p. 31-34.

An historical account and illustrated description of the city walls which the author considers can be traced back to the 5th century AD, though rebuilt and enlarged on various subsequent occasions, particularly in the 15th to 18th centuries. The history of the Bala Hissar, Kabul's great fort, is also outlined.

# 18th Century

### 314  The Abdalis - a study of the Dynasty.
Aminullah Stanakzai. *Afghanistan.* vol. 19, no. 1; no. 2. (1964), p. 37-39; p. 26-33.

An historical account derived from Pashto manuscripts, of the Abdalis, a Pashto-speaking tribe who later came to be called the Durranis.

### 315  Ahmad Shah Baba, father of the nation.
Mohammed Ali. *Afghanistan.* vol. 18, no. 2. (1963), p. 16-22.

This eulogy is in praise of the personal qualities of the founder of the Durrani Empire and the man who is credited with creating the Afghan state. He ruled from the death of Nadir Shah in 1747 until his own death twenty-six years later.

### 316  Ahmad Shah: the man and his achievements.
Ganda Singh. *Afghanistan.* vol. 8, no. 1. (1953), p. 1-19.

An illustrated article about the life and times of Ahmad Shah Baba (Ahmad Shah Durrani - 1722-72), founder of the Durrani Empire and father of the Afghan nation.

### 317  English East India Company and the Afghans, 1757-1800.
Birendra Varma. Calcutta: Punthi Pustak, 1968. 171p.

A history of the East India Company and the Moguls, with special emphasis on the various Afghan invasions of India in the 18th century.

### 318  Nadir Shah, a critical study based mainly on contemporary sources.
L. Lockhart. London: Luzac, 1938. 344p. maps. bibliog.

A scholarly though highly readable study, meticulously researched and clearly presented, tracing the life and times of the Persian ruler, Nadir Shah (1688-1747), who drove the Afghans out of Persia and led his armies across Afghanistan in 1736-37 to capture Kandahar and invade India.

319  **Two coronations.**
Ahmad Ali Kohzad. *Afghanistan.* vol. 6, no. 3. (1950), p. 38-40.
Brief historical account of the coronation ceremonies for Ahmad Shah Durrani in
the 18th century and Amir Dost Mohammed in the 19th century. There is an error
in the numbering of the journal; this should be vol. 5, not vol. 6.

# 19th Century

320  **The Afghan campaigns of 1878-80 (Biographical Division).**
Sydney H. Shadbolt. London: Sampson Low, Marston, Searle, and
Rivington, 1882. 274p.
A volume of portraits and biographical notes of the British officers who lost their
lives in the Second Afghan War, together with portraits and the service records of
those who were awarded the Victoria Cross. A gold-mine of information for the
historian.

321  **The Afghan campaigns of 1878-80, compiled from official and private
sources (Historical Division).**
Sydney H. Shadbolt. London: Sampson Low, Marston, Searle, and
Rivington, 1882. 352p. maps.
The first part, illustrated with six maps, provides a narrative account of the Second
Afghan War. The remainder of the volume is devoted to the service records of
British officers who took part and the regimental service records of all British units
which operated in Afghanistan, making this an invaluable source for the historian.

322  **The Afghan connection: the extraordinary adventures of Major Eldred Pottinger.**
George Pottinger. Edinburgh: Scottish Academic Press, 1983. 239p.
maps. bibliog.
A biography of one of the outstanding British figures in the 19th-century history of
Afghanistan. Pottinger's career placed him in the country as early as 1837 and from
then until the end of the First Afghan War his changing fortunes lay in that country.
He was among the few survivors of the 1841 retreat from Kabul but died of fever
in Hong Kong only two years later. His uncle, Major-General Sir Henry Pottinger,
who also served in the First Afghan War, was Governor of Hong Kong at the time
of his nephew's death.

323  **The Afghan frontier.**
G. Campbell. London 1879. 82p.
A critical look at Britain's policy regarding Afghanistan and the North-West Frontier
in which the author muses that it is 'strange to the generation that learned the
lessons of the first Afghan war...that a second similar war should have been waged
for precisely the same object, namely the establishment of a friendly power on the

north-west frontier of India'. The writer concludes 'that the difficulties and expense of any attempt to meddle with [Afghanistan] far outweigh the advantages'.

324 **The Afghan question from 1841 to 1878.**
The Duke of Argyll [George Douglas Campbell]. London: Strahan, 1879. 288p.

A formidable indictment of the British government's dealings with Afghanistan in which the author strips 'every vestige of sagacity and political morality off the reputation of a Ministry'. The author considers that in giving in to 'recurring fits of nervous panic on the subject of the advances of Russia' the British government indulged in conduct which was both immoral and injurious to its own interests. The Duke presents a compelling account of events.

325 **The Afghan war: Gough's action at Futtehabad.**
C. Swinnerton. London: W. H. Allen, 1880. 81p. maps.

A brief, but lively account of a battle that took place between the British and the Afghans near Jalalabad in 1879 during the Second Afghan War.

326 **The Afghan war of 1879-80, being a complete narrative of the capture of Cabul, the siege of Sherpur, the battle of Ahmed Khel, the brilliant march to Candahar, and the defeat of Ayub Khan, with the operations on the Helmund, and the settlement with Abdur Rahman Khan.**
Howard Hensman. London: W. H. Allen, 1881. 567p. maps.

An authoritative and highly readable account of the Second Afghan War by a news-paper correspondent who attached himself to General Roberts' command and accompanied the Kurram field force to Kabul via the Logar Valley, remaining with the British army throughout the winter, and witnessing the now famous engagements of Charasia, Sherpur, Asmai Heights, and other famous battles. General Roberts himself later said of Hensman's account: 'nothing could be more accurate or graphic'.

327 **The Afghan Wars, 1839-1842 and 1878-1880.**
Archibald Forbes. London: Seeley, 1892. 337p. maps.

The First and Second Anglo-Afghan wars, the events leading up to them, and their aftermath are clearly set out and discussed in this absorbing history.

328 **The Afghan Wars, 1839-1919.**
T. A. Heathcote. London: Osprey, 1980. 224p. maps. bibliog.

A compilation of events during the First, Second, and Third Afghan Wars which Britain fought beyond the North-West Frontier, this is drawn from first-hand accounts and official reports. It is complemented by numerous illustrations.

329 **Afghanistan and the Afghans, being a brief review of the history of the country and account of its people, with a special reference to the present crisis and war with the Amir Sher Ali Khan.**
Henry Walter Bellew. London: Sampson Low, Marston, Searle and Rivington, 1879. 230p.
An advocate of the Forward Policy, Bellew summarizes the history of Anglo-Afghan relations and warns of the threat of a Russian invasion of India. This book appeared on the eve of the Second Afghan War.

330 **Afghanistan: the buffer state. Great Britain and Russia in Central Asia; a comprehensive treatise on the entire Central Asian question with two maps specially prepared from the most recent information.**
Gervais Lyons. London; Madras: Luzac, 1910. 232p. maps.
An account of Russian expansion in Central Asia, seen from both the British point of view as a threat to the security of India, and from the Russian side. This is a valuable analysis of the subject, particularly as the author was a fluent Russian speaker and had travelled widely in that country in 1905 and 1906.

331 **Afghanistan (the Mohammedzai period), a political history of the country since the beginning of the nineteenth century with emphasis on its foreign relations.**
Mohammed Ali. Kabul: The Author, 1959. 211p. bibliog.
This study, written by Afghanistan's foremost contemporary historian, draws mainly on British sources since, as he admits, for 'this period of Afghan history there is very little literature either in Pashto or Persian'.

332 **The Ameer Abdur Rahman.**
Stephen Wheeler. London: Bliss, Sands & Foster, 1895. 251p. maps. (Public Men of Today, an International Series).
A well-crafted biography of the man, written, one assumes, from standard histories and British government records of the time, though no bibliography is provided and only now and then are passages illuminated by footnotes which reveal sources. A valuable study nonetheless and interesting to compare with 'The Life of Abdur Rahman, Amir of Afghanistan' (q.v.) published by Sultan Mohammed Khan five years later.

333 **Amir Sher Ali Khan.**
A. Ghani. *Afghanistan.* vol. 16, no. 1. (1961), p. 35-56.
This traces the historical events in the life of a son of Dost Mohammed, who was proclaimed Amir on June 12th, 1862, was defeated by his half brother Afzal Khan in 1867, and fled to Herat. Afzal Khan became Amir at Kabul, but the British Government recognized Sher Ali as Amir in 1868. He died in 1879 at the beginning of the Second Afghan War.

334 **Anglo-Russian relations concerning Afghanistan, 1837-1907.**
William Habberton. Urbana, Illinois: University of Illinois, 1937.
102p. maps. bibliog. (Illinois Studies in the Social Sciences, vol. 21,
no. 4 ).
A detailed study of the 'Central Asian Question', drawing on British government
documents, Foreign Office manuscripts, letters, memoirs, biographies, and histories.
A clear analysis of British and Russian imperial interests in Afghanistan and the
political and military consequences of those interests.

335 **The battle of Maiwand.**
Mohammed Ali. *Afghanistan.* vol. 10, no. 2. (1955), p. 26-38.
An account of a famous battle which took place in July 1880 during the Second
Afghan War. The Commander of the Afghan force was Mohammed Ayub Khan. He
faced a force of 2,500 men under the command of Brigadier Burrows and inflicted
a decisive defeat on the British at a place called Maiwand near Kandahar.

336 **A bibliography of Nuristan (Kafiristan) and the Kalash Kafirs of
Chitral, part two: selected documents from the secret and political
records, 1885-1900.**
Schuyler Jones. Copenhagen: Royal Danish Academy of Sciences
and Letters, 1969. 274p. (Hist. Filos. Medd. Dan. Vid. Selsk., vol.
43, no. 1).
This contains extracts of entries concerning the area now known as Nuristan, taken
from the confidential reports of the Government of India prepared by various British
political agents in Chitral, Peshawar, Gilgit, the Khyber, and Kabul. Taken together,
they provide an account of events in Kafiristan from 1885 to 1900, the period
during which the army of Amir Abdur Rahman invaded the region and converted
the population to Islam.

337 **British diplomacy in Afghanistan: an example.**
D. P. Singhal. *Afghanistan.* vol. 17, no. 2. (1962), p. 1-17.
An account of library research in London which revealed information about the
Turkish Mission to Kabul of 1877, the role of certain British officials in the affair,
and its repercussions in the Great Game.

338 **British India's northern frontier, 1865-1895. A study in imperial policy.**
Garry J. Alder. London: Longmans Green, 1963. 392p. maps. bibliog. (Imperial Studies).
A history of the political, military, and geographical manoeuvring that characterized
Anglo-Russian rivalries in Central Asia in the second half of the 19th century. The
events leading up to the formation of the modern Afghan state are traced, 'warts
and all'.

339 **Cabul, or Afghanistan, the seat of the Anglo-Russian question: being a pamphlet of facts about the country, the Ameer, and the people.**
Phil Robinson. London: Sampson, Low, Marston, Searle, and Rivington, 1878. 92p. map.
Starting with a geographical description of the country, the author goes on to explain why the people of Afghanistan do not form a nation and then provides information on Russian-Afghan and British-Afghan relations. The main cities and passes are also described.

340 **Central Asia and the Anglo-Russian frontier question: a series of political papers.**
Arminius Vambéry. London: Smith, Elder, 1874. 385p.
A series of articles, originally appearing in *Unsere Zeit*, on Anglo-Russian rivalry in Central Asia, Russia's conquests in that region, and Russian territorial ambitions. The author is convinced that there is a Russian threat to Afghanistan and India, and that Britain must be on her guard.

341 **Circumstances leading to the First Afghan War.**
Afzal Iqbal. Lahore, Pakistan: Research Society of Pakistan, 1975. 95p.
A study of the historical and political events surrounding Britain's defeat in Afghanistan in which the blame is put on the Earl of Aukland, then Governor General of India, for a war which need never have happened.

342 **Contributions to Islamic studies: Iran, Afghanistan, and Pakistan.**
Christel Braae, Klaus Ferdinand. Aarhus, Denmark: Danish Research Council for the Humanities, 1987. 155p. bibliog. (Research Programme on Contemporary Islam, vol. 3).
The second of the three papers in this volume is written by Asta Olesen and deals with 'The political use of Islam in Afghanistan during the reign of Amir Abdur Rahman (1880-1901)', providing an interesting insight into the workings of the Amir's government.

343 **Correspondence relating to Persia and Afghanistan.**
Official Correspondence. London: British Government, 1839. 524p.
Section five contains verbatim copies of correspondence between the Amir of Afghanistan and the Governor-General of India, along with letters to and from leading British representatives in Afghanistan and on the North-West Frontier. Altogether there are sixty-five documents relating to Afghanistan from such notables as Henry Pottinger, Amir Dost Mohammad, Alexander Burnes, and Shah Shuja.

344 **Diary of a march through Sinde and Afghanistan, with the troops under the command of General Sir William Nott, K.C.B., &c. and sermons delivered on various occasions during the campaign of 1842.**
I. N. Allen. London: J. Hatchard, 1843. 468p.

After offering a 'Sketch of the Dooraunee Empire' (the Durrani Empire [1747-93]), the author recounts his travels through Sindh and on up to the Bolan Pass, Kandahar, Ghazni, and then to Kabul. He subsequently follows the route of the retreat from Kabul which had taken place the previous year, making his way to Jalalabad and Peshawar.

345 **Dr. Brydon's report on the British retreat from Kabul in January 1842: an important historical document.**
Louis Dupree, Nancy Hatch Dupree. *Afghanistan.* vol. 20, no. 3. (1967), p. 55-65.

The introduction explains the context and there follows a transcript of the surgeon's report, together with comments and quotes from other sources. The Duprees correctly point out that Dr. Brydon did not die in Jalalabad as is sometimes reported, but as they do not appear to know what happened to him afterward, it may be recorded that he was present at the Siege of Lucknow during the Great Mutiny, retired with honours in 1858, and returned home to Scotland taking with him, if family legend is to be believed, the horse that had carried him to safety in Afghanistan. He died in 1873 and is buried in the churchyard in Rosemarkie in Ross-shire.

346 **The dropped stitch.**
Garry J. Alder. *Afghanistan Journal.* vol. 1, no. 4; vol. 2, no. 1. (1974; 1975), p. 105-13; p. 20-27.

This history of British expansion (at Sikh expense) across the Punjab towards Afghanistan begins in 1849 with the capture of Peshawar. The author goes on to relate the ups and downs of Anglo-Afghan relations between the First Afghan War and the Second.

347 **Eighteen years in the Khyber, 1877-1898.**
Robert Warburton. London: John Murray, 1900. 344p. map.

The life and times of a British officer who was Warden of the Khyber, served in the Second Afghan War, and was much involved in frontier affairs during a momentous period of its history. There is a good deal of interesting material about Amir Abdur Rahman and British frontier policy.

348 **England and Afghanistan, a phase in their relations.**
Dilip Kumar Ghose. Calcutta: World Press, 1960. 230p. map. bibliog.

An analysis of Britain's Forward Policy from the conquest of the Punjab in 1849 to the Anglo-Russian Agreement of 1887 in which the author shows that there was a fundamental unity in British foreign policy regarding Central Asia which is often overlooked.

349 **England and Russia in the East: a series of papers on the political and geographical condition of Central Asia.**
Henry G. Rawlinson. London 1875. 393p. map.
A geographical and political account of Central Asia's rôle in 19th century history which examines Russian territorial expansion and its effect on British policy and includes an interesting critique of the writings of European travellers who explored the region. As always in Central Asia, Afghanistan is in the middle, both geographically and politically.

350 **The expedition into Afghanistan: notes and sketches descriptive of the country contained in a personal narrative during the campaign of 1839 and 1840 up to the surrender of Dost Mahomed Khan.**
James Atkinson. London: Wm. H. Allen, 1842. 428p. map.
A personal account of the First Afghan War by the superintending surgeon of the Army of the Indus which includes a history of Shah Shuja, the military advance to Kandahar, the capture of Ghazni, the march to Kabul, the surrender of Amir Dost Mohammad, and the march to Jalalabad. The book ends prior to the 1841 retreat from Kabul and the destruction of the British force.

351 **The First Afghan War, 1838-1842.**
J. A. Norris. Cambridge, England: Cambridge University Press, 1967. 500p. maps. bibliog.
A thorough, scholarly, and readable history which begins by looking at Anglo-Russian rivalry and British policy regarding Central Asia before relating the events of 1838-1842. Despite formidable rivals, this is probably the best book on this period.

352 **The first Afghan war and its causes.**
Henry M. Durand. London: Longmans, Green, 1879. 445p.
An excellent history by Henry Marion Durand, one of the key figures in the British Government of India (not to be confused with his equally famous son, Henry Mortimer Durand) who was on the Viceroy's Council and, at the time of his death in 1870, Lieutenant-Governor of the Punjab. A background account of relevant events from 1799-1837 is followed by a narrative description, month by month, of occurrences, both in Afghanistan and in India, from 1838 to 1842. Durand provides fascinating insights into personalities and events, and he does not hesitate to criticize either individuals or government policies when the occasion calls for it.

353 **Forty-one years in India, from subaltern to Commander-in-Chief.**
Frederick S. Roberts, Lord Roberts of Kandahar. London: Macmillan, 1897. 2 vols. maps.
An engrossing autobiography by a man who sailed to India in 1852 at the age of twenty, saw active service during the Mutiny, was awarded the Victoria Cross, and held the rank of General by the time he was forty-seven. He was commander of the British Army in Afghanistan during the Second Afghan War. His accounts of this period are found in chapters 43-62.

354  **From Alexander Burnes to Frederick Roberts, a survey of Imperial frontier policy.**
J. L. Morison. *Proceedings of the British Academy.* vol. XXII. (1936), 32p. (Raleigh Lectures on History).
An historical assessment of Anglo-Afghan relations and the problem of the North-West Frontier from the First Afghan War to the Second.

355  **From Khyber to Oxus.**
Suhash Chakravarty. New Delhi: Orient Longman, 1976. 280p. map. bibliog.
A study which deals with the period of Anglo-Afghan history from 1869 to 1880. The 'Afghan problem' as seen from the British point of view is examined and diplomatic and military moves made in the light of Russia's real or imagined intentions are explained.

356  **Further postal history of the Second Afghan War, 1878-81, with Kandahar and Baluchistan, 1881-87: a review in the light of contemporary records.**
D. R. Martin. London: Postal History Society, 1961. 41p. maps. bibliog. (Special Series, no. 12).
A brief account of the war is followed by descriptions of field post offices, civil post offices, communications, and mail robberies. The author concludes with 'Hints on postal operations in the field'. This is a valuable account obtained by the painstaking sifting of many thousands of pages of published accounts and government reports of the war. Stamps, cancellations or strikes, and covers are illustrated.

357  **Government and society in Afghanistan: the reign of Amir 'Abd al-Rahman Khan.**
Hasan Kawun Kakar. Austin, Texas; London: University of Texas, 1979. 328p.
A detailed study of Abdur Rahman's life and reign with special emphasis on national and local government, taxation, the military, and the social and economic structure of the country.

358  **Gun-running and the Indian north-west frontier.**
Arnold Keppel. London: John Murray, 1911. 214p. maps.
The first six chapters of this book deal with an account of the problems which the British faced in their attempts to keep the peace on the North-West Frontier of India. The main problem was seen to be the Pushtuns and the policies of the Afghan government. Prior to World War I, according to the author, the British had no wish to see a free and independent government in Afghanistan. What was wanted was an Afghan government over which Britain could exercise control. Gun-running therefore posed a threat to British interests.

359 **The Hazaras and the British in the nineteenth century.**
Sarah Jones. *Afghanistan Journal.* vol. 5, no. 1. (1977), p. 3-5. map. bibliog.
A brief history of the Hazara peoples and their role in Anglo-Afghan relations as described by 19th century European writers. Some Hazaras served in the British Army as early as the First Afghan War. A battalion of Hazara Pioneers raised in 1904 was not disbanded until 1932.

360 **Herat: the granary and garden of Central Asia.**
G. B. Malleson. London: W. H. Allen, 1880. 196p. map. bibliog.
The author, an advocate of the 'Forward Policy' (a policy of moving forward from the Indus to Kabul, Kandahar and Herat to prevent the Persians, French and Russians from invading India), argues that Britain should extend her political and military influence over all of Afghanistan, including Herat, in order to check Russian advances in Central Asia. Herat is viewed as the key strategic city as regards the security of British India. This is an interesting blend of late Victorian attitudes and politics.

361 **History of the war in Afghanistan.**
John William Kaye. London; Calcutta: W. H. Allen, 1890. 3 vols.
An official history and standard work on the First Afghan War, with a detailed account of the political background to events beginning in 1800 and continuing through to the summer of 1839. The second volume covers the period from August 1839 to January 1842, while the third volume traces parallel events occuring beyond the immediate battle scenes in 1841 and on to the end of 1842.

362 **In the highlight of modern Afghanistan.**
Ahmad Ali Kohzad. Kabul: Historical Society of Afghanistan, [n.d.]. 144p. (Historical Society of Afghanistan, no. 56).
A collection of eight historical essays derived from various Dari manuscripts in Kabul libraries, among them: 'The siege of Ghazni', 'The [British] evacuation of Kabul', and 'The assassination of Shah Shuja'. These are of particular interest as they provide an Afghan view of the First Afghan War - a political and military event largely documented by British writers.

363 **India and Afghanistan, 1876-1907: a study in diplomatic relations.**
D. P. Singhal. St. Lucia, Queensland: University of Queensland, 1963. 216p. maps. bibliog.
An account of the events leading up to the Second Afghan War, the installation of Abdur Rahman as Amir of Afghanistan, and his subsequent reign. The British desire to create an independent buffer state between India and Russia is examined and the means of achieving it is described.

364 **The Indian borderland, 1880-1900.**
Thomas Hungerford Holdich. London: Methuen, 1901. 402p. map.
A thorough account of events beyond the North-West Frontier from the Second Afghan War to the twilight of Victoria's reign by one of the principal figures in

frontier affairs. The work of the various boundary commissions is described and political events are placed in historical perspective.

365  **Indo-Afghan relations, 1880-1900.**
Ram Sagar Rastogi. Lucknow, India: Nav-Jyoti, 1965. 256p. maps. bibliog.
This is essentially a history of Abdur Rahman's reign, which tells how he came to power, describes his relationship with the British Government of India, and tells of the various boundary commissions which demarcated his frontiers.

366  **Journal of the disasters in Affghanistan, 1841-2.**
Lady Florentia Sale. London: John Murray, 1843. 451p. map.
This famous journal begins in September 1841, three years after the beginning of the First Afghan War, and continues through to September 21st, 1842 when Florentia Sale was released from captivity and reunited with her husband General Sir Robert Sale. It thus includes the nine-month period during which the author was a prisoner of the Afghans.

367  **The Kabul insurrection of 1841-42, revised and corrected from Lieutenant Eyre's original manuscript by Major-General Sir Vincent Eyre.**
Vincent Eyre. London: Wm. H. Allen, 1879. 335p. maps.
Together with the more famous journal kept by Lady Florentia Sale (q.v.), this gives a full and accurate picture of events leading up to the First Afghan War and the diplomatic and military incidents which culminated in the Kabul insurrection and subsequent disasters which overtook the British Army in Afghanistan. In addition it contains the personal experiences of the author, himself a prisoner of the Afghans at the time.

368  **Kabul to Kandahar.**
Maud Diver. London: Peter Davies, 1935. 192p. map. bibliog. (Great Occasions).
This is the story of the Second Afghan War, written for those who like a good true adventure, rather than for the military history buff or the Afghan history specialist.

369  **The life of Abdur Rahman, Amir of Afghanistan.**
Edited by Sultan Mahomed Khan. London: John Murray, 1900. 2 vols. map.
The story of the Amir's life, written partly by himself (eleven of the twelve chapters of volume I), and partly edited and translated by the Amir's Secretary of State 'from the Amir's own words'. The impression gained from a reading of this is that the Amir was a kindly, benevolent old soldier and avuncular ruler, but the historical record shows that he was a cruel despot who ordered the deaths of tens of thousands of his fellow citizens.

370 **Life of the Amir Dost Mohammed Khan of Kabul.**
   Mohan Lal. London: Longman, Brown, Green, and Longmans, 1846.
   2 vols.
Dost Mohammed occupied the throne of Kabul from 1819 to 1839 and from 1842
to 1863, during which time he succeeded in expanding and unifying the nation
by adding the territories between the Hindu Kush and the Amu Darya as well as
Kandahar and Herat to those already under his rule. This was written by the well-
known Kashmiri traveller and biographer who was in the service of the East India
Company and who personally knew most of the men and participated in many of
the events he describes.

371 **A memoir of India and Avghanistaun with observations on the present
   exciting and critical state and future prospects of those countries, comprising remarks on the massacre of the British army in Cabul, British
   policy in India, a detailed descriptive character of Dost Mahomed and
   his court, etc.**
   Josiah Harlan. Philadelphia, Pennsylvania: J. Dobson, 1842. 208p.   ·
   map.
Written in an ornamental and florid style this is, nevertheless, from the pen of a
man who spent nearly twenty years during the first half of the 19th century in the
Punjab and Afghanistan in regions seen by few Europeans at the time. Harlan, an
adventurer in the great Kipling tradition, served under both Ranjit Singh and the
Amir Dost Mohammad. His account is part personal experience, part history, and
part political criticism.

372 **Memoirs of Major-General Sir Henry Havelock, K.C.B.**
   John Clark Marshman. London: Longman, Green, Longman, and
   Roberts, 1860. 462p.
Chapters two and three (p. 43-136) deal with Havelock's experiences as a British of-
ficer during the First Afghan War and provide interesting and informative sidelights
on the official accounts.

373 **Memorials of Affghanistan, being state papers, official documents,
   dispatches, authentic narratives, etc., illustrative of the British expedition to and occupation of Affghanistan and Scinde between the years
   1838 and 1842.**
   J. H. Stocqueler. Calcutta: Ostell & Lepage, 1843. 468p. maps.
A particularly interesting volume on the First Afghan War consisting of reports
written at the time by those who experienced at first-hand the events they describe.
The editor has linked individual accounts by narrative passages which place each
report in its historical context. Included are 164 pages of appendices.

374 **The military operations at Kabul, which ended in the retreat and destruction of the British Army, January 1842, with a journal of imprisonment in Affghanistan.**
Vincent Eyre. London: John Murray, 1843. 436p. map.
First-hand account of the events which marked the end of the First Afghan War in which Britain 'lost six entire regiments of infantry, three companies of sappers, a troop of European horse artillery, half the mountain train battery, nearly a whole regiment of cavalry, and four squadrons of regular horse...'- five thousand fighting men in all, including more than 100 officers, and some 12,000 camp followers.

375 **My God - Maiwand! Operations of the south Afghanistan field force, 1878-1880.**
Leigh Maxwell. London: Leo Cooper, 1979. 277p. maps. bibliog.
A lively and engaging history of the military operations carried out during the Second Afghan War in the Girishk-Kandahar region where, on July 27th, 1880, British forces suffered a defeat at the hands of the Afghans, losing nearly a thousand men.

376 **Narrative of the war in Affghanistan in 1838-39.**
Henry Havelock. London: Henry Colburn, 1840. 2 vols.
Personal experiences of the author (later Major-General Sir Henry Havelock of Lucknow) and a military history of the First Afghan War. As the author took part in the capture of Ghazni, the occupation of Kabul, and the forcing of the Khurd Kabul (the route taken by the British army in 1841 on its retreat from Kabul), he was better placed than most historians to write an account of what took place. The book was published just before disaster struck the British force in Afghanistan in 1841.

377 **The pacification of the Hazaras of Afghanistan.**
M. Hasan Kakar. New York: Afghanistan Council, Asia Society, 1973. 16p. (Occasional Paper, no. 4).
An account of Amir Abdur Rahman's 1891-93 conquest of the Hazara peoples of central Afghanistan written by an Afghan historian.

378 **Papers relating to military operations in Affghanistan presented to both Houses of Parliament by command of Her Majesty, 1843.**
Parliamentary Papers. Calcutta: William Rushton, 1843.
These papers contain verbatim correspondence between the principal officers, government officials, and government representatives in India and Afghanistan from December 1841 to December 1842. There are 547 documents in all, which represent valuable source material for the historian.

379  Personal narrative of the campaigns in Affghanistan, Sinde, Beloochis-
     tan, etc. detailed in a series of letters.
     William H. Dennie, edited by William E. Steele. Dublin: William
     Curry, 1843. 223p. map.
A lively account of the author's experiences during the First Afghan War, all the
more readable for having been originally written for the eyes of personal friends
only.

380  Playing the great game, a Victorian cold war.
     Michael Edwardes. London: Hamish Hamilton, 1975. 167p. maps.
     bibliog.
An account of political intrigues in Central Asia and the men who wandered into its
mountain ranges and deserts to further the interests of their respective governments
in the 19th century. As Afghanistan was very much in the geographical middle of
all this, the book is mainly concerned, directly and indirectly, with that country.

381  The postal history of the First Afghan War, 1838-1842.
     D. R. Martin. London: Postal History Society, 1964. 60p. maps.
     bibliog. (Special Series, no. 18).
Describes the setting up of a postal service from India to Afghanistan, the routes
chosen, postal rates, stamps, covers, cancellations, and administration of the system.
It is illustrated with examples of the stamps and cancellations used, and route maps.

382  The predictions of Amir Abdur Rahman Khan and the present Soviet
     invasion.
     Azmat Hayat Khan. WUFA, Quarterly Journal of the Writers Union of
     Free Afghanistan. vol. 1, no. 3. (1986), p. 63-70.
A selection of 19th-century quotes about Imperial Russia's expansionist policies in
Central Asia, together with suggestions for putting a stop to them, from Amir Abdur
Rahman's autobiography The life of Abdur Rahman, Amir of Afghanistan (q.v.),
which was published in London in 1900 by Mir Munshi Sultan Mahomed Khan.

383  Prison sketches, comprising portraits of the Cabul prisoners and other
     subjects adapted for binding up with the journals of Lieut. V. Eyre
     and Lady Sale.
     Vincent Eyre. London: Dickinson, 1843. 34p.
Contains twenty-five lithographed portraits of some of the main actors, both Afghan
and British, in the First Afghan War. Most of the portraits were originally drawn
by Lieut. Eyre, himself a prisoner, but some are by Godfrey Vigne and others. In
addition there is a lithograph of Alexander's column (Minar-i-Chakri), The prison at
Shewukee, The fort where General Elphinstone died, and three views of Bamiyan.

384 **Recollections of the Kabul campaign, 1879 amd 1880.**
Joshua Duke. London: W. H. Allen, 1883. 424p. maps.
A medical officer's personal account of life in mountain artillery, cavalry and in-
fantry units during the Second Afghan War as a member of General Sir Frederick
Roberts' staff.

385 **The rival powers in Central Asia, or the struggle between England
and Russia in the East.**
Joseph Popowski. London: Archibald Constable, 1893. 235p.
Originally published in German in 1890, this examines political events in
Afghanistan as they were caused, or at least influenced, by Britain's worries about
the course of Russian expansion in Asia. The author asserts that Russia desires to
possess India, examines political relations between Britain and Russia from the be-
gining of the 19th century, and maintains that 'England is powerless to arrest Russia
in Asia by means of diplomacy'. The author concludes that a war between Russia
and England in Asia is only a matter of time. The obvious battlefield is Afghanistan.

386 **La rivalité Anglo-Russe en Perse et en Afghanistan jusqu'aux accords
de 1907.**
(Anglo-Russian rivalry in Persia and Afghanistan up to the agreements
of 1907.)
Pio-Carlo Terenzio. Paris: Arthur Rousseau, 1947. 179p. bibliog.
This examines the origins, nature, and extent of the rivalry in South and Central
Asia between Russia and England which occupied so much of the time and energies
of the two nations in the 19th century.

387 **The romance of the Indian frontiers.**
George MacMunn. London: Jonathan Cape, 1931. 352p. maps.
About half of this book is devoted to an account of the peoples, places, and wars
in Afghanistan in the 19th century. As such, it offers a brief history of British
trans-frontier adventures in the land of the Afghans.

388 **Rough notes of the campaign in Sinde and Affghanistan in 1838-1839,
being extracts from a personal journal kept while on the staff of the
Army of the Indus.**
James Outram. Bombay: American Mission, 1840. 232p. maps.
An account of the opening rounds of the First Afghan War as told by the ADC to
Lord Keane, Commander-in-Chief of the Army in Bombay. James Outram was on
active service in Kandahar and took part in the capture of Ghazni. During the Indian
Mutiny in 1857, by which time he held the rank of Lieutenant-General, he was in
command of the forces in Lucknow and for his distinguished services was created
a baronet. He died in Paris at the age of sixty and is buried in Westminster Abbey.

389 **Russian correspondence with Kabul, 1870-1879.**
D. P. Singhal. *Afghanistan.* vol. 19, no. 3; no. 4. (1963), p. 12-36; p. 23-43.
A detailed, scholarly, and thorough examination of relevant historical documents for the period in question throws light on Russian intentions and British fears in the decade that preceded the Second Afghan War.

390 **The Russians at the gates of Herat.**
Charles Marvin. London; New York: Frederick Warne, 1885. 178p. map.
In the 19th century the author was one of the few British observers of the Central Asian scene who spoke Russian fluently and had travelled widely in the region. He is sceptical of the British idea that Afghanistan might serve as an effective buffer state, preventing Russia's further advance toward India, and is convinced by the geography of western and southern Afghanistan that Herat is the key to British security in South Asia.

391 **The Russians in Afghanistan in the 1830's.**
Mikhail Volodarsky. *Central Asian Survey.* vol. 3, no. 1. (1984), p. 63-86.
An account of Anglo-Russian rivalry seen mainly from an economic viewpoint - a Victorian trade war in which both sides strove to dominate the markets of Central Asia. The author maintains that 'A study of the map would convince objective observers that no hostile intent dominated Russian policy in Asia'.

392 **Sale's Brigade in Afghanistan, with an account of the seizure and defence of Jellalabad.**
G. R. Gleig. London: John Murray, 1846. 182p.
An account of the First Afghan War and in particular the part played in it by the 13th Queen's Infantry and the 35th Bengal Native Infantry which, under the leadership of Sir Robert Sale, was in the thick of the action from first to last. The march from the Indus to Kandahar, the march to Ghazni, the march to Kabul, the occupation of Kabul, and the march to Jalalabad are recounted, as is the defence of Jalalabad.

393 **The savage frontier: a history of the Anglo-Afghan Wars.**
D. S. Richards. London: Macmillan, 1990. 214p. map. bibliog.
This traces the uneasy and frequently disastrous relations between Afghanistan and Britain from 1838 through to the start of the Second World War. Although based mostly on 19th century histories and personal accounts, this also includes a chapter on the Soviet invasion of 1979.

394 **Sayid Jamal-ud-din Afghani: politician, reformer, journalist, and orator.**
Mohammed Ali. *Afghanistan.* vol. 17, no. 1. (1962), p. 1-9.
A brief biographical sketch of the life (ca. 1838-97) and times of a controversial figure who campaigned for Islamic unity and acted as advisor to the rulers of Afghanistan, Egypt, and the Ottoman Empire. Although Sayyid Jamal-ud-din

Afghani claimed to be an Afghan, research by different historians indicates that he was Iranian.

395 **The Second Afghan War, 1878-79-80, its causes, its conduct, and its consequences.**
H. B. Hanna. London: Archibald Constable, 1899. 3 vols. maps.
A critical history of the war designed to awaken the British public to the dangers and follies of the Forward Policy. The author shows that the Second Afghan War was a direct outcome of the First, both being caused by Britain's fear of Russia, and neither serving any purpose. He concludes that, as Britain could not succeed in holding Afghanistan by military force, neither can Russia. This is major work by a British officer who served in Afghanistan.

396 **The Second Afghan war, 1878-80, official account produced in the Intelligence Branch, Army Headquarters, India.**
Government of India Report. London: John Murray, 1908. 734p. maps.
A comprehensive account of the entire campaign from the autumn of 1876 to the evacuation of Kandahar in May, 1880, lavishly illustrated with photographs, maps, and plans.

397 **Signal catastrophe: the story of the disastrous retreat from Kabul, 1842.**
Patrick Macrory. London: Hodder & Stoughton, 1966. 288p. maps. bibliog.
A well-researched and absorbing account of the 1842 destruction of the British forces in Afghanistan in what came to be called the First Afghan War. In a foreword, written more than a decade before the Soviet invasion of Afghanistan, Field-Marshal Sir Gerald Templer writes: 'There is another aspect of this tragedy which should perhaps be mentioned - the impossibility of controlling, by force of arms alone, a country where the mass of the people are against the "foreigner". It could perhaps be said that this lesson has not yet been entirely learnt in the modern world'.

398 **Sir Alfred Lyall and the understanding with Russia.**
H. Mortimer Durand. *Journal of the Central Asian Society.* vol. 1, pt. 3. (1914), p. 20-45.
An examination of Russian and British interests during the 19th century in Central Asia and the nature of the consequent political tensions involving Afghanistan.

399 **The strategic principles of Lord Lytton's Afghan policy.**
James J. Allan. *Journal of the Royal Central Asian Society.* vol. 24, pt. 3. (1937), p. 429-36.
An examination of the leading figures, events, and policies that led to the Second Afghan War. Lytton is credited with having sincere regard for the interests of Britain's Empire in the East, but, according to the author, acted with undue haste and thus courted '...the very insult which became his famous *casus belli* for the Second Afghan War'.

400 **Strategies of British India: Britain, Iran, and Afghanistan, 1798-1850.**
M. E. Yapp. Oxford: Oxford University, 1980. 682p. maps. bibliog.
The author tells us that 'the subject of this book is the search for a system which
would safeguard British India from the dangers of attack from the north-west'. In
part three, 'The Afghan System', (p. 307-460) he deals with Anglo-Afghan relations
from 1839 to 1842 and closely examines the political events, both real and imagined,
which shaped British policy and actions at that time.

401 **The survival of Afghanistan: two imperial giants held at bay in the
nineteenth century.**
N. D. Ahmad. Lahore, Pakistan: People's Publishing House, 1973.
92p. maps. bibliog.
The author identifies and examines both the internal and external factors which have
been responsible for Afghanistan's survival as an independent nation and goes on
to look at the nature of Russian imperialism.

402 **To Caubul with the cavalry brigade, a narrative of personal experiences with the force under General Sir F. S. Roberts.**
Reginald W. Mitford. London: W. H. Allen, 1881. 212p. map.
This presents the personal experiences of the Second Afghan War by a Major in the
14th Bengal Lancers who saw action in most of the engagements of that conflict.

403 **Twenty years on the North-West Frontier.**
G. B. Scott. Allahabad, India: Pioneer Press, 1906. 272p. maps.
Among other things, this contains an account of the author's personal experiences
during the Second Afghan War and an essay assessing the likelihood of a Russian
invasion of India.

404 **The Victoria Cross in Afghanistan and on the frontiers of India during
the years 1877-1880; how it was won.**
W. J. Elliott. London: Dean & Sons, 1882. 248p. map.
Presents graphic accounts of military engagements and incidents in the First and
Second Afghan Wars and the British soldiers (eighteen in all) whose gallantry was
rewarded with Britain's highest military honour. Numerous engravings illustrate
people and places.

# Modern Period (1900-1979)

**405 Afghanistan, 1900-1923: a diplomatic history.**
Ludwig W. Adamec. Berkeley, California; Los Angeles: University of California, 1967. 245p. bibliog.
This study presents a history of Afghan foreign relations and describes and analyses the country's foreign policy under three Afghan rulers: Abdur Rahman, Habibullah, and Amanullah.

**406 Afghanistan 1919: an account of operations in the Third Afghan War.**
G. N. Molesworth. London: Asia Publishing House, 1962. 183p. maps.
This contains background chapters on the First and Second Afghan Wars and then deals with the Third Afghan War in some detail with sections on 'Operations in the western Khaibar', 'Eastern Khaibar', 'Thal and Kurram', 'Upper Kurram', 'Chitral', 'South Baluchistan' and 'North Baluchistan and Zhob Valley'. The author was Adjutant of the 2nd Battalion, Somerset Light Infantry and was on active service throughout the period described. He remarks that 'the official account [of the Third Afghan war] is more interesting for what it omits than for what it contains. So many senior commanders who saw it in draft, blue-pencilled it so much, that only the bare bones remain'.

**407 Afghanistan, the war of independence, 1919.**
Mohammed Ali. Kabul: The Author, 1960. 62p. map.
An account of the Third Afghan War written by an Afghan historian which shows once again that, while foreign powers audacious enough to send their armies into Afghanistan may win some battles, they always fail to win the war.

**408 Amanullah, ex-king of Afghanistan.**
Roland Wild. London: Hurst & Blackett, 1933. 288p.
A highly-coloured journalistic-style summary of the King's early years, his visit to Europe, and the author's visit to Kabul. It continues with the close of Amanullah's reign and an account of Bacha Saqao's regime, ending with Nadir Shah's accession and a glimpse of Amanullah's life in exile.

**409 Britain and Afghanistan in historical perspective.**
Cyriac Maprayil. London: Cosmic, 1983. 164p. map. bibliog.
An essay on British imperialism precedes an account of the Third Afghan War. Political events of the 1930s are outlined as background to a description of the Afghan position during the Second World War. The texts of various treaties between Britain and Afghanistan from 1879 to 1923 are set out in appendices.

410  **British imperialism and Afghanistan's struggle for independence, 1914-1921.**
Abdul Ali Arghandawi. New Delhi: Munshiram Manoharlal, 1989. 406p. map. bibliog.
A political history of the country and its relations with Britain during the First World War and the immediate postwar years.

411  **The emergence of modern Afghanistan: politics of reform and modernization, 1880-1946.**
Vartan Gregorian. Stanford, California: Stanford University Press, 1969. 586p. map. bibliog.
A political history spanning nearly seventy eventful years from the end of the Second Afghan War to the end of the Second World War. In particular, the author is concerned to trace socioeconomic developments and to examine the policies that led to them. This is a thorough study and a useful source of information.

412  **The frontier scouts.**
Charles Chenevix Trench. London: Jonathan Cape, 1985. 298p. maps. bibliog.
This is the story, from the 1870s to the end of the Second World War, of the British-led corps of Afghans, known as 'Scouts', who served on the North-West Frontier under various political agents in a bid to guard British India's most turbulent border. Chapter five deals with the part played by the Frontier Corps in the Third Afghan War.

413  **H.M. King Nadir Shah-i-Ghazi, of Afghanistan: Naji-i-Millat (Saviour of the Nation).**
Ronald M. S. Morrison. *Journal of the Royal Central Asian Society.* vol. 21, pt. 3. (1934), p. 170-75.
A tribute to the King following his assassination by Abdul Khaliq. The author describes Nadir Shah as '...the greatest ruler who has ever reigned over Afghanistan' and cites some of the progressive reforms which he implemented.

414  **Iran, Turkey, and Afghanistan: a political chronology.**
Lawrence Ziring. New York: Praeger, 1981. 230p. bibliog.
Afghanistan is discussed in chapter three, 'The origins and development of Afghanistan' and chapter six, 'Afghanistan in the 1970s'. The author, having identified a 'Northern Tier' of countries from north-west Pakistan to the eastern Mediterranean, views them as forming a political 'shatterbelt' where 'centuries of conflict have failed to resolve either local or regional issues'. He sees the Soviet invasion of Afghanistan as a direct consequence of the collapse of US influence in Iran.

415  **My life: from brigand to king, the autobiography of Amir Habibullah.**
Habibullah Ghazi. London: Sampson Low, Marston, [n.d.]. 276p.
This purports to be the life story of the Tadjik rebel, bandit, and soldier of fortune who ruled Afghanistan for nine months in 1929 after the collapse of Amanullah's

government. He is not to be confused with Amir Habibullah, son of Amir Abdur Rahman. The book is quite possibly fiction.

416 **Reform and rebellion in Afghanistan, 1919-1929: King Amanullah's failure to modernize a tribal society.**
Leon B. Poullada. Ithaca, New York: Cornell University Press, 1973. 318p. maps. bibliog.
A history written from the point of view that the study of Afghan politics should be understood within the context of tribal politics and that Amanullah's failure to modernize the country was largely due to the fact that the powers of the central government did not extend into tribal areas - a condition which is as true in the 1990s as it was in the 1920s.

417 **The Third Afghan war, 1919. Official account compiled in the General Staff Branch, Army Headquarters, India.**
Calcutta: Government of India, 1926. 174p. maps.
A concise account of Afghanistan and its history. An analysis of both British and Afghan forces in 1919 precedes a detailed description of military movements and engagements from May 6th, 1919 to the end of July that same year. Concluding sections describe the cholera epidemics, water supplies, rations, and finally 'Lessons of the war'. This last chapter could have been read with profit by the Soviet government in 1979.

418 **Wings over Kabul: the first airlift.**
Anne Baker, Ronald Ivelaw-Chapman. London: William Kimbe, 1975. 190p.
An account of the Kabul evacuations of 1929 - 'the first major airlift of civilians and officials from one country to another in circumstances of acute political stress'. The eighty-four missions lifted 586 civilians from Kabul following the downfall of King Amanullah and the subsequent take-over by Bacha Saqao, the rebel king (Habibullah Ghazi). Included are many photographs and extracts from letters and diaries plus personal reminiscences.


**A geographical introduction to the history of Central Asia.**
*See* item no. 53.

# The Soviet Invasion and Occupation (1979-1989)

419 **The Afghan armed resistance.**
Nasrullah Safi. *WUFA, Quarterly Journal of the Writers Union of Free Afghanistan.* vol. 1, no. 2. (1986), p. 27-37.
The author's thesis is that the April 1978 *coup d'état* (known as the 'Saur [April] Revolution') was planned by the Russians as a prelude to the Soviet invasion. It therefore had no popular support, as evidenced by the fact that armed resistance to the Kabul regime and later to the Russians was immediate and spontaneous. The author, himself an army officer, analyses the nature of armed resistance and the strategies employed by the *Mujahideen.*

420 **The Afghan brain drain.**
A. Rasul Amin. *WUFA, Quarterly Journal of the Writers Union of Free Afghanistan.* vol. 1, no. 3. (1986), p. 3-8.
The editor of *WUFA* examines the loss to Afghanistan of many of her best-trained people as a result of the Soviet invasion and appeals to leaders of the *jehad* to make the best use of these exiles in order to produce an efficient organization and to coordinate the leadership of the resistance movement.

421 **The Afghan crisis.**
Gary Gamer. New York: Task Force on Militarization in Asia and the Pacific, 1988. 47p.
The first part of this report offers an historical background to the Soviet invasion and occupation of Afghanistan, the second outlines the political crisis, the third examines humanitarian concerns, and the fourth considers prospects for peace. There are some recommendations and an annotated bibliography.

## The Soviet Invasion and Occupation (1979-1989)

422 **Afghan resistance and Soviet occupation: a five-year summary.**
Craig Karp. Washington, DC: Department of State, Bureau of Public Affairs, 1984. 4p. (Special Report, no. 118).
A brief position report for members of the government and the public alike which summarizes the circumstances of the Soviet invasion, the political background, the military situation, the strengths of the Soviet military presence, and the political situation as it stood nearly five years after the war started.

423 **Afghan resistance: the politics of survival.**
Edited by Grant M. Farr, John G. Merriam. Lahore: Vanguard, 1988. 235p. map. bibliog.
A collection of papers which examine anti-Soviet movements, arms shipments, the Afghan refugee problem in Pakistan, and the world response to the Afghan refugee question.

424 **The Afghan syndrome: how to live with Soviet power.**
Bhabani Sen Gupta. London: Croom Helm, 1982. 296p.
A survey of the political climate in which the Soviet invasion occurred, an examination of Soviet policy, and the wider implications for India, Pakistan, and China. The author considers that at this time the world had yet to adjust to the fact that the Soviet Union was a major world power.

425 **The Afghan war in 1983: strengthened resistance versus Soviet 'Nazi' tactics.**
Borje Almqvist. *Central Asian Survey*. vol. 3, no. 1. (1984), p. 23-46.
An examination of the progress of the Fourth Afghan War, based partly on published accounts and partly on first hand observations, which includes an account of the military successes of Ahmad Shah Massoud's operations in the Panjshir Valley, an appraisal of Soviet tactics, and the problems faced by the Karmal regime and the Afghan Army.

426 **Afghanistan.**
George Arney. London: Mandarin, 1990. 276p. maps.
The first six chapters trace the history of Afghanistan from the Mogul period to the Soviet invasion. The remainder of the book deals with the decade of war and its aftermath. It is a useful survey.

427 **Afghanistan, 1980-1989.**
Ed Grazda. Zurich; Frankfurt; New York: Der Alltag, [n.d.]. 139p.
A book of black-and-white photographs, mostly taken behind Soviet lines during the occupation of the country, adding up to an album of despair through which there are occasional glimpses of the undaunted spirit of the people of Afghanistan.

428 **Afghanistan, 1980: the world turned upside down.**
Louis Dupree. Hanover, New Hampshire: American Universities Field Staff Reports, 1980. 13p. (AUFS Reports, 1980, no. 37, Asia).
A brief examination of the Soviet invasion, its effects, and the political situation in Afghanistan both before and after.

429 **Afghanistan: a decade of Sovietisation.**
Edited by Yusuf Elmi. Peshawar, Pakistan: Afghan Jehad Works Translation Centre, 1988. 375p.
A collection of papers by various Afghan authors examining the effects of the Soviet invasion on the Afghan legal system, education, and the press. Includes accounts by victims of torture, brainwashing, and propaganda.

430 **Afghanistan as a victim of Soviet penetration, manipulation, domination, and exploitation.**
S. Kaimur. *WUFA, Quarterly Journal of the Writers Union of Free Afghanistan*. vol. 2, no. 4. (1987), p. 1-14.
A discussion of the reasons why Moscow decided to invade the country, several of which are considered and then rejected in favour of a strategic reason, combined with a desire to appropriate Afghanistan's natural resources.

431 **Afghanistan crisis: implications and options for the Muslim world, Iran and Pakistan.**
Ijaz S. Gilani. Islamabad, Pakistan: Institute of Policy Studies, 1982. 158p. map. bibliog.
This traces the rise of communist influence in Afghanistan, changing Soviet-Afghan relations, and Soviet strategies prior to the invasion. The rôle of various *Mujahideen* groups, both political and military is examined.

432 **Afghanistan, from tragedy to triumph.**
Sadhan Mukherjee. Karachi: Pakistan Publishing House, 1984. 258p.
The tone of this book, published four years after the Soviet invasion of Afghanistan, is set by the author's assertion that 'with the unstinted help of the Soviet Union, other socialist countries, and also non-aligned countries like India, Afghanistan has, at the fag end of the 20th century, suddenly emerged into the 20th century having remained for long virtually at the medieval stage'. The book begins with the Saur revolution in April 1978 and carries through into 1984. There is no bibliography and the author's sources are not revealed.

433 **Afghanistan in crisis.**
Edited by K. P. Misra. London: Croom Helm, 1981. 150p. bibliog.
A collection of eight papers by as many Indian scholars on the political events leading up to and immediately following the Soviet invasion, which includes discussions of US policy and reaction, India and the crisis in Afghanistan, Pakistan's policy, the United Nations and the Afghan crisis, and the military action taken inside the country.

## The Soviet Invasion and Occupation (1979-1989)

434 **Afghanistan in crisis: a review article.**
Anthony Hyman. *Central Asian Survey*. vol. 1, no. 1. (1982), p. 133-40.
A critical review and discussion of several 1981 publications concerning the crisis in Afghanistan resulting from the Soviet invasion. It is by a journalist well-informed about the country.

435 **Afghanistan: inside a rebel stronghold; journeys with the Mujahiddin.**
Mike Martin. Poole, England: Blandford, 1984. 256p. map.
A personal account by a journalist who spent four months behind Soviet lines in Afghanistan in 1983, travelling to *Mujahideen*-held areas east and north of Kabul, and then on to Bamiyan north-west of the capital. Three maps and seventy-nine photographs accompany the text.

436 **Afghanistan, key to a continent.**
John C. Griffiths. London; Boulder, Colorado: Andre Deutsch, 1981. 225p. maps. bibliog.
The bulk of this is a rehash of the standard histories of Afghanistan interspersed with the author's journalistic account of his own travels in the region. It offers an summary of the historical and political events prior to and immediately following the 1979 Soviet invasion of Afghanistan.

437 **Afghanistan: puppets without props.**
Christina Dameyer. *WUFA Quarterly Journal of the Writers Union of Free Afghanistan*. vol. 4, no. 2. (1989), p. 95-100.
A discussion of the political situation in the country following the Soviet withdrawal, viewed in the light of the agents, the weapons, and the military equipment left behind to prop up the Najibullah regime.

438 **Afghanistan: seven years against a superpower.**
Barnett R. Rubin. *WUFA, Quarterly Journal of the Writers Union of Free Afghanistan*. vol. 1, no. 4. (1986), p. 26-34.
A survey of political events in Afghanistan and the Soviet Union and an evaluation of various political possibilities in the light of the Soviet military stalemate resulting from Afghan resistance.

439 **Afghanistan: the Soviet invasion in perspective.**
Anthony Arnold. Stanford, California: Hoover Institution Press, Stanford University, 1985. 179p. map. bibliog. (Hoover International Studies).
The first eight chapters trace political events in Afghanistan from the turn of the century up to the Soviet invasion. The last three examine the internal and external problems created by the Soviet Union as a result of their occupation of the country, US policy toward the Soviet Union, and the forces at work in occupied Afghanistan. The author argues that Afghanistan is not necessarily lost to the Soviet Union and that Russian troops might be withdrawn from the country under certain conditions.

He believes that changes within the Soviet Union, combined with world opinion, might achieve withdrawal and would be of great benefit to Russia.

### 440 Afghanistan: the Soviet war.

Edward Girardet. London: Croom Helm, 1985. 259p. maps.

An examination of the state of the country since the Soviet invasion, this provides an appraisal of the conflict based on the author's experiences inside Afghanistan, as well as those of other journalists, doctors, refugees, and resistance sources.

### 441 Afghanistan today.

Edited by A. Rasul Amin. Peshawar, Pakistan: Writers Union of Free Afghanistan, 1986. 68p.

An album of colour photographs showing victims of the Soviet invasion and the Communist-inspired war. The title, no doubt deliberately chosen, is the same as that of an official Democratic Republic of Afghanistan periodical which has as its subtitle: *Magazine of peace, solidarity and friendship organization of the Democratic Republic of Afghanistan* (q.v.). Designed to shock, this contains depressing photos of refugee camps and men, women, and children in hospital with terrible wounds.

### 442 Afghanistan, travels with the Mujahideen.

Sandy Gall. London: Hodder & Stoughton, 1988. 226p. maps.

A first-hand account of the war by a noted British journalist who travelled widely in Soviet-occupied Afghanistan in 1982, 1984, and 1986 for the purpose of reporting a tragedy that was in danger of being forgotten by the Western world.

### 443 Afghanistan under Soviet domination, 1964-81.

Anthony Hyman. London: Macmillan, 1982. 223p. maps. bibliog.

A readable and well-researched assessment of the crisis in Afghanistan, the opposition to the Soviet invasion, and the outlook for the future, written by one of the more astute observers of the Afghan scene.

### 444 Afghanistan under Soviet domination, 1964-83.

Anthony Hyman. London: Macmillan, 1984. 247p. maps. bibliog.

A specialist in South Asian history and in Islamic Studies, the author examines the political changes leading up to the Saur revolution, traces the events of that period, and follows developments up to and including the Soviet invasion. This comprises a thorough and reliable study by one who knows the country at first hand.

### 445 Afghanistan: whose war?

Syed Shabbir Hussain, Absan Husain Rizvi. Islamabad, Pakistan: El-Mashriqi, 1987. 105p. bibliog.

Describes the nature of Afghan resistance, the Sovietization of the country, the destruction caused by the Soviet invasion and occupation, and the nature of the Geneva talks.

## The Soviet Invasion and Occupation (1979-1989)

### 446  Afghanistan's role in Soviet strategy.
David Rees. London: Institute for the Study of Conflict, 1980. 18p. maps. (Conflict Studies, no. 118.).

The author considers that the Soviet invasion was a result of 'years of economic, political and subversive measures, including the building [in Afghanistan] of strategic highways and airfields', pointing out that this facilitates possible operations against Iran and Pakistan. The paper describes Soviet preparations, deceptions and motives, and the weaknesses of US policy. The author concludes that 'only the western deployment of effective counterforce - military, political, economic - will affect the Kremlin's will in Afghanistan or anywhere else'.

### 447  Afghanistan's troubled capital: Kabul.
Mike Edwards. *National Geographic Magazine.* vol. 167, no. 4. (1985), p. 494-505.

A former Peace Corps employee returns to visit Kabul during the Soviet occupation. This illustrated article describes life in the city under war conditions.

### 448  Afghans meet Soviet challenge.
Fath-ur-Rahman, Bashir A. Qureshi. Peshawar, Pakistan: Institute of Regional Studies, 1981. [n.p].

Describes Islamic movements in the country, offers a history of Soviet-Afghan relations, and asks who it is that the Russians have come to defend. The authors provide accounts of Soviet atrocities in Afghanistan and speculate about Soviet plans for South Asia.

### 449  Among the Afghans.
Arthur Bonner. Durham, North Carolina: Duke University, 1987. 366p.

An American journalist pays an uncomfortable visit to the *Mujahideen*, finding the food, transportation, and arrangements in general unsatisfactory, but presses on, determined to get a story. This contains the usual historical summary of the country which here serves as a backdrop for the author's personal experiences.

### 450  An analysis of the present situation in Afghanistan, January 1985.
Mohammad Eshaq. Oxford: Society for Central Asian Studies, [1985]. 23p. (Central Asian Survey, Incidental Papers Series, no. 2).

A document written by the political assistant to Ahmad Shah Massoud and issued by the Peshawar office of *Jamiat-e Islami*, this examines the Soviet decision to invade the country, dissects the mistake, and outlines the Soviet military plan. It then analyses the change in Soviet military tactics that took place in the winter of 1983-84, the morals and behaviour of Soviet troops, the progress made by the *Mujahideen*, and the nature of the Afghan resistance.

### 451  Behind Russian lines: an Afghan journal.
Sandy Gall. London: Sidgwick & Jackson, 1983. 194p. maps.

First-hand account of a two-month journey on foot made in 1982 inside Afghanistan to meet *Mujahideen* leaders and to record on film and tape the war that the Soviet

Union waged against the villagers of Panjshir Valley. A highly readable account of a difficult journey which turned out to be a successful film-making enterprise.

452 **A brief appraisal of war in Jalalabad.**
Nasrullah Safi. *WUFA, Quarterly Journal of the Writers Union of Free Afghanistan.* vol. 4, no. 2. (1989), p. 12-21.
An army officer evaluates the problems, both military and political, facing the *Mujahideen* in their attempts to take Jalalabad.

453 **Brief responses to questions concerning the Afghanistan problem.**
Louis Dupree. *WUFA, Quarterly Journal of the Writers Union of Free Afghanistan.* vol. 1, no. 3. (1986), p. 25-32.
A résumé of the profound problems facing the Soviet Union in its attempts to maintain a puppet regime in Kabul and to pacify the remainder of the country.

454 **Caught in the crossfire; a woman journalist's breathtaking experiences in war-torn Afghanistan.**
Jan Goodwin. London: Macdonald, 1987. 330p. map.
This first-hand personal narrative of a woman journalist's experiences in Pakistan, Soviet-occupied Afghanistan and, briefly, the Soviet Union, is well summarized by the book's subtitle. It includes graphic accounts, many of them at second hand, of Soviet atrocities, recounts the physical and mental strain of participating in military operations over difficult terrain with Afghans on their home ground, and provides insights as to why the Soviets cannot win in Afghanistan.

455 **Causes of Soviet invasion.**
Azmat Hayat Khan. *WUFA, Quarterly Journal of the Writers Union of Free Afghanistan.* vol. 2, no. 2. (1987), p. 51-60.
An examination of what the author sees as the short-term and long-term Soviet objectives in South Asia and the options open to Moscow once Afghanistan is pacified.

456 **The conflict in Afghanistan.**
John C. Griffiths. Hove, England: Wayland, 1987. 78p. maps. bibliog. (Flashpoints).
A brief account, illustrated with numerous black-and-white photographs, of the Soviet invasion and its consequences. It includes an historical chapter to outline the place of Afghanistan in Anglo-Russian rivalries in the 19th century.

457 **The different stages of Afghanistan's jehad.**
Nasrullah Safi. *WUFA, Quarterly Journal of the Writers Union of Free Afghanistan.* vol. 3, no. 1. (1988), p. 83-93.
The author identifies three phases of the Afghan *jehad* against the Russians: the seizure of political power by the *Khalq-Parcham* factions, the Soviet invasion of the country, and the 1987 proclamation of the national reconciliation programme

by the puppet government. He concludes with an explanation of why the Afghan *Mujahideen* had not achieved victory over their enemies after eight years of fighting.

## 458 Dust of the saints: a journey to Herat in time of war.
Radek Sikorski. London: Chatto & Windus, 1989. 274p. maps.

Account by a young Polish journalist of a journey made in 1987 across Afghanistan from the Bolan Pass and Kandahar area to Herat and back again during the Soviet occupation. Understanding what Russian domination means from his own experiences at home and, himself a political refugee, he brings a sharp edge and sharper focus to his report of life and death in Soviet-occupied Afghanistan.

## 459 Failure of Sovietization in Afghanistan.
Nake M. Kamrany. *WUFA, Quarterly Journal of the Writers Union of Free Afghanistan.* vol. 1, no. 3. (1986), p. 9-23.

An evaluation of the strength of Afghan resistance after six years of Soviet occupation, together with an examination of Soviet strategy, political policies, economic plans, and military campaigns.

## 460 A general reflection on the stealthy Sovietisation of Afghanistan.
A. Rasul Amin. *Central Asian Survey.* vol. 3, no. 1. (1984), p. 47-61.

An examination of the ideological aims and methods used by Soviet Communists in Afghanistan as viewed against the historical background of Russian expansion into and political domination of Central Asia.

## 461 Gorbachev bringing Ivan home: a complicated superpower game.
Rahmat D. Zirakyar. *WUFA, Quarterly Journal of the Writers Union of Free Afghanistan.* vol. 3, no. 1. (1988), p. 13-33.

The author considers that the Soviet Union is anxious to strengthen its relations with both Arab states and Israel in order to challenge US influence in the Middle East and 'to thwart any effective international backing for the Afghan Mujahideen'. He outlines what he considers to be the main difficulties of ending the war in Afghanistan.

## 462 The hidden war: a Russian journalist's account of the Soviet war in Afghanistan.
Artyom Borovik. London; Boston, Massachusetts: Faber & Faber, 1990. 288p.

A personal and unvarnished account of the war as seen and experienced by a journalist who travelled with Soviet forces and saw a good deal of military action 'in a foreign land against an unseen enemy for unclear purposes'.

463 **Human rights violations in Afghanistan.**
Mohammed Asef Ikram. *WUFA, Quarterly Journal of the Writers Union of Free Afghanistan.* vol. 1, no. 4. (1986), p. 35-52.
Case studies of the killing of civilians in rural and urban areas by Soviet troops, KHAD (secret police) agents, and members of the Kabul regime. The report gives names, dates, and other details of nearly 100 victims, plus accounts of many more.

464 **Importance of the Nuristan region as a base.**
Abdul Hai Warshan. *WUFA, Quarterly Journal of the Writers Union of Free Afghanistan.* vol. 1, no. 3. (1986), p. 71-78. bibliog.
The writer argues that, as the war with the Soviet Union is going to be a long one, there is an urgent need for the Afghan resistance forces to establish secure bases in remote parts of the country. He considers that Nuristan is of vital strategic importance in this regard.

465 **International politics and Afghanistan today.**
Rahmat Djan Zirakyar. *WUFA, Quarterly Journal of the Writers Union of Free Afghanistan.* vol. 1, no. 4. (1986), p. 13-25. bibliog.
An examination of the cost of the Soviet invasion, the PDPA regime, diplomatic moves, the Islamic unity of the *Mujahideen*, the situation in Iran, and US proposals for an end to the war. The author points out that in 1986 the Soviets had already been fighting the people of Afghanistan for twice as long as they fought the Germans in the Second World War.

466 **Liberation and social emancipation: the modernization of the Afghan resistance movement.**
Jan Heeren Grevemeyer. *WUFA, Quarterly Journal of the Writers Union of Free Afghanistan.* vol. 1, no. 4. (1986), p. 69-78. bibliog.
An examination of changes in the Afghan resistance movement as it evolved '...from peasant revolt to guerilla group and then to a social emancipation movement'.

467 **L'URSS en Afghanistan: de la coopération à l'occupation, 1947-1984.**
(The Soviet Union in Afghanistan: from cooperation to occupation, 1947-1984.)
Pierre Metge. Paris: Centre interdisciplinaire de recherches sur la paix et d'études stratégiques, 1984. 186p. maps. bibliog. (Cahiers d'Études Stratégiques).
This study considers that, given Soviet interests in the area, the progression from economic and military cooperation to intervention in the political arena was inevitable, as was the subsequent Soviet invasion, once a regime which they had helped into power began to fail.

The Soviet Invasion and Occupation (1979-1989)

468 **Mujahideen and air defense weapons.**
Nasrullah Safi. *WUFA, Quarterly Journal of the Writers Union of Free Afghanistan.* vol. 2, no. 4. (1987), p. 40-47.
An analysis of the changes in Soviet air tactics following *Mujahideen* access to sophisticated ground-to-air missiles.

469 **'A nation is dying': Afghanistan under the Soviets, 1979-1987.**
Jerl Laber, Barnett R. Rubin. Evanston, Illinois: Northwestern University, 1988. 179p. bibliog.
Based on some 400 interviews with Afghan refugees in Pakistan, this documents human rights violations, massacres, theft, torture, executions, rape, forced conscription, murder of children and the elderly, and suppression of civil liberties by both the Soviets and Afghan government forces.

470 **NGO's and the Afghan war: the politicisation of humanitarian aid.**
Helga Baitenmann. *Third World Quarterly.* vol. 12, no. 1. (1990), p. 62-85.
NGOs are non-governmental organizations and according to the author there are nearly 300 of them providing aid in response to the crisis in Afghanistan. It is the writer's view that they have been used for political purposes and, in the case of those working inside Afghanistan, they 'were conscious agents of political interests'.

471 **On the diplomatic and political front: Afghanistan from April, 1978 through February, 1989.**
Rahmat Rabi Zirakyar. *WUFA, Quarterly Journal of the Writers Union of Free Afghanistan.* vol. 4, no. 2. (1989), p. 65-80.
A chronological summary of political events with wry comments by the author.

472 **Opposition in the USSR to the occupation of Afghanistan.**
Taras Kuzio. *Central Asian Survey.* vol. 6, no. 1. (1987), p. 99-117.
This study shows that opposition within the USSR to the occupation of Afghanistan comes from those with varying political views, from those of different nationalities, and those belonging to various other groups. 'It is an area of opposition neglected and ignored by many commentators of the Soviet scene'. The author concludes that 'this type of opposition is potentially explosive for the USSR'.

473 **Panjshir - the seventh offensive.**
Mohammad Eshaq. Oxford: Society for Central Asian Studies, [1984]. 11p. (Incidental Papers Series, no. 1).
A summary of the fighting in Panjsher prior to the seventh offensive on 20 April, 1984 is followed by an account of both Soviet and *Mujahideen* tactics, successes, and failures.

474 **Pashtun tribes and the Afghan resistance.**

Hakim Taniwal, Ahmad Yusuf Nuristani. *WUFA, Quarterly Journal of the Writers Union of Free Afghanistan.* vol. 1, no. 1. (1985), p. 35-49.

An article by an anthropologist and a sociologist in which they examine the nature of social structure in the country and the relationship between the tribes and various political parties, in order to provide a context in which to view the Pushtun tribes and Afghan resistance.

475 **The policy of 'national reconciliation' or 'national submission'!**

Ahmad Yusuf Nuristani. *WUFA, Quarterly Journal of the Writers Union of Free Afghanistan.* vol. 2, no. 4. (1987), p. 75-85.

An interview with Professor Mohammed Hasan Kakar of Kabul University after his release from Pul-i-Charkhi prison. The historian describes his feelings about the Soviet invasion, the circumstances of his arrest, his imprisonment, eventual release, and gives an assessment of the political situation.

476 **The present situation in Afghanistan (June 1986).**

Mohammad Eshaq. *Central Asian Survey.* vol. 6, no. 1. (1987), p. 119-39.

A general summary of the military, political, educational, medical, and cultural situation in Afghanistan as of 1986, with information on refugees, both internal and external, food shortages, the Geneva talks, and morale.

477 **The price of liberty, the tragedy of Afghanistan.**

Sayed Qasim Reshtia. Rome: Bardi Editore, 1984. 141p. maps.

An important account of the country and its people, mostly dealing with the period from the Saur revolution to the invasion and occupation of Afghanistan by the Soviets. Written by one of the most distinguished Afghans of this century, the author, editor, cabinet member, and ambassador now living in exile in Switzerland.

478 **Propaganda posters of the Afghan resistance.**

Anthony Hyman. Oxford: Society for Central Asian Studies, 1985. 55p. (Incidental Papers Series, no. 3).

A collection of fifty anti-Communist posters, with captions, selected and discussed by a British journalist.

479 **Report from Afghanistan.**

Gérard Chaliand. New York: Viking, 1982. 112p. maps. bibliog.

A French journalist who made two journeys into Afghanistan in 1980 examines the geographical and ethnic characteristics of the country, the economics of agriculture, and the political realities of Russo-Afghan relations as a background to the Soviet invasion and its aftermath. The author travelled in Paktia and Kunar in June, October, and November, 1980 and thus what he has to say mostly applies to the earliest stages of the Soviet occupation. It is his view that the Russians are there to stay.

The Soviet Invasion and Occupation (1979-1989)

480  **Report on Afghanistan.**
     Kuldip Nayar. New Delhi: Allied, 1981. 212p. map. bibliog.
This describes the Soviet invasion, the political crisis in Kabul, the international reaction to Soviet intervention, and events in Afghanistan in the first months of the Soviet occupation.

481  **Report on massacres and destruction of villages by the Russian/Karmal forces in Kunar Province (1985-86).**
     Mohammed Asef Ikram. *WUFA, Quarterly Journal of the Writers Union of Free Afghanistan.* vol. 1, no. 3. (1986), p. 89-105.
A description of Communist military action against rural agricultural settlements in eastern Afghanistan, with lists of the names and ages of 323 men, women, and children killed, and the names of seventy-nine villages destroyed in the period covered by the report.

482  **Report on the massacres by the Russian/Karmal forces in Nangrahar Province (1984-85).**
     Shamshad Kokozai. *WUFA, Quarterly Journal of the Writers Union of Free Afghanistan.* vol. 1, no. 2. (1986), p. 47-59.
An account of six joint Soviet-Karmal regime military raids carried out on rural villages in eastern Afghanistan in 1984 and 1985, together with lists of the names of 227 men, women, and children killed.

483  **Russian new military tactics.**
     Nasrullah Safi. *WUFA, Quarterly Journal of the Writers Union of Free Afghanistan.* vol. 1, no. 3. (1986), p. 33-40.
An Afghan army officer examines changes in Soviet military tactics against the *Mujahideen* and links these with the changes in Soviet leadership which brought Gorbachev into power.

484  **Russian roulette: Afghanistan through Russian eyes.**
     Gennady Bocharov. London: Hamish Hamilton, 1990. 187p.
A first-hand and rather critical account of life and death in the country during the Soviet occupation by a Russian journalist with a gift for asking awkward questions and then for recording the politically awkward conversations that follow. The existence of this book is a graphic illustration of the changes that have occurred in the Soviet Union during recent years.

485  **Russia's war in Afghanistan.**
     Edward Girardet. *Central Asian Survey.* vol. 2, no. 1. (1983), p. 83-109.
A general account of the progress of the war and of the part played in it by the Afghan resistance forces concludes with speculation about possible growing dissatisfaction among the peoples of the USSR with Soviet involvement.

486  Situation of human rights in Afghanistan: note by the Secretary General.
New York: General Assembly, United Nations, 1985-86. 43p. 14p. maps. (Report of the Economic and Social Council: A/40/843 and A/41/778).
These two reports describe the progress of the war, the bombardment of the civilian population, acts of brutality committed by the armed forces, use of anti-personnel mines and booby-trap toys, treatment of prisoners, and a range of other crimes against the civilian population.

487  Some thoughts on the Afghan jehad in the wake of the Reykjavik summit.
Abdul Kayyeum. WUFA, Quarterly Journal of the Writers Union of Free Afghanistan. vol. 3, no. 1. (1988), p. 1-12.
A caustic examination of Soviet policies and political action in Afghanistan and an explanation of why the Soviet occupation of the country cannot be dealt with by negotiation. Written by a former Minister of Education and Deputy Premier of Afghanistan.

488  South Asian security after Afghanistan.
G. S. Bhargava. Lexington, Massachusetts: D. C. Heath, 1983. 198p.
The author, an Indian journalist, examines the implications for Pakistan and India of the Soviet invasion of Afghanistan and analyses the geography and politics of the 'India-Pakistan-Afghanistan Triangle' in the light of US foreign policy. He traces the history of events in Afghanistan from April 1978 to 1982, concluding that '...it is doubtful that the Soviets will succeed...' and seeing the Soviet presence in the country as a result of the Afghan Government having abandoned its policy of neutrality. The politically sensitive issue concerning the creation of an independent homeland for Pathans (Afghans) in Pakistan (the Pushtunistan Issue) is discussed in detail.

489  A Soviet Estonian soldier in Afghanistan.
Introduced by Peter Philips. Central Asian Survey. vol. 5, no. 1. (1986), p. 101-15.
An interview with a Soviet conscript from the Baltic who describes his experiences in Afghanistan, including his doubts and fears.

490  The Soviet intervention in Afghanistan is put to trial.
Lennart Edelberg, Ulf Timmermann. Afghanistan Journal. vol. 9, no. 1. (1982), p. 20.
A brief report of the Permanent People's Tribunal which met in Stockholm (1-3 May 1981) to examine legal aspects of the Soviet invasion in the light of international law and the Universal Declaration of the Rights of Peoples adopted in Algiers in 1976. A list of Tribunal materials and papers can be ordered from Oktober Stencilservice AB, Holländargatan 9A, 111 36 Stockholm, Sweden.

491 **Soviet military tactics in Afghanistan.**
Nasrullah Safi. *WUFA, Quarterly Journal of the Writers Union of Free Afghanistan.* vol. 1, no. 1. (1985), p. 1-8.
An army officer concludes that the Soviet invasion was long-planned and miscalculated, and creates a political and military dilemma for Moscow.

492 **The Soviet occupation of Afghanistan.**
John Fullerton. Hong Kong: Far Eastern Economic Review, 1984. 205p. maps. bibliog.
A British journalist's account of the Soviet invasion, the subsequent war, the *Mujahideen*, human rights in Afghanistan, and the politics of the Soviet occupation.

493 **The Soviet withdrawal from Afghanistan.**
Edited by Amin Saikal, William Maley. Cambridge, England: Cambridge University Press, 1989. 177p.
A collection of nine papers prepared by Western scholars for an international symposium held in 1988 in Canberra. The authors are experts in the fields of international relations, political science, and international law. Writing from these perspectives they examine the Soviet presence in Afghanistan and discuss the practical and political implications of Soviet withdrawal. According to the notes on contributors, only one of them (Louis Dupree) had any first-hand experience in Afghanistan.

494 **The struggle for Afghanistan.**
Nancy Peabody Newell, Richard S. Newell. Ithaca, New York; London: Cornell University Press, 1981. 236p. map.
A work which examines the Afghan struggle against the Soviet invasion and occupation of their country. The authors argue that the world's failure to respond effectively to the invasion was due to the widely held view that, once launched, Soviet control was inevitable. History has shown, however, that the destiny of Afghanistan has never for long been in the hands of a foreign power.

495 **Talking about peace: after Geneva.**
Anthony Hyman. *WUFA, Quarterly Journal of the Writers Union of Free Afghanistan.* vol. 1, no. 3. (1986), p. 41-46.
A British journalist surveys five years of attempts by the United Nations to bring about a peaceful settlement in the country, pointing out that agreement between negotiators, if achieved, is not necessarily to be regarded as the agreement of the peoples of Afghanistan.

496 **This is what happens when Soviets visit your country: a few pages from my diary.**
Shahra. *WUFA, Quarterly Journal of the Writers Union of Free Afghanistan.* vol. 1, no. 3. (1986), p. 79-82.
An eye-witness account of the Soviet air and ground attack on the undefended city of Kandahar and its civilian population which was carried out from the 16th to the 22nd of January 1982.

497 **Through the looking glass: a look at the official Soviet version of the war in Afghanistan.**

Anthony Hyman. *WUFA, Quarterly Journal of the Writers Union of Free Afghanistan.* vol. 1, no. 2. (1986), p. 39-45.

An examination of the image of contemporary Afghanistan which has been created by the Soviet novelist Aleksandr Prokhanov in his books and essays - an idealized, romantic, and imperialistic image, one central theme of which is the duty of Soviet man to civilize the backward, undisciplined, and independent-minded Afghans. Prokhanov's novel *A tree in the centre of Kabul* is examined in particular.

498 **The tragedy of Afghanistan: a first-hand account.**

Raja Anwar. London: Verso, 1988. 286p.

Following a sketch of the country's early history, including a chapter on British relations with Afghanistan, the author examines the 'Pushtun problem', 'The birth of Afghan Communism', 'The Karmal-Taraki break', 'The end of kingship', 'The take-over plan', and 'The April Revolution'. Also described are Taraki's downfall, the rise of Hafizullah Amin, his brief period in power, the installation of Babrak Karmal by the Soviets in 1979, and the Soviet invasion.

499 **The tragedy of Afghanistan; the social, cultural, and political impact of the Soviet invasion.**

Edited by Bo Huldt, Erland Jansson. London; New York; Sydney: Croom Helm, 1988. 270p. bibliog.

A collection of papers by European and Afghan scholars organized under subject headings: 'Ethnicity and the new nationalism', 'Afghan learning and education',' The war', 'Ecology', 'The exile'. The book is a result of a 1985 seminar held by the Swedish Institute of International Affairs.

500 **The truth about Afghanistan: documents, facts, eyewitness reports.**

Edited by V. Ashitkov, K. Gevorkyan, A. Polonsky, V. Svetozarov. Moscow: Novosti, 1981. 202p.

The opening paragraph of the introduction - with unconscious irony - sets the tone of this example of Soviet propaganda: 'Profound changes have taken place in the life of the Afghan people in the few years following the overthrow of the Daoud dictatorship in April, 1978. Shaking off the age-old fetters of feudalism the working people of Afghanistan have taken the path of building a truly free, democratic and just society.'

501 **Unity is the remedy.**

A. Rasul Amin. *WUFA, Quarterly Journal of the Writers Union of Free Afghanistan.* vol. 1, no. 1. (1985), p. 9-15.

An examination of the underlying causes of disunity among the peoples of Afghanistan and an explanation of why it is difficult for them to work together even in the face of a common enemy.

## The Soviet Invasion and Occupation (1979-1989)

502 **War in a distant country; Afghanistan: invasion and resistance.**
David C. Isby. London: Arms & Armour, 1989. 128p. maps. bibliog.
A picture-book with a newsmagazine format and style, offering the obligatory sketch
of Afghan history, an outline of political developments leading up to the Soviet
invasion, and an account of the various resistance groups. The author then provides
a chronological summary, year by year, of the course of the war, an analysis of
the conflict from the Soviet perspective, a run-down of *Mujahideen* leaders, and a
discussion of the fragmentary nature of Afghan resistance.

503 **War in Afghanistan.**
Mark Urban. London: Macmillan, 1988. 248p. maps.
In the author's Preface we read that 'this book is a description of the military struggle
for Afghanistan. It concerns the objectives, operations, tactics and effectiveness of
the forces involved in that struggle. The aim is to describe the war as objectively
and in as much detail as possible'. This statement is a fair summary; Urban takes
the reader through events from 1978 to 1986 and provides a résumé of political
events prior to 1978 as background.

504 **The war in Afghanistan: an account and analysis of the country, its
people, Soviet intervention and the resistance.**
Andre Brigot, Olivier Roy. New York; London: Harvester Wheat-
sheaf, 1988. 157p. maps. bibliog.
French authors inform the reader that most Western observers of the country's plight
are French, that French reports are the most comprehensive, and that French research
has shown that the Soviets have made major gains at little cost to themselves by
occupying the country. As this came out shortly before the Soviet withdrawal, which
the authors clearly did not anticipate, it was somewhat dated almost from the start.
It is, however, a good introduction to the country and its problems since the Soviet
invasion. Unfortunately there is no index.

505 **Western stakes in the Afghanistan war.**
Robert L. Canfield. *Central Asian Survey.* vol. 4, no. 1. (1985), p.
121-35. bibliog.
It is the author's view 'that Soviet and Western interests manifestly collide in
Afghanistan where the *mujahidin,* by opposing the Soviet occupation of their country, restrain developments that could endanger the wellbeing of many Western bloc
nations, and even of some, such as India, that are nonaligned'. The developments to
which he refers are in communications: roads, railways, bridges, and in the changes
that these bring.


**Victims of torture in Afghanistan.**
*See* item no. 527.

# Refugees

**506  The Afghan refugee family abroad: a focus on Pakistan.**
Nancy Hatch Dupree. *WUFA, Quarterly Journal of the Writers Union of Free Afghanistan.* vol. 2, no. 4. (1987), p. 15-30. bibliog.
The writer considers that '...family cohesiveness still functions as the single most powerful sustaining force among Afghan refugees' and that, on the whole, it has survived the turmoil of the Soviet invasion and occupation.

**507  Afghan refugee women in Pakistan, the psychocultural dimension.**
Nancy Hatch Dupree. *WUFA, Quarterly Journal of the Writers Union of Free Afghanistan.* vol. 3, no. 1. (1988), p. 34-45.
The author estimates that over seventy-five per cent of the Afghan refugees in Pakistan are women and children, but points out that women have been little involved in special refugee assistance programmes and that too little is known about the special problems they face and the resulting psychological consequences. She draws on research carried out by Dr. Mohammad Azam Dadfar.

**508  Afghan refugees in Pakistan: from emergency towards self-reliance, a report on the food relief situation and related socio-economic aspects.**
Hanne Christensen. Geneva: United Nations Research Institute for Social Development, 1984. 87p.
A report which deals with the socio-economic conditions of both Afghan refugee communities and those of the surrounding host area, intending to show that some groups are more self-reliant than others, and drawing attention to the ways in which refugees and local people interact in social and economic terms.

**509  The Afghan tragedy, a report by British voluntary agencies.**
Edited by Margi Bryant. London: British Refugee Council, 1988. 39p. map.
Ten different British voluntary agencies, all of them working with Afghan refugees or with Afghans who stayed on in war zones inside the country, joined forces to produce this illustrated report. It contains a survey of conditions in the country,

the personal experiences of several refugees, an overview of what aid agencies are doing, descriptions of conditions in the camps, and a list of eight recommendations.

### 510 Afghanistan, a portrait: guide for resettling Afghan refugees.
Patrick A. Taran. New York: Church World Service, 1982. 36p. (Immigration and Refugee Program).

The first part of this gives a general introduction to the land, the people, and their culture. There are sections on geography, resources and livelihoods, people and languages, religion, society and family, history, literature, folklore and games, and foods and diet. The second part is devoted to information on the refugee problem and examines employment, education, health and other related topics in context.

### 511 Afghanistan's Kirghiz in Turkey.
M. Nazif Shahrani. *Cultural Survival Quarterly.* vol. 8, no. 1. (1984), p. 31-34.

An account of the move from north-eastern Afghanistan to eastern Anatolia of 1,138 Afghan Kirghiz pastoral nomads in the summer of 1982. A rare, if not unique, well-documented example of the voluntary and politically-inspired emigration of an entire community of nomads from one country to another in modern times.

### 512 Afghans in exile: refugees - a threat to stability?
Tom Rogers. In: *Conflict studies 202.* London: Centre for Security and Conflict Studies, 1987. p. 1-19. map. bibliog.

Viewing the Afghan refugee problem in a global and historic context, the author concludes that there is an impending crisis for political stability in Pakistan due to encouragement by the Soviets of 'secessionist sentiments among ethnic separatists', particularly in already unstable Baluchistan.

### 513 Along Afghanistan's war-torn frontier.
Debra Denker. *National Geographic Magazine.* vol. 167, no. 6. (1985), p. 772-97.

An illustrated account of a journey made among Afghan refugees along the North-West Frontier of Pakistan.

### 514 An analysis of residential choice among self-settled Afghan refugees in Peshawar, Pakistan.
Kerry Margaret Connor. Ann Arbor, Michigan: University Microfilms International, 1987. [n.p.].

This investigation shows that Afghan refugees, when given a choice, tended to settle in groups according to area of geographical origin and shared political attitudes.

515 **Colloque international sur le probleme des refugies Afghans.**
(International colloquium on the problem of Afghan refugees.)
Jean-Paul Gay, Marina Isenburg, Annick Recolin, Marie-Odile Terrenoire, Jean-Pierre Turpin, Michel Verron. Paris: Bureau International Afghanistan, 1984. 56p. maps. (Numéro spécial de *La lettre
du BIA*, mars 1984).
A series of papers presented by various writers involved with the country and her
problems; in this case focusing on those with observations and recommendations to
make about refugees. The occasion was a colloquium held in Geneva in November
1983.

516 **The crisis of migration from Afghanistan: domestic and foreign implications. A summary of the proceedings of an international symposium.**
Edited by Barbara Harrell-Bond. Oxford: Refugee Studies Programme, 1987. 36p.
An account of the symposium held in Oxford from 29 March to 2 April, 1987
which was attended by representatives of the former government of Afghanistan,
aid agencies, *Mujahideen*, anthropologists, journalists, and others.

517 **The cultural basis of Afghan nationalism.**
Ewan Anderson, Nancy Hatch Dupree. London; New York: Pinter,
1990. 264p.
A collection of twenty papers from two conferences: The Crisis of Migration from
Afghanistan: Domestic and Foreign Implications, held in Oxford in March-April,
1987 and the Conference on Muslim Refugees held in Bellagio, Italy. The published
results by Afghan, Pakistani, and European contributors cover a range of social,
economic, and political topics, but the main focus is on the refugees.

518 **Honour in exile: continuity and change among Afghan refugees.**
Inger W. Boesen. *Folk, Journal of the Danish Ethnographic Society.*
vol. 28. (1986), p. 109-24. bibliog.
An examination of the cultural problems facing Afghan refugees which focuses
on the majority Pushtuns, discussing the concept of *Pushtunwali* with its code of
honour, its attitudes, and its ideals.

519 **The impared mind.**
Edited by M. Azam Dadfar. Peshawar, Pakistan: Psychiatric Centre
for Afghans, 1990. 48p.
A collection of five papers recording the work of the psychiatric centre and the
problems they have faced in dealing with victims of the Soviet invasion. The papers
include a report on victims of torture, post traumatic stress disorders, epilepsy, and
the general psychological effects of the war on a largely rural civilian population.
An earlier report in the series, dated 1988, contains ten articles by different medical doctors who have worked extensively with mentally ill Afghan refugees at the
psychiatric centre in Peshawar.

520  **International humanitarian enquiry commission on displaced persons in Afghanistan.**
Michael Barry, Johan Lagerfelt, Marie-Odile Terrenoire. *Central Asian Survey.* vol. 5, no. 1. (1986), p. 65-100. map. bibliog.
This begins with an Introduction, general information about the country, an historical summary, and an attempt to sum up the 'present situation' in two pages. A short bibliography precedes a report of a 'field mission inside' which occupied four weeks in September and October, 1985. The villages that were visited are listed, together with numbers of households. Information gained in the course of 'A 700-kilometer trek through the four eastern Afghan provinces of Paktyâ, Lôgar, Wardak and Ghazni yields a rate of depopulation of over 50% by Autumn 1985...' There are also sections on 'the agricultural outlook' and 'atrocities'.

521  **Pakistan under pressure.**
William S. Ellis. *National Geographic Magazine.* vol. 159, no. 5. (1981), p. 668-700. map.
An illustrated article which, in part, discusses the plight of Afghan refugees in Pakistan and the problems which their presence brings to the government of that country.

522  **Preliminary report on conditions affecting the repatriation of Afghan refugees.**
Richard English. Geneva: United Nations High Commissioner for Refugees, 1988. 103p. maps.
The main part of this report deals with United Nations High Commissioner for Refugees (UNHCR) 'concerns and activities' in Afghanistan and in Pakistan. These include medical assistance and planning, agricultural assistance, and just about everything else from clearing land mines to food and shelter.

523  **Refugee camp syndrome.**
Mohammad Azam Dadfar. *WUFA, Quarterly Journal of the Writers Union of Free Afghanistan.* vol. 2, no. 2. (1987), p. 1-9.
A preliminary report by the medical doctor who runs a Psychiatric Centre for Afghan refugees in Peshawar.

524  **Refugee camps and torture victims.**
Mohammad Azam Dadfar. *WUFA, Quarterly Journal of the Writers Union of Free Afghanistan.* vol. 3, no. 1. (1988), p. 53-66.
The doctor in charge of the Psychiatric Centre for Afghans in Peshawar reports that between January, 1986 and February, 1988 his centre dealt with 406 victims of torture, whose ages ranged from twelve to eighty, and included eleven women. Among other things, his study lists the methods used by the Kabul Regime for both physical and psychological torture.

525 **Refugee syndrome.**
    Mohammad Azam Dadfar. *WUFA, Quarterly Journal of the Writers
    Union of Free Afghanistan.* vol. 1, no. 2. (1986), p. 61-75.
This is a result of a medical survey carried out among Afghan refugees in the
Peshawar area in the second half of 1985 which focuses on mental conditions arising
from stress caused by the war, the loss of family members, forced migration, a
prolonged stay in refugee camps, economic insecurity, and a lack of incentive for
future planning.

526 **Refugees syndrome.**
    M. Azam Dadfar. *WUFA, Quarterly Journal of the Writers Union of
    Free Afghanistan.* vol. 1, no. 3. (1986), p. 83-88.
A report, by the doctor in charge, on patients treated in the Psychiatric Centre for
Afghan Refugees, with case studies and a summary of the disorders suffered by
those being treated.

527 **Victims of torture in Afghanistan.**
    Mohammed Azam Dadfar. *WUFA, Quarterly Journal of the Writers
    Union of Free Afghanistan.* vol. 2, no. 4. (1987), p. 48-52.
A medical report on 265 cases of torture treated in the Psychiatric Centre for Afghans
in Peshawar during 21 months in 1986-87.

528 **Voluntary agencies role in provision of humanitarian assistance to
    Afghan refugees in North West Frontier Province, Pakistan.**
    Shah Zaman Khan. Peshawar, Afghanistan: Afghan Refugee Com-
    mission, 1987. 136p.
This lists forty-seven aid agencies in Peshawar, outlines the work that each agency
has been set up to deal with, and provides their addresses.

529 **The wind blows away our words.**
    Doris Lessing. London: Picador, 1987. 172p.
A novelist takes an interest in Afghan refugees and, in 1986, travels to Pakistan to
see refugee camps at first hand. The book recounts her experiences in making that
journey.

**Afghan resistance: the politics of survival.**
*See* item no. 423.

**A pilot study of the displacement, loss of human life, and disablement of
the population in three Afghan villages.**
*See* item no. 610.

**Some observations on and assessment of the population losses in
Afghanistan.**
*See* item no. 611.

**Refugees**

First consolidated report, office of the United Nations co-ordinator for humanitarian and economic assistance programmes relating to Afghanistan (UNOCA/1988/1).
*See* item no. 687.

Operation Salam: first consolidated report, up-date February, 1989 (UNOCA/1988/1 Add.1).
*See* item no. 692.

From mental peace to an impaired mind.
*See* item no. 701.

Ten years of war and civil war in Afghanistan: an educational catastrophy for an entire generation.
*See* item no. 869.

# Anthropology

530 **Growing in respect: aging among the Kirghiz of Afghanistan.**
M. Nazif Shahrani. In: *Other ways of growing old.* Edited by P. T.
Amoss, S. Harrell. Stanford, California: Stanford University, 1981.
p. 175-91. bibliog.
The author, an anthropologist from Afghanistan, concludes his study by remarking
that 'growing old in Kirghiz society is viewed essentially as a process of growing
wise, of gaining in respect and authority...Old age is cherished as a triumph and
rarely, if ever, considered a problem'.

531 **The retention of pastoralism among the Kirghiz of the Afghan Pamirs.**
M. Nazif Shahrani. In: *Himalayan anthropology: the Indo-Tibetan
interface.* Edited by James Fisher. The Hague: Mouton, 1978. p.
233-50. map. bibliog.
An account of the physical environment of the Wakhan Corridor and the traditional
economy of the Kirghiz is followed by a discussion of why these nomads have not
been tempted to abandon pastoralism and adopt some other mode of livelihood.

532 **Ethnic relations under closed frontier conditions: northeast
Badakhshan.**
M. Nazif Shahrani. In: *Soviet Asian ethnic frontiers.* Edited by William
O. McCagg, Brian D. Silver. New York; Oxford: Pergamon, p. 174-
92. (Pergamon Policy Studies on the Soviet Union and Eastern Eu-
rope).
An historical account of Afghan Turkestan is followed by one which describes the
relations between the peoples of northern Afghanistan and the Kabul government.
Finally, the author shows how the closing of the Soviet and Chinese borders along
the Wakhan Corridor has affected the lives of the Wakhi and the Kirghiz peoples.

533 **Nomadic pastoralists and sedentary hosts in the central and western Hindukush Mountains, Afghanistan.**
Daniel Balland. In: *Human impact on mountains.* Edited by Nigel J. R. Allan, Gregory W. Knapp, Christoph Stadel. Totowa, New Jersey: Rowman & Littlefield, 1988. p. 265-94. maps. bibliog.
A study of the relationships 'between pastoral nomads and their agro-pastoral host populations in the mountains' using Gujar pastoralists and Pushtun nomads as examples.

534 **Nomadism in Afghanistan, with an appendix on milk products.**
Klaus Ferdinand. In: *Viehwirtschaft und Hirtenkultur: Etnographische Studien.* L. Földes. Budapest: Akadémiai Kiadó, 1969. p. 127-60. bibliog.
A concise illustrated account of various pastoral nomadic groups in the country, the regions they inhabit, their languages, and their economic systems, to which is added accounts of the nomad traders (*tejâr*), the nomad harvesters (*laugar*), and a special section on milk products.

535 **Afghan Studies.**
V. A. Romodin, edited by B. G. Gafurov, Y. V. Gankovsky. Moscow: Nauka, Central Department of Oriental Literature, USSR Academy of Sciences, Institute of the Peoples of Asia, 1968. 32p. (Fifty Years of Soviet Oriental Studies (Brief Reviews)).
An interesting and valuable survey of the principal Soviet scholars and their works on Afghanistan, which cover anthropology in the main, but also include historical archaeological and linguistic studies among them.

536 **Agnates, affines and allies: patterns of marriage among Pakhtun in Kunar, north-east Afghanistan.**
Asger Christensen. *Folk, Dansk Etnografisk Tidsskrift.* vol. 24. (1982), p. 29-63. bibliog.
A discussion of marriage and the determinants of marriage patterns among sedentary Pakhtun (Pushtun) agriculturalists in the Kunar Valley, the most common pattern being 'a combination of marriages with patrilateral parallel cousins and exogamous affines (mostly matrilateral cross-cousins)'.

**537 Anthropological researches from the 3rd Danish Expedition to Central Asia.**

H.R.H. Prince Peter of Greece and Denmark, L. Edelberg, J. Balslev Jorgensen, K. Paludan, H. Siiger. Copenhagen: The Royal Danish Academy of Sciences and Letters, 1966. 76p. bibliog. (Hist. Filos. Skr. Dan. Vid. Selsk.).

This volume contains a section on 'Physical anthropological investigations from Afghanistan' where anthropometrical data for a total of 105 males are given on p. 47-56. Six photographs of men from different ethnic groups are shown in Plate III.

**538 An anthropologist in Afghanistan.**

J. P. Singh. *Afghanistan.* vol. 16, no. 1. (1961), p. 1-8.

Personal account of a Manchester-trained Sikh anthropologist who chose Andarab as the location for his fieldwork in the late 1950s. Much of the article is concerned with the problem of explaining what it is that anthropologists study and why, and to this end he provides an interesting outline of topics. The author's subsequent publications appeared under the name J. P. Singh Uberoi.

**539 Les Aryans au nord et au sud de l'Hindou-Kouch.**

(The Aryans north and south of the Hindu Kush.)

Charles de Ujfalvy. Paris: G. Masson, 1896. 488p. map. bibliog.

Having identified the Aryans north of the Hindu Kush as the Tadjiks, the Iranians of the Pamirs, and the 'Sarts' (Uighurs), the author provides an account of these peoples before moving to the southern side where he identifies the Dardic peoples, the Chitralis, and the 'Kafirs', among others, as Aryans, and provides ethnographic descriptions derived from various authors.

**540 Les bazars de Kaboul.**

(The bazaars of Kabul.)

André Velter, Emmanuel Delloye, Marie-José Lamothe. Milan, Italy: Hier et Demain, 1979. 255p. maps.

Beautifully illustrated with fine photographs, this is a description of the various bazaars and craft centres of Kabul as they were on the eve of the Soviet invasion. Together with similar, though more detailed, studies carried out in Tashkurghan by C. J. Charpentier (q.v.) and P. Centlivres (q.v.), this is a valuable record of a traditional Central Asian bazaar. The illustrations successfully evoke the winter atmosphere of Afghanistan's capital.

**541 The blood groups of the Timuri and related tribes in Afghanistan.**

Robert B. Woodd-Walker, Harry M. Smith, Victor Alan Clarke. *American Journal of Physical Anthropology.* vol. 27. p. 195-204. map. bibliog.

A study of blood groups carried out by the Oxford University Expedition in 1963 showed investigators that 'the Timuri appear to be intermediate in allele frequencies between Caucasoid and Mongoloid populations, with unmistakable evidence of both in their ancestry'.

111

542 **The Central Asian Arabs of Afghanistan: pastoral nomadism in transition.**
Thomas J. Barfield. Austin, Texas: University of Texas Press, 1981. 182p. maps. bibliog.
A social and economic study, based on fieldwork carried out in 1975 and 1976, of an Arab nomad group living in the Kunduz region of north-east Afghanistan. The author states that the 'research design was aimed at coming to an understanding of the pastoral economy and its relationship to nomadic social structure'. As relatively little field research of this kind has been carried out in Afghanistan, or elsewhere in Central Asia for that matter, this is an important contribution to our understanding of the region.

543 **The changing herding economy of the Kom Nuristani.**
Richard F. Strand. *Afghanistan Journal.* vol. 2, no. 4. (1975), p. 123-34. map. bibliog.
An account of the role of livestock and livestock management in the transhumant economy of a community of Nuristanis in the Bashgal Valley.

544 **The conflict of tribe and state in Iran and Afghanistan.**
Edited by Richard Tapper. London: Croom Helm, 1983. 463p. maps.
A collection of papers, most of which were presented at a conference at the School of Oriental and African Studies at the University of London in 1979, examine the relationships between traditional 'tribal' political groups and state governments. With the notable exception of the Pathan scholar Dr. Akbar S. Ahmed, all the contributors are European academics.

545 **Cousin marriage in context: constructing social relations in Afghanistan.**
Jon W. Anderson. *Folk, Dansk Etnografisk Tidsskrift.* vol. 24. (1982), p. 7-28. bibliog.
An examination, of marriage between cousins related through parents of the same sex, in this case the father (patrilineal parallel cousin marriage), among the Ghilzai.

546 **Cultural values and family relations in Kamari, Afghanistan.**
M. Jamil Hanifi. *Afghanistan Journal.* vol. 9, no. 2. (1982), p. 48-52. bibliog.
Some results of anthropological fieldwork carried out in 1970, with information as described in the title, by an anthropologist from Afghanistan.

547 **Cultures of the Hindukush.**
Edited by Karl Jettmar, Lennart Edelberg. Wiesbaden, Germany: Franz Steiner, 1974. 146p. map. bibliog. (Beiträge zur Südasienforschung, Südasien-Institut, Universität Heidelberg, vol. 1).
A collection of some twenty-three papers by various scholars who had carried out research in north-east Afghanistan and Chitral. The fields of study represented are linguistics, oral traditions, pre-Muslim religions, political anthropology, kinship,

folklore, mythology, calender festivals, and traditional architecture. The First Hindu Kush Cultural Conference, at which these papers were presented, took place at Moesgaard in Denmark in 1970. The Second Hindu Kush Cultural Conference was held in Chitral in 1990.

### 548  Danish scientific mission in Kabul.
*Afghanistan.* vol. 2, no. 4. (1947), p. 52-56.
Announces the arrival of a Danish Scientific Mission in Kabul under the leadership of Henning Haslund-Christensen to undertake anthropological research. A *curriculum vitae* of the leader and the other members - Halfdan Siiger, Knud Paludan, and Lennart Edelberg - together with their portraits, is given. Haslund-Christensen died in Kabul in September 1948. For an obituary by Halfdan Siiger, see *Afghanistan*, vol. 3, no. 3, 1948, p. 33-35.

### 549  Demuta, folk-hero of Nisheigrom: myth and social structure.
Schuyler Jones. *Acta Orientalia.* vol. 34. (1972), p. 17-30. map. bibliog.
This is an analysis of a village folk-hero myth in the light of the social structure of the community concerned, illustrating the rôle of genealogical information in the society.

### 550  Deutsche im Hindukusch, Bericht der deutschen Hindukusch-Expedition 1935 der deutschen Forschungsgemeinschaft.
(Germans in the Hindu Kush, report of the German Hindu Kush Expedition of 1935 of the German Research Society.)
Edited by Arnold Scheibe. Berlin: Karl Siegismund, 1937. 351p. maps.
A detailed account of surveys carried out on the agricultural systems, forests, physical and cultural anthropology, and languages of Nuristan by a team of scientists, most of whom were also busy writing another chapter in the history of the Great Game.

### 551  The ecology of rural ethnic groups and the spatial dimensions of power.
Robert L. Canfield. *American Anthropologist.* vol. 75, no. 5. (1973), p. 1511-28. maps. bibliog.
An article in which the author seeks to account for the geographical locations of certain rural ethnic groups in terms of the physical environment and in light of the relations the groups have with each other.

### 552  An enquiry into the ethnography of Afghanistan.
Henry Walter Bellew. Woking, England: Oriental University Institute, 1891. 208p.
The author's approach is historical and his purpose is to identify the present inhabitants of the country with historical accounts of earlier peoples. The text is thus a blend of ethnographic information (mainly tribal names, clan names, and place

names), and references to Greek historians. As the book is not divided into chapters and as there is no index it requires considerable patience to make use of it.

553  **Environment and history in Pashai world-view.**
Jan Ovesen. *Folk, Dansk Etnografisk Tidsskrift.* vol. 25. (1983), p. 167-84. map. bibliog.
The Pashai live in eastern Afghanistan, many of them in isolated valleys along the southern fringes of Nuristan. This study examines certain features of Pashai culture in an attempt at a better understanding of their world-view.

554  **Ethnic origins and tribal history of the Timuri of Khurasan.**
André Singer. *Afghan Studies.* vol. 3-4. (1982), p. 65-76. bibliog.
An anthropologist's attempt to reconstruct the history of the Timuri of Khurasan from manuscript and published sources as well as discussions with informants in the field.

555  **Ethnographic notes on clan/lineage houses in the Hindukush and 'clan temples' and descent group structure among the Kalasha ('Kalash Kafirs') of Chitral.**
Schuyler Jones, Peter S. C. Parkes. In: *Proceedings of the Sixth International Symposium on Asian Studies, 1984: Vol. IV, South and Southwest Asia.* Edited by K. N. Au, Nelson H. H. Leung. Hong Kong: Asian Research Service, 1985. p. 1155-76. map. bibliog.
An anthropological discussion of the purpose and significance of certain pre-Islamic structures found in some Nuristani villages, together with an account of similar structures in Kalasha villages in some adjacent valleys in Chitral.

556  **Ethnographical notes on Chahâr Aimâq, Hazâra and Moghôl.**
Klaus Ferdinand. *Acta Orientalia.* vol. 28. (1965), p. 175-203. bibliog.
An anthropologist's illustrated review article of H. F. Schurmann's book *The Mongols of Afghanistan: an ethnography of the Moghôls and related peoples of Afghanistan* (q.v.), with detailed information on dwelling types.

557  **Ethnologie und Geschichte, Festschrift für Karl Jettmar.**
(Ethnology and History, a festschrift for Karl Jettmar.)
Edited by Peter Snoy. Wiesbaden, Germany: Franz Steiner, 1983. 654p. maps. bibliog. (Beiträge zur Südasienforschung, Südasien-Institut, Universität Heidelberg, Band 86).
A collection of fifty-six papers by as many scholars on historical, anthropological, linguistic, and archaeological subjects, many of them concerning research in Afghanistan.

558 **Faction and conversion in a plural society: religious alignments in the Hindu Kush.**
Robert L. Canfield. Ann Arbor, Michigan: University of Michigan Press, 1973. 142p. maps. bibliog. (Anthropological Papers, Museum of Anthropology, University of Michigan, no. 50).

The author states that 'this study attempts to explain why three Islamic sects are distributed in a regular way across the landscape of Bamian....and why the village communities of Shibar, its eastern part, have internally divided into opposing religious sects'. This work thus examines a set of fundamental problems in one region which are to be found to some degree over much larger areas of the country. It provides an insight into the extraordinarily complex ethnic and religious patterns existing within Afghanistan.

559 **The German Hindu Kush expedition, 1935.**
*Journal of the Royal Central Asian Society.* vol. 23, pt. 3. (1936), p. 465-68.

A summary account of the expedition and its official objectives (botanical, linguistic, anthropological) with a description of the Nuristan region. What is not mentioned, probably because it was only suspected and not known at the time, is that, except for Wolfgang Lentz, all members of the expedition were on a Nazi intelligence-gathering mission.

560 **Guardians of the North-West Frontier: the Pathans.**
André Singer. Amsterdam: Time-Life, 1982. 168p. map. bibliog. (Peoples of the Wild).

This deals in words and pictures with those Afghans (i.e., Pashto-speakers) who live between the Indus and the North-West Frontier, the subjects of the 'Pushtunistan' debate. The main focus is on the Mohmands living along the Kabul River northwest of Peshawar. Afghans distinguish two main groups of Pashto-speakers: the Durranis and the Ghilzais. The Mohmands belong to the Durrani group.

561 **Hazara integration into the Afghan nation: some changing relations between Hazaras and Afghan officials.**
Robert L. Canfield. New York: Afghanistan Council of the Asia Society, [n.d.]. 14p. bibliog. (Occasional Paper, no. 3).

An examination of relations between the Hazara peoples and the Afghans (Pashto-speakers) with a look at the changes in these relations that have taken place in recent years.

562 **Horses and women: some thoughts on the life cycle of Ersari Türkmen women.**
Anneliese Stucki. *Afghanistan Journal.* vol. 5, no. 4. (1978), p. 140-49.

A discussion of the importance of the horse in the lives of the Ersari Turkmens (Turkomans), the role of women, attitudes toward women and horses, and an account of birth practices and rules governing the behaviour of females during adolescence. Numerous colour and black-and-white photographs illustrate the article.

563 **The inquiry into the history of the Hazara Mongols of Afghanistan.**
Elizabeth E. Bacon. *Southwestern Journal of Anthropology*. vol. 7.
(1951), p. 230-47. maps.

The writer, interested in comparing the culture of the Hazaras with that of the
medieval Mongols, searches the historical records in order to trace the origins of the
former.

564 **Kinship and ethnicity in the Nahrin area of northern Afghanistan.**
Hugh Beattie. *Afghan Studies*. vol. 3-4. (1982), p. 39-51. maps.
bibliog.

An anthropological analysis, based on fieldwork carried out in 1978, of a community
whose population is divided into three groups: Pushtun, Tadjik, and Hazara.

565 **Die Kirghisen des afghanischen Pamir.**
(The Kirghiz of the Afghan Pamirs.)
Rémy Dor, Clas M. Naumann. Graz, Austria: Akademische Druck
und Verlagsanstalt, 1978. 124p. maps. bibliog.

Written for the non-specialist reader, this account of the Kirghiz includes chapters
on the environment, the daily life of these mountain nomads, their traditional *yurt*
dwellings, and a general overview of their culture. Many fine colour illustrations
are included.

566 **The Kirghiz and Wakhi of Afghanistan: adaptation to closed frontiers.**
M. Nazif Shahrani. Seattle, Washington; London: University of
Washington, 1979. 264p. maps. bibliog. (Publications on Ethnicity and Nationality of the School of International Studies, University
of Washington).

A study of high altitude pastoralism in the north-eastern part of the country and of
the ways in which traditional seasonal movements of the Kirghiz people and their
livestock are affected by the closing of political frontiers. The author, an Uzbek
from northern Afghanistan, carried out fieldwork among the Wakhi and Kirghiz
peoples during 1972-75.

567 **The Kirghiz Khans: styles and substance of traditional local leadership in Central Asia.**
M. Nazif Shahrani. *Central Asian Survey*. vol. 5, no. 3-4. (1986), p.
255-71. map. bibliog.

The author considers that there is a need, largely unfulfilled to date, of detailed
studies of the nature of traditional local level leadership and the rôle which such
leaders play in political conflicts. As an example he offers an analysis of leadership
from his fieldwork among the Kirghiz.

568 **Kirghiz pastoral nomads of the Afghan Pamirs: an ecological and ethnographic overview.**
M. Nazif Shahrani. *Folk, Dansk Etnografisk Tidsskrift.* vol. 18. (1976), p. 129-43. map. bibliog.
A study which examines the various pressures brought to bear upon the Kirghiz of the Wakhan Corridor by international political developments.

569 **Légendes et coutumes Afghanes.**
(Afghan legends and customs.)
Ria Hackin, Ahmad Ali Kohzad. Paris: Presses Universitaires de France, 1953. 204p. (Publications du Musée Guimet, Bibliothèque de Diffusion, vol. LX).
A collection of some thirty myths and legends and a selection of customs relating to *rites de passage* such as birth, marriage, and death, assembled in Begram, Kabul, and Bamiyan by Ria Parmentier Hackin of the Musée Guimet in 1930.

570 **Livestock symbolism and pastoral ideology among the Kafirs of the Hindu Kush.**
Peter Parkes. *Man, Journal of the Royal Anthropological Institute.* vol. 22, no. 4. (1987), p. 637-60. bibliog.
An analysis of 'indigenous ritual and moral values surrounding transhumant livestock husbandry in Central Asia', with particular reference to the peoples of Nuristan and the neighbouring Kalasha people of Chitral.

571 **Marriage among Pakhtun nomads of eastern Afghanistan.**
Klaus Ferdinand. *Folk, Dansk Etnografisk Tidsskrift.* vol. 24. (1982), p. 65-87. bibliog.
A study of marriage among the Pashto-speaking Tara Khel pastoral nomads who spend their winters in Laghman, Kunar, and Ningarhar and their summers near Kabul.

572 **Marriage and social groupings among the Pashai.**
Jan Ovesen. *Folk, Dansk Etnografisk Tidsskrift.* vol. 24. (1982), p. 143-56. bibliog.
An examination of marriage as an alliance-creating institution and a discussion of the fact that among the Pashai marriage rules tend towards endogamy 'on almost all social levels'.

573 **Marriage norms and practices in a rural community in north Afghanistan.**
Asta Olesen. *Folk, Dansk Etnografisk Tidsskrift.* vol. 24. (1982), p. 111-41. bibliog.
The author carrried out fieldwork in the Khulm or Tashkurghan region with its mixed population of Tadjiks, Pushtuns, Uzbeks, Arabs, and Turkomans, and his study shows 'how the institution of marriage is conditioned by varying political, economic and social factors'. Case studies and an account of a marriage are given.

Anthropology

574 **Marriage preferences and ethnic relations among Durrani Pashtuns of Afghan Turkestan.**
Nancy Tapper, Richard Tapper. *Folk, Dansk Etnografisk Tidsskrift.* vol. 24. (1982), p. 157-77. bibliog.

Aims to show that 'the Durrani ethnic group in the region studied consititutes an "aristocracy" who attempt to use marriage and the control of women to consolidate and increase their privileged relation to productive resources'.

575 **Men of influence in Nuristan: a study of social control and dispute settlement in Waigal Valley, Afghanistan.**
Schuyler Jones. London; New York: Seminar, 1974. 299p. maps. bibliog. (Seminar Studies in Anthropology).

A study in political anthropology, this book is based on fieldwork carried out in the 1960s. It deals with a group of communities in central Nuristan, a culturally complex region in the Hindu Kush mountains of north-east Afghanistan, where the people engage in mixed farming with a cultural emphasis on transhumant livestock herding. It provides a brief historical background to the region and then describes the social, economic, and political organization of the Wai-ala-speaking communities of the Waigal Valley.

576 **The Mongols of Afghanistan: an ethnography of the Moghôls and related peoples of Afghanistan.**
H. F. Schurmann. 'S-Gravenhage, The Netherlands: Mouton, 1962. 435p. map. bibliog. (Central Asian Studies).

Based on fieldwork carried out in 1954 and 1955, this provides an historical-linguistic overview of the peoples of Afghanistan (Afghans, Aimâqs, Tadjiks, Turkmens, Uzbeks, Turkic Moghôls, Arabs, Sayyids, Jews, Hindus, Kazakhs, and the Hazaras) and then gives data on the Moghôls or Mongols. Tribal organization, social structure, local government, law and litigation, inheritance, trade, agriculture, land tenure, dwellings, and religion are covered in some detail. For critical comment see Klaus Ferdinand's *Ethnographical notes on Chahâr Aimâq, Hazâra and Moghôl* (q.v.) in which he sheds more light on the subject.

577 **Nomaden von Gharjistan: Aspekte der wirtschaftlichen, socialen, und politischen Organisation nomadischer Durrani-Paschtunen in Nordwestafghanistan.**
(Nomads of Gharjistan: aspects of economic, social, and political organization of the Durrani Pashtun nomads of North-West Afghanistan.)
Bernt Glatzer. Wiesbaden, Germany: Franz Steiner, 1977. 236p. map. bibliog. (Beiträge zur Südasienforschung, Südasien-Institut, Universität Heidelberg, Vol. 22.).

A geographical, historical, and ethnographic account of the Pashto-speaking nomads of north-west Afghanistan, with an emphasis on economic, political, and social organization and the politics of water rights, land rights, and kinship. The information was derived from seven months of fieldwork in 1970 and 1971. A three-page English summary is included.

118

578 Nomadic expansion and commerce in central Afghânistân: a sketch of some modern trends.
Klaus Ferdinand. *Folk, Dansk Etnografisk Tidsskrift*. vol. 4. (1962), p. 123-59. maps. bibliog.
A study of east Afghan nomads (mainly Ghilzai) and south and west Afghan nomads (mainly Durrani), showing how these groups differ from each other, socially, culturally, and linguistically, but with the main emphasis on their occupational and economic differences.

579 Nomadism in Afghanistan.
Ahmad Ali Motamedi. *Afghanistan*. vol. 12, no. 1. (1957), p. 17-22.
As a young student the author travelled with the Danish nomad specialist Klaus Ferdinand on field trips in the country and made extensive notes about nomad culture, economy, material culture, and technology. Motamedi later became Director of the Kabul Museum.

580 Notes on Afghanistan and part of Baluchistan, geographical, ethnographical, and historical, extracted from the writings of little known Afghán and Tájzík historians, geographers, and genealogists; the histories of the Ghúrís, the Turk sovereigns of the Dihlí Kingdom, the Mughal sovereigns of the house of Tímúr, and other Muhammadan chronicles; and from personal observations.
Henry George Raverty. London: Eyre & Spottiswoode, 1888. 734p.
A unique volume requiring much patience to use as it has no table of contents, no maps, and no bibliography. Although containing a great deal of information, this tome is difficult to evaluate as the translator/compiler usually neglects to cite his sources. A detailed index just manages to save the volume for research purposes. Raverty, always quick to point out the errors of other authors, remains blissfully unaware of his own.

581 Notes on nomad tribes of eastern Afghanistan.
J. A. Robinson. New Delhi: Government of India Press, 1935. 202p. map.
An account of the Powindah and Ghilzai nomads, with detailed information on their migration routes, grazing grounds, and winter encampments, as well as the names of group leaders, their tribal/clan affiliations, the numbers of families in each group, and the numbers and kinds of livestock which they took through certain named passes between 1929 and 1934. This provides invaluable background information for the anthropologist or geographer studying present-day nomads of the area.

582 **Nouveaux ouvrages sur les langues et civilisations de l'Hindou-Kouch (1980-1982).**
(New works on the languages and cultures of the Hindu Kush [1980-1982].)
Gérard Fussman. *Journal Asiatique.* vol. 271, no. 1-2. (1983), p. 191-206.

The noted French linguist here provides another descriptive and critical overview of newly-published works on the Hindu Kush region. This, together with his 1980 survey (q.v.), constitutes a valuable source of information for researchers.

583 **Nuristan.**
Lennart Edelberg, Schuyler Jones.   Graz, Austria: Akademische Druck- u. Verlagsanstalt, 1979. 186p. maps. bibliog.

Lavishly illustrated with colour and black-and-white pictures as well as drawings and plans, this provides an overview of social, economic, linguistic and techno-logical aspects of the cultures of Nuristan, with an emphasis on the geographical environment, livestock herding and agriculture, arts and crafts, and oral traditions. The very large number of illustrations, combined with data obtained in the course of fieldwork, makes this a unique historical record of the area as it was prior to the Soviet invasion of Afghanistan.

584 **Nuristan: mountain communities in the Hindu Kush.**
Schuyler Jones. *Afghan Studies.* vol. 1. (1978), p. 79-92. bibliog.

A brief historical account of early travellers and explorers who were in, or claimed to have been in, the Hindu Kush region, followed by a geographical and anthropological description of the country and its people. There are eight black-and-white plates.

585 **Nuristan: 'the land of light' seen darkly.**
Louis Dupree. New York: American Universities Field Staff Reports Service, 1971. 24p. maps. bibliog. (South Asia Series, vol. 15, no. 6 (Nuristan)).

A brief general account of Nuristan, both historical and cultural, with an emphasis on material culture, but also containing information on the pre-Muslim religions of the region, which was known as 'Kafiristan' prior to the forcible conversion of the population to Islam during the period from 1895-1900.

586 **The Nuristanis are Aryans and not Greek remnants.**
Ahmad Ali Kohzad. *Afghanistan.* vol. 9, no. 2. (1954), p. 36-40.

The author, in keeping with a period in which ardent nationalism was the order of the day, takes up some points raised by Lennart Edelberg in the course of a lecture at the Ministry of Education in Kabul: for nationalistic reasons (which are not mentioned) he is pleased to learn that the Nuristanis are considered to be of Aryan origin, rather than Greek and hopes that the Greek myth will be laid to rest.

587 **On the distribution of Turk tribes in Afghanistan: an attempt at a preliminary classification.**
Gunnar Jarring. *Lunds Universitets Arsskrift.* vol. 35, no. 4. (1939), p. 3-104. bibliog.

The author, having carried out fieldwork in 1935 and having studied published materials in several languages, including Russian, describes the distribution of the Turkish-speaking peoples in the country 'in order to make the task easier for those who will in the future investigate the Turks of this area linguistically and ethnologically'. His research provides information on the Turkmen, Uzbek, and other peoples of northern and central Afghanistan. There is a useful index of tribes and peoples and another of geographical names as well as a bibliography.

588 **The Orakzai country and clans.**
L. White King. Lahore: Vanguard, 1984. 262p.

A reprint of L. W. King's *Monograph on the Orakzai country and clans* first published as an official British Government report in 1900. This contains an introduction by Pakistan's foremost anthropologist, Dr. Akbar S. Ahmed. Although the book describes the land and the Orakzai people who lived in tribal territory within the British sphere of interest, many Orakzais lived and still live in Afghanistan. This is a unique source of valuable social, economic, and political background information.

589 **Pashai; Landschaft, Menschen, Architektur.**
(Pashai; landscape, people, architecture.)
Karl Wutt. Graz, Austria: Akademische Druck und Verlaganstalt, 1981. 141p. maps. bibliog.

A valuable study of a little-known people who inhabit certain isolated valleys on the southern slopes of the Hindu Kush in eastern Afghanistan. The author, an architect and ethnologist, provides information on the cultural anthropology, and the material culture and technology of this society. This is a useful contribution to Hindu Kush cultural studies.

590 **The Pashtuns of Kunar: tribe, class and community organization.**
Asger Christensen. *Afghanistan Journal.* vol. 7, no. 3. (1980), p. 79-92. maps. bibliog.

The author points out that most anthropological studies of the Pushtun (Pathan) peoples have concentrated on pastoral nomads; few have been concerned with sedentary agricultural Pushtuns. This report presents data on tribal distribution and local community organization among the Pushtuns of Kunar.

591 **Pathans.**
R. T. I. Ridgway. Calcutta: Superintendent Government Printing, India, 1910. 252p. (Handbooks for the Indian Army).

A detailed survey of the language, culture, and social organization of the Pashto-speaking peoples of the North-West Frontier and Afghanistan compiled by an officer of the 40th Pathan Regiment. Valuable data on Pathan tribes and clans in eastern Afghanistan and what was then the North-West Frontier of India. Chapter eight in particular is devoted to an account of the Pushtuns in Afghanistan. Though salted with generalizations and the author's value judgements, this provides useful background material on the peoples of the area.

592  **Peoples of Central Asia.**
Lawrence Krader. Bloomington, Indiana: Indiana University, 1963. 319p. maps. bibliog. (Uralic and Altaic Series, vol. 26).
An anthropological survey providing linguistic, historical, social, economic, religious, physical, and demographic information about the Kirghiz, Uzbek, Kazakh, Tadjik, and Turkmen peoples of the region. Although the study concentrates on those living north of the Amu Darya, they are to be found south of the river as well, and the study therefore serves as a useful introduction to the peoples of northern Afghanistan.

593  **Preliminary notes on Hazâra culture.**
Klaus Ferdinand. Copenhagen: Royal Danish Academy of Sciences and Letters, 1959. 51p. bibliog. (Hist. Filos. Medd. Dan. Vid. Selsk. 37, no.5).
Results of a preliminary study of the Hazaras by an anthropologist who was a member of the 1953-55 Danish Scientific Mission to Afghanistan. The geographical setting, the economic system, settlements, tribal government, and calender system are described. Linguistic information on the Hazara language (Hazâragî) is also given.

594  **Pukhtun economy and society: traditional structure and economic development in a tribal society.**
Akbar S. Ahmed. London: Routledge & Kegan Paul, 1980. 406p. maps. bibliog. (International Library of Anthropology).
A social and economic study of the Pashto-speaking peoples who live along the North-West Frontier of Pakistan. As the boundary with Afghanistan cuts through this cultural area, members of the Pushtun tribes discussed live on both sides of the border. Until such time as there may be a comparable study undertaken west of the Durand Line, this remains the best that is available on the subject.

595  **Quelques ouvrages récents sur les langues et civilisations de l'Hindou-Kouch (1976-1979).**
(Some recent works on the languages and cultures of the Hindu Kush [1976-79].)
Gérard Fussman. *Journal Asiatique.* vol. 268. (1980), p. 451-65. bibliog.
A critical survey of published works by one of Europe's foremost experts on the languages of the Hindu Kush region.

596 **The races of Afghanistan, being a brief account of the principal nations inhabiting that country.**
Henry Walter Bellew. Calcutta: Thacker, Spink, 1880. 124p.
This apparently draws upon published histories and official reports (there is no bibliography, however), but the author states '...that the work has been written f··· the most part from memory at odd intervals of leisure from official duties ⟨·ur-ing...the present campaign in Kabul'. He must have had a formidable memory, for this account covers the history of the Afghans, an essay on British relations with Afghanistan, another on Amir Sher Ali, and goes on with a further eight essays on the various tribes of the country.

597 **The red Kafirs.**
M. A. Shakur. Peshawar, Pakistan: The Author, 1946. 68p. map. bibliog.
A brief examination of the history and the cultures of the peoples living in Kafiristan (present day Nuristan) by the then curator of the Peshawar Museum.

598 **Revolutions & rebellions in Afghanistan: anthropological perspectives.**
Edited by M. Nazif Shahrani, Robert L. Canfield. Berkeley, California: Institute of International Studies, University of California, 1984. maps. bibliog. (Research Series, no. 57).
A collection of fourteen papers presented at the American Anthropological Association Meeting held in Washington, DC in December 1980. The sections are mostly divided up regionally: Nuristan and Eastern Afghanistan, Qataghan and Badakhshan, Bamiyan and Turkistan, and Western and Southern Afghanistan. The final section is 'The Saur Revolution and the Afhgan [sic] woman'.

599 **The Sheikh Mohammadi - a marginal trading community in east Afghanistan.**
Asta Olesen. *Folk, Dansk Etnografisk Tidsskrift.* vol. 27. (1985), p. 115-46. bibliog.
A study of a low-status migrating minority peoples generally known as *Jat, Jogi,* or *Qawal* by other peoples in Afghanistan.

600 **Sir George Robertson: an early field worker.**
Adam Curle. *Man, a Monthly Record of Anthropological Science.* vol. 61, arts. 1-25. (1961), p. 15-18. bibliog.
A biographical sketch of the career of George Scott Robertson, the British MD and political agent who wrote *The Kafirs of the Hindu Kush* (q.v.), a work which remains to this day the best book ever written about the people and the region known today as Nuristan.

601 **Socio-economic change among a group of east Afghan nomads.**
Gorm Pedersen. *Afghanistan Journal.* vol. 8, no. 4. (1981), p. 115-22.
Report of a study of nomad traders in which the author suggests that certain factors
are contributing to the settlement of nomads and thus the eventual elimination of
the nomadic way of life.

602 **Some notes on the mythology of the Kafirs of the Hindu Kush (before
1898).**
Ahmad Ali Motamedi. *Afghanistan.* vol. 12, no. 3; no. 4. (1957), p.
9-15; p. 7-12.
A selection of oral traditions gathered in the course of a 1953 field trip to Nuristan
with Lennart Edelberg and Klaus Ferdinand.

603 **The Tâjiks, a brief history.**
V. V. Bartol'd, translated by J. M. Rogers. *Afghan Studies.* vol. 3-4.
(1982), p. 53-64.
This is an English translation of a Russian article which appeared in *Tadzhikistan*.
Published in Tashkent in 1925, this deals with the Tadjiks both north and south of
the Amu Darya.

604 **Temple of Imra, temple of Mahandeu: a Kafir sanctuary in Kalasha
cosmology.**
Peter Parkes. *Bulletin of the School of Oriental and African Studies.* vol.
54, pt. 1. (1991), p. 75-103. maps. bibliog.
This is an important contribution to our present understanding 'of religious knowledge in the Hindu Kush, particularly the comparative mythology of the Afghan
Kafirs and of their Dardic-speaking neighbours in northern Pakistan'. The author,
who carried out fieldwork among the Kalasha of Chitral, is an expert on the pre-
Islamic systems of belief and oral traditions of the region and his work has greatly
increased our understanding of the social, economic, and political institutions of
Hindu Kush communities.

605 **Träger medialer Begabung im Hindukusch und Karakorum.**
(Possessors of mediumistic skills in the Hindu Kush and Karako-
rums.)
Erika Friedl. Vienna: Österreichische Ethnologische Gesellschaft,
1965. 127p. bibliog. (Acta Ethnologica et Linguistica, no. 8).
A German-language study, based on published accounts from the 19th and 20th
centuries, of shamanistic skills and practices in north-eastern Afghanistan, northern
Pakistan, Ladakh and Tibet. The material from Afghanistan relates to the Kafirs and
Kafiristan (present-day Nuristan).

606 **USAID and social scientists discuss Afghanistan's development prospects.**
Louis Dupree. New York: American Universities Field Staff Reports Service, 1977. 19p. (South Asia Series, vol. 21, no. 2 (Afghanistan)).
A report on a USAID-sponsored conference on rural life in Afghanistan with special emphasis on development possibilities. Some thirty-two specialists attended: four historians, three geographers, eleven anthropologists, one economist, two linguists, two sociologists, one law expert, one demographer, and six unclassifiable. The author summarizes their contributions.

607 **Vergleichende Kulturgeographie der Hochgebirge des Südlichen Asien.**
(Comparative cultural geography of the high-mountain regions of southern Asia.)
Edited by Carl Rathjens, Carl Troll, Harald Uhlig. Wiesbaden, Germany: Franz Steiner, 1973. 186p. maps. (Erdwissenschaftliche Forschung, vol. 5).
This volume, written mostly in German, contains four important papers on Afghanistan: 'Common field systems in the Hindukush of Afghanistan' and 'Types of peasant economy at the upper limit of permanent settlements in the Hindukush of Afghanistan' by Erwin Grötzbach; 'Highland pasture economy of the Pashtuni nomads in Afghanistan' by Christoph Jentsch; and 'The Palae in Nuristan, a type of cooperative dairy farming' by Ahmad Yusuf Nuristani.

608 **Women, honour and love: some aspects of the Pashtun woman's life in eastern Afghanistan.**
Inger W. Boesen. *Afghanistan Journal.* vol. 7, no. 2. (1980), p. 50-59.
A study of women in Pashtun society based on fieldwork carried out in the Kunar Valley in 1977-78.

609 **Zeitrechnung in Nuristan und am Pamir.**
(Calendar systems in Nuristan and the Pamirs. )
Wolfgang Lentz. Berlin: Deutsche Akademie der Wissenschaften, 1939. 211p. maps. (Abhandlungen der Preussischen Akademie der Wissenschaften, Jahrgang 1938. Phil.-hist. Klasse Nr. 7.).
The fieldwork which resulted in this pioneering study was carried out by the author while taking part in the Soviet-German Alai-Pamir Expedition of 1928 and the German Hindu Kush Expedition of 1935. In it he presents, analyses, and compares calender systems from numerous villages in north-west India (now Pakistan), Nuristan, northern Afghanistan, and the southern Soviet Union. The work was reprinted in 1978 by ADEVA (Graz, Austria) and the author took the opportunity to write a fifty-two page text to include more recent research. This is a major study by an incisive mind.

Anthropology

**Afghanistan.**
*See* item no. 6.

**Völkerschicksale am Hindukusch: Afghanen, Belutschen, Tadshiken.** Destiny of the Hindu Kush Peoples: Afghans, Beluchis, Tadjiks.
*See* item no. 42.

**Afghanische Studien.**
*See* item no. 43.

**Kafiristan: Versuch einer Landeskunde auf Grund einer Reise im Jahre 1928.** Kafiristan: an attempt at a general study of the country based on an expedition in 1928.
*See* item no. 62.

**The Kafirs of the Hindu Kush.**
*See* item no. 112.

**Leaves from an Afghan scrapbook.**
*See* item no. 113.

**The road to Kabul, an anthology.**
*See* item no. 126.

**The political organization of the Kam Kafirs: a preliminary analysis.**
*See* item no. 274.

**The romance of the Indian frontiers.**
*See* item no. 387.

**The Hazara farmers of central Afghanistan: some historical and contemporary problems.**
*See* item no. 613.

**Kafiristan.**
*See* item no. 616.

**Atlas linguistique des parlers Dardes et Kafirs.** Linguistic atlas of Dard and Kafir speakers.
*See* item no. 620.

**A comparative dictionary of the Indo-Aryan languages: indexes compiled by D. R. Turner.**
*See* item no. 623.

**Some Kati myths and hymns.**
*See* item no. 668.

**Some Paruni myths and hymns.**
*See* item no. 669.

**Militant Islam and traditional warfare in Islamic South Asia.**
*See* item no. 680.

**The religions of the Hindukush. Vol. I, the religion of the Kafirs; The pre-Islamic heritage of Afghan Nuristan.**
*See* item no. 682.

**Some aspects of family life in an Afghan village.**
*See* item no. 698.

**The continuity of Pashai society.**
*See* item no. 731.

**'From tribe to *Umma*': comments on the dynamics of identity in Muslim Soviet Central Asia.**
*See* item no. 735.

**The Baluchistan barrel-vaulted tent and its affinities.**
*See* item no. 919.

**Women and music in Herat.**
*See* item no. 941.

**Die Firuzkuhi-jurte des Museums für Völkerkunde in Wien.** The Firozkohi *yurt* in the Anthropological Museum in Vienna.
*See* item no. 956.

**Buzkashi: game and power in Afghanistan.**
*See* item no. 963.

# Population

610 **A pilot study of the displacement, loss of human life, and disablement of the population in three Afghan villages.**
Mohammad Wasim Lodin. *WUFA, Quarterly Journal of the Writers Union of Free Afghanistan.* vol. 3, no. 3. (1988), p. 45-71.
A sample survey, designed and conducted by an Afghan statistician, to assess the impact of the war on rural Afghanistan. He provides detailed information in a wide range of categories: household composition, age structure, sex, education, forced displacement, numbers imprisoned, numbers killed or wounded, etc.

611 **Some observations on and assessment of the population losses in Afghanistan.**
M. Siddieq Noorzoy. *WUFA, Quarterly Journal of the Writers Union of Free Afghanistan.* vol. 3, no. 3. (1988), p. 6-14.
An attempt, on the basis of the acknowledged shortcomings of available data, to assess the demographic situation in Afghanistan after eight years of war. There are useful footnotes citing UN documents.

**Anthropological researches from the 3rd Danish Expedition to Central Asia.**
*See* item no. 537.

# Nationalities, Minorities

### 612  The Abul camp in central Afghanistan.

H.R.H. Prince Peter of Greece and Denmark. *Journal of the Royal Central Asian Society.* vol. 41. (1954), p. 44-53.

A preliminary account, written in narrative style, of an annual event in which nomads from all over the country gather to elect a government, to choose a 'king' and to transact business.

### 613  The Hazara farmers of central Afghanistan: some historical and contemporary problems.

Marek Gawęcki. *Ethnologia Polona.* vol. 6. (1980), p. 163-75. bibliog.

This study describes the rural economy of the Hazaras and identifies the causes of the disadvantaged socioeconomic conditions in which they live.

### 614  History of former Kafiristan.

A. R. Palwal. *Afghanistan.* vols. 21-24. (1968-71),

Based partly on fieldwork and partly on library research, this extended essay runs through no less than four years of the journal's issues and attempts to reconstruct the social, economic, political, and religious history of the non-Muslim peoples who lived in isolated valleys on the southern slopes of the Hindu Kush in that part of eastern Afghanistan now known as Nuristan.

### 615  Is Hazara an old word?

M. Husain Shah. *Afghanistan.* vol. 17, no. 4. (1962), p. 32-38.

An examination of historical works by Asian and European writers reveals that the term 'Hazara' (which is thought to be derived from the Farsi for 'one thousand' *hazar*), although much used, is ill-defined. The author goes on to trace the linguistic origins of the word which describes an ancient people descended from the followers of Chingiz Khan and Amir Timur.

616 **Kafiristan.**
George Scott Robertson. *The Geographical Journal.* vol. 4. (1894), p. 193-218. map.
One of the earlier general accounts of the region, covering matters geographical, social, political, and religious, by one of the very few Western observers to visit the area prior to the invasion by the army of Afghanistan (1895-1900) and the conversion of the population to Islam.

617 **Nooristan.**
A. H. Waleh. *Afghanistan.* vol. 6, no. 3. (1951), p. 20-29.
A general illustrated account of Nuristan and its people, their manners, customs, and their way of life.

618 **The Uzbeks in Afghanistan.**
Eden Naby. *Central Asian Survey.* vol. 3, no. 1. (1984), p. 1-21.
A general account, covering demography, geography, and history of the Uzbeks, with an up-to-date appraisal of the contemporary situation since the Soviet invasion. The political complications arising from the fact that there are Uzbek populations on both sides of the Oxus (Amu Darya) is discussed.

**Bold horsemen of the steppes: Afghanistan's Turkomans hold fast to traditions of their nomadic forefathers, who once terrorized Central Asia.**
*See* item no. 150.

**The Hazaras of central Afghanistan.**
*See* item no. 154.

**The Sheikh Mohammadi - a marginal trading community in east Afghanistan.**
*See* item no. 599.

# Languages and Dialects

**619  Afghanistan 1989 in sociolinguistic perspective.**
Jadwiga Pstrusinska. London: Society for Central Asian Studies, 1990. 80p. bibliog. (Central Asian Survey, Incidental Papers Series, no. 7).
Contains a catalogue of forty-five languages said to be spoken in the country today. This is followed by an essay on Dari, another on Pashto ('Pashto in offensive'), and a third called 'The sociolinguistic epilogue', which comprises a survey of refugees and political events since the Soviet invasion.

**620  Atlas linguistique des parlers Dardes et Kafirs.**
(Linguistic atlas of Dard and Kafir speakers. )
Gérard Fussman. Paris: École Française d'Extrême-Orient, 1972. 451p. maps. bibliog. (Publications de l'École Française d'Extrême-Orient, vol. LXXXVI).
This work is in two volumes: the first consisting of 171 linguistic maps of eastern Afghanistan and northern Pakistan (culturally, an unusually complex region, even for Asia), and the second providing a detailed commentary on the nature of the linguistic characteristics of these Indo-Aryan languages. The author is one of Europe's foremost experts in the field.

**621  The Balochi language, a grammar and manual.**
George Waters Gilbertson. Hertford: Gilbertson, 1923. 310p. bibliog. A textbook for students which begins with a section on the adjective and goes on to the adverb, alphabet, articles, conjunctions, gender, idioms, interjection, the noun, prepositions, pronouns, and ends with the verb. Part two consists of texts, conversational sentences, and longer text examples. All Baluchi words are written in transliteration rather than Arabic script.

### 622 A comparative dictionary of the Indo-Aryan languages.

R. L. Turner. London: Oxford University Press, 1966. 841p. bibliog.

A monumental work which, among other things, lists and analyses words in 287 languages and dialects, including the 'Dardic' and 'Kafiri' languages. Not very portable, but invaluable for the researcher who has collected texts in the field, or is carrying out research on these languages.

### 623 A comparative dictionary of the Indo-Aryan languages: indexes compiled by D. R. Turner.

R. L. Turner, D. R. Turner. London: Oxford University Press, 1969. 357p.

This valuable word index accompanies the main volume (q.v.). Here words are arranged alphabetically within each language grouping. The languages of Afghanistan, some thirty in all, are scattered across several of these groups: New Indo-Aryan, Iranian, and 'Other Non-Indo-European', for example.

### 624 A comparative dictionary of the Indo-Aryan languages: phonetic analysis.

R. L. Turner, D. R. Turner. London: Oxford University, 1971. 235p.

A volume of sound-units and word-lists intended to assist in determining the relationship between a sound in an Old Indo-Aryan word and the corresponding sound in the Middle or New Indo-Aryan word from which it is derived. Stemming from *A comparative dictionary of the Indo-Aryan languages* (q.v.), these sounds and words are those considered to be the most relevant to the phonetic history of Indo-Aryan languages.

### 625 A course in Baluchi.

Muhammad Abd-al-Rahman Barker, Aqil Khan Mengal. Montreal: Institute of Islamic Studies, McGill University, 1969. 2 vols. maps.

Although these are language textbooks, they also attempt to place the language in its socio-cultural context by introducing material on social customs, history, tribal laws, and political systems. Designed as a one-year course, volume one concentrates on the spoken language; while volume two focuses on the written. The work deals with the Rakshani dialect of Baluchi.

### 626 The Dardic and Nuristani languages.

D. I. Edelman. Moscow: Nauka, 1983. 343p. bibliog. (Languages of Asia and Africa).

This is a major linguistic study by an eminent Russian scholar. Edelman systematically examines the individual languages belonging to Dardic and Nuristani linguistic groups, discussing the finer points of grammar, vocalization, consonant shifts, morphology, and phonetics. The text has been written for students and specialists, but the introduction which traces the history of linguistic studies in the region, and the bibliography at the end are in themselves worth the price.

627 **A dictionary of some languages and dialects of Afghanistan.**
Shah Abdullah Badakhshi. Kabul: Pashto Tolana, 1960. 225p.
Words from the different languages treated are arranged in columns for comparative
purposes. The languages (Shughni, Sanglechi, Wakhi, Ishkashmi, Munji, etc.) are
those of northern Afghanistan. The entire text is presented in Arabic script.

628 **A dictionary of the Pukhto, Pushto, or Language of the Afghans
with remarks on the originality of the language and its affinity to
the Semitic and other Oriental tongues.**
Henry George Raverty. London: William & Norgate, 1867. 1115p.
Compiled by one of Britain's foremost 19th-century students of the languages, manners, and customs of Afghanistan and the North-West Frontier, with a preface and
introductory remarks in which the author, in his usual caustic style, criticizes British
policy in the region.

629 **A dictionary of the Pukkhto or Pukshto language in which the words
are traced to their sources in the Indian and Persian languages.**
Henry Walter Bellew. London: Wm. H. Allen, 1867. 355p.
The Pashto-English section gives words in both Arabic script and transliteration,
together with their meanings; the English-Pashto section gives them in transliteration
only.

630 **The distribution of the Parachi language.**
Mohammed Nabi Kohzad. *Afghanistan.* vol. 12, no. 2. (1957), p.
39-41.
A brief discussion of Parachi with information on the localities where it is spoken:
Shutul (80 kilometres north of Kabul), and Patcharan (120 kilometres north-east
of Kabul). The author estimates that there are between 7,000 and 8,500 Parachi-
speakers in the country.

631 **An etymological vocabulary of Pashto.**
Georg Morgenstierne. Oslo: Det Norske Videnskaps-Akademi, 1927.
120p. (Hist.-Filos. Klasse, no. 3).
The introduction provides a useful summary of linguistic work by various scholars
on the Pashto language and serves to put into context new research in the field. In
the half century that followed the publication of this work Morgenstierne established
himself as Europe's foremost expert on the languages of Central Asia.

632 **Etymologie und Lautlehre des Afghänischen.**
(Etymology and phonology of the Afghan language.)
Wilhelm Geiger. Munich: Königlich Bayerish Akademie der Wis-
senschaften, 1893. 56p.
An early European work on the etymology and phonology of Pashto which remained
one of the chief Western sources on Pashto linguistics for some three decades.

633 **Factors influencing the development of modern literary ('Darri') Persian in Khorassan and Transoxiana in the tenth and eleventh centuries, A.D.**
Richard N. Frye. *Afghanistan.* vol. 13, no. 3. (1958), p. 1-7.
A linguistic and historical discussion showing how the dialect of Fars developed into modern Persian in Khorassan, Bactria, and Transoxiana during the 3rd century AH.

634 **Georg Morgenstierne.**
Prods O. Skjaervø. *Acta Orientalia.* vol. 40. (1979), [n.p.].
An obituary of and tribute to Europe's foremost expert on the languages of Afghanistan and neighbouring areas, together with a summary of his scholarly contributions. Georg Morgenstierne died in 1979.

635 **A grammar of Pashto: a descriptive study of the dialect of Kandahar, Afghanistan.**
Herbert Penzl. Washington, DC: American Council of Learned Societies, 1955. 131p. (Program in Oriental Languages, Publications Series B).
A grammar prepared with the intention of facilitating instruction in Pashto by the understanding of its structure.

636 **Grammar of the Pašto or language of the Afghans, compared with the Iranian and North-Indian idioms.**
Ernest Trumpp. London: Trübner, 1873. 412p.
A pioneering example of European linguistic scholarship on the Pashto language, providing not only a grammar, but also presenting comparative data derived from a study of other South Asian languages.

637 **A grammar of the Pukhto, Pushto, or language of the Afghans in which the rules are illustrated by examples from the best writers, both poetical and prose, together with translations from the articles of war and remarks on the language, literature, and descent of the Afghan tribes.**
Henry George Raverty. London: William & Norgate, 1867. 204p.
This contains essays on 'The alphabet', 'The parts of speech', 'The noun', 'The adjective', 'The pronoun', 'The verb', 'The separate particles', 'The derivation of words', 'The numerals', and 'The syntax'. Includes a thirty-five-page introduction in Raverty's rambling, critical, and occasionally caustic style.

638 **The Hazaragi dialect of Afghan Persian.**
G. K. Dulling. London: Central Asian Research Centre, 1973. 99p. map. bibliog.
A preliminary study of the language of the Hazara peoples who inhabit the Hazarajat - the central highlands of Afghanistan lying between Herat and Kabul. The study includes sections on orthography, phonology, grammar, Hazara texts, and notes on

lexical material. There is a Hazaragi-English vocabulary and an English-Hazaragi index.

639 **Indo-Iranian frontier languages, vol. I: Parachi and Ormuri.**
Georg Morgenstierne. Oslo: Instituttet for Sammenlignende Kultur-forskning, 1929. 419p. map. (Serie B: Skrifter, vol. 11).

At the time of Morgenstierne's fieldwork in 1924 Western scholars knew almost nothing about either Parachi or Ormuri, both Iranian languages spoken in certain villages in the Kabul region. This volume remains the most complete study of these languages published to date, providing a grammar, phonology, morphology, vocabulary, and texts for each.

640 **Indo-Iranian frontier languages, vol. II: Iranian Pamir languages (Yidgha-Munji, Sanglechi-Ishkashmi, and Wakhi).**
Georg Morgenstierne. Oslo: Instituttet for Sammenlignende Kultur-forskning, 1938. 562p. map. (Serie B: Skrifter, vol. 35).

A linguistic analysis of languages spoken in northeast Afghanistan, some of which are also spoken across the frontier in what is today northern Pakistan. The work contains texts, translations, vocabulary, phonology, and morphology for each language treated.

641 **Indo-Iranian frontier languages, vol. III: the Pashai languages, 2: texts and translations.**
Georg Morgenstierne. Oslo: Instituttet for Sammenlignende Kultur-forskning, 1944. 304p. (Serie B: Skrifter, vol. 40).

A linguistic analysis of Pashai, 'the North-Westernmost outpost of the Indo-Aryan group of languages'. Its geographical spread reaches from the Kunar Valley to the Panjshir Valley, each community embedded in and surrounded by communities of non-Pashai speakers. Morgenstierne cautiously suggests that Pashai may have been the language of the Hindu and Buddhist inhabitants of eastern Afghanistan in pre-Islamic times. Part one of this work (published separately) is devoted to the grammar of Pashai; part three (published separately in 1956) contains the vocabulary. A bibliography of Morgenstierne's published work (1903-72) appears in his 'Kalasha language, text and translations, vocabulary and grammar' which was published as volume four of his monumental 'Indo-Iranian frontier languages' series (Oslo, 1973).

642 **Indo-Iranica: mélanges présentés à Georg Morgenstierne à l'occasion de son soixante-dixième anniversaire.**
(Miscellaneous studies presented to Georg Morgenstierne on the occasion of his 70th birthday.)
Edited by Georges Redard. Wiesbaden, Germany: Otto Harrassowitz, 1964. 195p. bibliog.

A few papers in this volume are concerned with research problems relating to Afghanistan, notably those by Fredrik Barth and Olaf Hansen, but for the student of the languages of Afghanistan, this book's chief interest is in the seven page bibliography of Professor Morgenstierne's published works.

## Languages and Dialects

643 **Iranian languages as a source of history.**

Georg Morgenstierne. *Afghanistan.* vol. 20, no. 4. (1968), p. 20-26.

A discussion of the importance for linguistic and historical studies of the Iranian branch of Indo-European languages. Professor Morgenstierne suggests that a comprehensive etymological dictionary of Iranian is one of the most pressing needs in Indo-European studies.

644 **Kabul Museum stone inscription of the year 83.**

Sten Konow. *Acta Orientalia.* vol. 16. (1938), p. 234-40.

A description of a stone found near Jalalabad bearing a five line inscription in 'well executed Kharosthi' script, the language being northwestern Prakrit, with a date equivalent to 25 AD. The inscription commemorates the building of a water reservoir. A photograph of the stone with its inscription accompanies the article.

645 **The language of the Ashkun Kafirs.**

Georg Morgenstierne. *Norsk Tidsskrift for Sprogvidenskap.* vol. 2. (1929), p. 192-289.

A linguistic analysis of Ashkun, one of the languages of western Nuristan, which is spoken in an area between the Pech River and the Alingar. Based on data obtained in Afghanistan in 1924, it offers remarks on the characteristics of the language, its position among other Nuristani languages, a grammar, some texts and sentences, and a fifty-two page vocabulary. Although more than six decades have elapsed since its publication, it is still the main work on this language.

646 **The languages of Afghanistan.**

Georg Morgenstierne. *Afghanistan.* vol. 20, no. 3. (1967), p. 81-90.

In this lecture, delivered at Kabul University in September, 1966, Professor Morgenstierne ranges over a score or more of the thirty languages spoken in the country, dropping in here and there to throw light on obscure but fascinating linguistic anomalies, problems, and connections, as perhaps only he could do.

647 **Linguistic gleanings from Nuristan.**

Georg Morgenstierne. *Norsk Tidsskrift for Sprogvidenskap.* vol. 16. (1951), p. 117-35. map.

Written by the doyen of linguistic research in Afghanistan, this offers information about the the Ashkun language with emphasis on the dialect spoken in Wama in the Pech Valley of Nuristan and the languages of Tregam to the north-west of Chaga Sarai in the Kunar Valley.

648 **The linguistic stratification of Afghanistan.**

Georg Morgenstierne. *Afghan Studies.* vol. 2. (1979), p. 23-33. bibliog.

A survey of the languages and linguistic problems of Afghanistan by Europe's foremost expert on the subject.

649 **A manual of Pushtu.**
G. Roos-Keppel, Abdul Ghani Khan. London: Sampson Low, Marston, 1901. 310p.

A textbook for students, consisting of three parts: a concise grammar; a course of sixty lessons and exercises, graded according to difficulty; and a list of colloquial sentences. The whole has been prepared for British civil service and military personnel who wish to pass the Lower and/or Higher Standard examinations.

650 **Notes on the Arabic dialect spoken in the Balkh region of Afghanistan.**
Abdul-Sattār Sīrat. *Acta Orientalia.* vol. 35. (1973), p. 89-101.

This was the first study in a European language of Afghan Arabic. It reveals that the Arabic spoken in the northern part of the country is closely related to Soviet Central Asian Arabic and, as such, belongs to a clearly defined dialect group. The article provides notes on phonology, semantics, morphology, and syntax.

651 **Notes on the Bashgali (Kafir) Language.**
John Davidson. *Journal of the Asiatic Society of Bengal.* vol. 71, pt. 1, extra no. 1. (1902), 192p. bibliog.

A more thorough study than its title suggests, this contains information on the grammar and provides a vocabulary of the language now known as Kati. Very useful bibliography.

652 **Notes on the Pashto Tolana vocabulary of Munji.**
Georg Morgenstierne. *Acta Orientalia.* vol. 30. (1966), p. 177-88.

A discussion of the little-known language of Munji based on information derived from Shah Abdullah Badakhshi's *A dictionary of some languages and dialects of Afghanistan* (q.v.) published in Kabul in 1960 by the Pashto Academy.

653 **Notes on Tirahi.**
Georg Morgenstierne. *Acta Orientalia.* vol. 12. (1934), p. 161-89.

The author presents linguistic information, gathered in the field in 1929, about what he classified as a 'Dardic' dialect spoken in some villages southeast of Jalalabad in eastern Afghanistan. Despite the fact that his one Tirahi-speaker 'was old and nearly toothless, very slow-minded, [and] rather short-tempered', he gained a good deal of information about the language, including a fifteen-page vocabulary.

654 **The orbit of Afghan studies, a lecture given at the Society's inaugural meeting (in London).**
Harold W. Bailey. *Afghan Studies.* vol. 1. (1978), p. 1-8.

This presidential address, delivered by the Cambridge Professor of Sanskrit (1936-67), who is also one of Europe's foremost scholars and leading expert on the ancient languages of Central Asia, constitutes an erudite overview of the subject.

655 **Pashto basic course.**
O. L. Chavarria-Aguilar. Ann Arbor, Michigan: University of Michigan, 1962. 159p.

A course book for classroom use containing fourteen lessons for the student of the spoken language. The materials are those for the dialect of Pashto spoken in eastern Afghanistan, which differs considerably from, for example, that spoken in Peshawar.

656 **Pashto instructor's handbook.**
O. L. Chavarria-Aguilar. Ann Arbor, Michigan: University of Michigan, 1962. 73p.

'The materials contained in this Handbook consist chiefly of the drills on those sounds which it is expected will cause some degree of difficulty to speakers of English learning Pashto.'

657 **'Pashto', 'Pathan' and the treatment of *r*+ sibilant in Pashto.**
Georg Morgenstierne. *Acta Orientalia*. vol. 18. (1940), p. 138-44.

A linguistic discussion regarding the transition of certain sounds in Pashto which leads on to historical considerations and an attempt to identify Pashto-speakers with certain peoples mentioned in the early history of the region.

658 **Pashtu, part I, syntax of colloquial Pashtu, with chapters on the Persian and Indian elements in the modern language.**
D. L. R. Lorimer. Oxford: Clarendon, 1915. 377p.

A major work by one of Britain's foremost 20th-century soldier/scholars. Systematic, detailed, and thorough, it remains a valuable study for students of the language. The second part was never published.

659 **Persian texts from Afghanistan.**
Georg Morgenstierne. *Acta Orientalia*. vol. 6. (1928), p. 308-28.

Texts, collected in the field in 1924 by the famous Norwegian linguist, of Dari, the popular language of Kabul and the surrounding country. These serve to illustrate differences between Modern Persian (Farsi) and Dari.

660 **Pushto instructor: a grammar of the Pukkhot [Sic] or Pukshto language on a new and improved system, combining brevity with practical utility and including exercises and dialogues intended to facilitate the acquisition of the colloquial.**
Henry Walter Bellew. London: W. H. Allen, 1867. 155p.

Bellew, like Henry George Raverty (q.v.), was a Victorian soldier/scholar with wide anthropological and linguistic interests. This contains a preface and sections on 'Pukkhto or Pukshto grammar', 'The parts of speech', 'The verb', 'The particle', and forty pages of exercises.

661 **A reader of Pashto.**
Herbert Penzl. Ann Arbor, Michigan: University of Michigan, 1962.
274p.
A textbook which provides a graded introduction to the reading of Pashto texts,
intended for both classroom use and private study. It has been prepared by North
America's foremost Pashto scholar.

662 **Report on a linguistic mission to Afghanistan.**
Georg Morgenstierne. Oslo: H. Aschehoug, 1926. 101p. maps.
(Instituttet for Sammenlignende Kulturforskning).
An account of the author's 1924 linguistic field research in which he set out to
study the Aryan dialects on both sides of the Indo-Iranian linguistic frontier, 'a very
promising field of investigation for the student of comparative philology, who could
here hope to come across the last of the unknown Indo-European languages which
are still spoken'. Happily for linguistic studies, Professor Morgenstierne was still
carrying out research on these languages half a century later.

663 **Report on a linguistic mission to Helmand and Nīmrūz.**
J. Elfenbein. *Afghan Studies.* vol. 2. (1979), p. 39-44. bibliog.
A report on the Bal (Baluchi) speaking peoples and their geographical distribution
by one who, like Morgenstierne before him, regards Afghanistan as 'linguistically
one of the most interesting countries on earth'. See William Trousdale, 'A note on
Elfenbein's Linguistic Mission to Helmand and Nimruz' in *Afghan Studies*, vols. 3
and 4, 1982, and Elfenbein's reply on p. 104 of that same volume.

664 **A short grammatical outline of Pashto.**
D. A. Shafeev. The Hague: Mouton, 1964. 89p.
Translated from the Russian by Herbert Paper, this is arranged into sections dealing
with phonetics, morphology, and syntax, with lists of the most common verbs, con-
jugation tables of verbs, and a list of eighteen published works on Pashto grammar.

665 **A sketch of the Bashgeli Kafirs and of their language.**
G. W. Leitner. *Journal of the United Service Institution of India.* 1881.
p. 142-90.
Written in 1879 from materials collected in 1866 and 1867 from Kafir prisoners
taken by the Maharaja of Kashmir, this includes brief notes about the difficulties of
linguistic field studies and gives miscellaneous ethnographic notes before offering a
vocabulary and grammar of the language (24 pages), a sketch of Kalasha grammar
(9 pages), and three pages of tables in which Kalasha is compared with the Gilgiti
and Arnyia languages. There is a map and some drawings of Kafirs. Today the
language of the Bashgal Valley is known as Kati, while 'Kalasha' is the term used
for the non-Muslim peoples of the Rumbur, Bomboret, and Berir Valleys of Chitral.

666 **A sketch of the northern Balochi language, containing a grammar, vocabulary, and specimens of the language.**
M. Longworth Dames. Calcutta: Asiatic Society, 1881. 174p.
This deals with Baluchi as spoken on the present Afghanistan-Pakistan frontier in the Kandahar-Quetta area. It differs significantly from the southern dialect of Baluchi. This volume was published as an extra number of the *Journal of the Asiatic Society of Bengal*, part 1, Calcutta, 1880.

667 **Sociolinguistic factors in Afghanistan.**
M. Alam Miran. *Afghanistan Journal.* vol. 4, no. 3. (1977), p. 122-27. bibliog.
A discussion of the ways in which language functions in a society and how it is used by members of society, with reference to the linguistic complexity of the country (more than thirty languages are spoken in Afghanistan today), and the need for a national language or languages (Dari and Pashto).

668 **Some Kati myths and hymns.**
Georg Morgenstierne. *Acta Orientalia.* vol. 21. (1953), p. 161-89.
Examples of oral traditions in the East Kati language of Nuristan, together with English translations and information about the pre-Islamic dieties and spirits of the Kafirs of the Hindu Kush.

669 **Some Paruni myths and hymns.**
Lennart Edelberg. *Acta Orientalia.* vol. 34. (1972), p. 31-94. map. bibliog.
A collection of oral traditions from the pre-Islamic period and an even earlier legendary past, obtained in north-central Nuristan in the course of field research in 1947-49. Traditional village calendars are given and there are numerous illustrations.

670 **Some remarks on Pashto etymology.**
Jarl Charpentier. *Acta Orientalia.* vol. 7. (1929), p. 180-97.
A critical examination of Georg Morgenstierne's *Etymological vocabulary of Pashto* (q.v.) in which suggestions are put forward regarding possible etymological connections for certain words. This is followed (on p. 198-200) by Morgenstierne's remarks concerning Charpentier's etymologies.

671 **A specimen of Bashgali from Kamdesh.**
W. Ivanow. *Acta Orientalia.* vol. 10. (1932), p. 154-57.
This is a text obtained in Bombay during an interview with a Mulla from Kamdesh. The author comments on this dialect of Kati in the light of information given in Morgenstierne's *Report on a linguistic mission to Afghanistan* (q.v.).

672  **Standard Pashto and the dialects of Pashto.**
Herbert Penzl. *Afghanistan.* vol. 14, no. 3. (1959), p. 8-14.
The author considers that syntactic differences between various Pashto dialects are insignificant; the inflectional endings are, however, striking, as are the phonemes. There is a generally accepted written standard for the language, but not a spoken standard. He remarks that 'The special symbols of the Pashto alphabet...show that the cradle of the alphabet must have been in Kandahar'.

673  **A text-book of the Balochi language, consisting of miscellaneous stories, legends, poems and Balochi-English vocabulary.**
M. Longworth Dames. Lahore: Government Printer, Punjab, 1922. 221p.
This contains a thirty-eight-page grammar and thirty-three short stories in Baluchi, though rendered in the Latin alphabet rather than the Arabic. Part two is a 'legendary history of the Baloches' similarly presented. Part three consists of Baluchi poems, and part four is a vocabulary - a Baluchi-English dictionary with the words arranged alphabetically in Arabic script. No English translations of the stories and poems are given.

674  **Uzbek texts from Afghan Turkestan, with glossary.**
Gunnar Jarring. *Lunds Universitets Arsskrift.* vol. 34, no. 2. (1938), p. 1-246. bibliog.
A collection of eighteen Uzbek texts collected in the field between October and December 1935. The stories are given both in the Uzbek dialect of Andkhui and in English and are of interest to both linguists and those who study oral traditions.

675  **The Waigali language.**
Georg Morgenstierne. *Norsk Tidsskrift for Sprogvidenskap.* vol. XVII. (1954), p. 146-324. map. bibliog.
A study of the Wai-ala language which is spoken in the Waigal Valley in south-central Nuristan. Written by the noted Norwegian linguist, this remains the most authoritative analysis of the language published to date. It includes an extensive vocabulary, a list of mythological names, and a list of place names.

**The Hephthalite inscriptions of Uruzgan.**
*See* item no. 212.

**Is Hazara an old word?**
*See* item no. 615.

**The Ghulshan-i-Roh: being selections, prose and poetical, in the Pushto, or Afghān language.**
*See* item no. 877.

**The *Kalid-i-Afghani*, being selections of Pushto prose and poetry for the use of students.**
*See* item no. 881.

## Languages and Dialects

**Popular poetry of the Baloches.**
*See* item no. 889.

**A short history of Pashto prose.**
*See* item no. 891.

**Translation of the *Kalid-i-Afghani*, the text book for the Pakkhto examination, with notes, historical, geographical, grammatical, and explanatory.**
*See* item no. 892.

**Two Pashai popular songs.**
*See* item no. 939.

# Religion

### 676 The implications of the Islamic question for Soviet domestic and foreign policy.
Hans Bräker. *Central Asian Survey*. vol. 2, no. 1. (1983), p. 111-28. bibliog.

An examination of Soviet policy towards Iran and Afghanistan following the spread of militant Islamic renewal movements and the fear, on the part of the Soviets, that such political activity might spill over into the Soviet Central Asian states.

### 677 Islam as a binding force in Afghan resistance.
Z. A. Mumtaz. *WUFA, Quarterly Journal of the Writers Union of Free Afghanistan*. vol. 2, no. 2. (1987), p. 61-76.

Discusses Muslim attitudes towards Communism and the Soviet Union as expressed by *Mujahideen* members interviewed by the author.

### 678 Islam reawakening in Central Asia.
Shafaq Stanezai. *WUFA, Quarterly Journal of the Writers Union of Free Afghanistan*. vol. 2, no. 2. (1987), p. 10-32.

An account of the Muslim republics of Soviet Central Asia and the difficulties facing Moscow as a result of the Soviet invasion of Afghanistan. The author identifies four main problems which he suggests will face the Soviet Union in the year 2000, and he concludes that the Muslim republics should be allowed to leave the union 'before it is too late'.

### 679 Islamic sources of resistance.
Robert L. Canfield. *Orbis, a Journal of World Affairs*. (1985), p. 57-71.

This issue of the journal is devoted to a forum on Afghanistan with articles by four different authors, of which Canfield is one. His thesis is that 'It is the conjunction of political and religious qualities in Afghan Islam that provides the *mujahidin* with certain advantages for their resistance against the Afghan Marxist-Soviet regime'.

680 **Militant Islam and traditional warfare in Islamic South Asia.**
Louis Dupree. Hanover, New Hampshire: American Universities Field Staff Reports, 1980. 12p. map. bibliog. (AUFS Reports, 1980, no. 21, Asia).

A look at modern trends in Islam and traditions of conflict between the Shiite and Sunni Muslims, with examples from Afghanistan of clan or tribal feuding and tribal warfare.

681 **Notes on Afghan Sufi orders and Khanaqahs.**
Bo Utas. *Afghanistan Journal.* vol. 7, no. 2. (1980), p. 60-67. bibliog.

A study of traditional Afghan Sufi retreats and centres of religious learning (*khanaqahs*) and their shrines, mosques, schools, and guest houses. Four Sufi orders were active in Afghanistan at the time of the study in 1978: Naqshbandiya, Qadiriya, Chishtiya, and Suhravardiya.

682 **The religions of the Hindukush. Vol. I, the religion of the Kafirs; The pre-Islamic heritage of Afghan Nuristan.**
Karl Jettmar. Warminster, England: Aris & Phillips, 1986. 172p. map. bibliog.

A review and analysis of what is known of the pre-Muslim religious beliefs of an isolated people who lived on the southern slopes of the Hindu Kush in what is today north-east Afghanistan. Forcibly converted to Islam following the Afghan invasion of those remote valleys in 1895-1900, their descendants are today known as the Nuristanis. This work includes sections on the people, their history, and the 'Environment, Economy, and Social Order', in addition to outlining their religious concepts, the rôle of priests, and a calendar of feasts. There is a good bibliography and a useful glossary of 'Kafiri deities and mythological terms' by Peter Parkes.

683 **Soviet Islam since the invasion of Afghanistan.**
Alexandre Bennigsen. *Central Asian Survey.* vol. 1, no. 1. (1982), p. 65-78.

This is a discussion of the problems facing the Soviet government from her own Muslim peoples as a result of the invasion of Afghanistan and of the consequent anti-religious campaign launched in the Soviet Union in an attempt to contain this potentially disruptive political situation.

684 **The structure and position of Islam in Afghanistan.**
Donald N. Wilber. *The Middle East Journal.* vol. 6, no. 1. (1952), p. 41-48.

An examination of religious organization and religious education in the country and an evaluation of the rôle of Islam in the future of Afghanistan in the light of political changes and an increased Soviet presence.

**Islam and resistance in Afghanistan.**
*See* item no. 268.

**Faction and conversion in a plural society: religious alignments in the Hindu Kush.**
*See* item no. 558.

**Afghanistan: the trajectory of internal alignments.**
*See* item no. 724.

**The Imami Sayyed of the Hazarajat: the maintenance of their elite position.**
*See* item no. 738.

**Problems in the integration of the Afghan nation.**
*See* item no. 752.

**Islamic studies review: Sharia and Islamic education in modern Afghanistan.**
*See* item no. 865.

# Social Conditions

685 **The administrative and social structure of Afghan life.**
Arthur V. Huffman. *Journal of the Royal Central Asian Society.* vol.
38, pt. 1. (1951), p. 41-48.
This deals briefly with the 'structure of government', 'tribal organization - principal
tribes', and 'social stratification, culture and education'.

686 **Afghanistan: torture of political prisoners.**
London: Amnesty International, 1986. 51p. map.
This report documents examples of widespread torture in the country, most of the
victims being in the hands of KHAD (Khedamat-i Etela'at-i Dawlati), the State
Information Services known as the secret police. There are, moreover, 'consistent
accounts of the complicity of Soviet personnel through their presence during inter-
rogation under torture'. The report records the reasons for arrest, the nature of the
torture inflicted, involvement of Soviet personnel, trials, and conditions of detention.

687 **First consolidated report, office of the United Nations co-ordinator
for humanitarian and economic assistance programmes relating to
Afghanistan (UNOCA/1988/1).**
Edited by Sadruddin Aga Khan. Geneva: United Nations, 1988. 206p.
maps.
A thorough and detailed report which brings home to a horrifying extent the damage
which the Soviet war has inflicted on the country and its people. There are, for
example, three pages of information on twenty different types of mines known to be
widely deployed. Information is also supplied on the following: displaced persons,
nomads, refugees, food aid, agriculture, health, education, industry, transport, and
planning.

688 **International Seminar on Social and Cultural Prospects for Afghanistan.**

Edited by A. Rasul Amin. *WUFA, Journal of Afghan Affairs.* (special issue) vol. 5, no. 4. (Oct.-Dec. 1990), 215p.

A seminar was organized and this memorial volume prepared to mark the passing of Louis Dupree. Seven different panels were set up within which both Afghan and European participants discussed a range of social, economic, and political problems facing the country.

689 **Manners and customs of the Afghans.**

Mohammed Ali. *Afghanistan.* vol. 12, no. 3. (1957), p. 1-8.

This briefly covers such cultural traits as hospitality, the family, marriage, belief in spirits, sense of humour, and social life.

690 **The modernization of Afghanistan.**

F. R. Farid. *Afghanistan.* vol. 17, no. 3. (1962), p. 7-22.

This begins with a summary history of the country, examining progress made under various rulers, and ending with an account of present government structure and educational and economic plans for the future.

691 **Operation Salam: donor dossier.**

Edited by Sadruddin Aga Khan. Geneva: United Nations, 1989. 27p.

A record of where the money comes from to pay for Operation Salam - the UN programme of aid to Afghanistan. Each donor country is listed and the amounts provided by each are given.

692 **Operation Salam: first consolidated report, up-date February, 1989 (UNOCA/1988/1 Add.1).**

Edited by Sadruddin Aga Khan. Geneva: United Nations, 1989. 55p. map.

Operation Salam is the name given to the UN programme for assistance to Afghanistan. This report provides a table, based on information from Kabul, of returning refugees with the numbers given for each province in the country. The total given is 169,912. The second part lists all the donations to the assistance fund, country by country. The largest pledge (US$660 million) was from the Soviet Union.

693 **Operation Salam News.**

Edited by Sadruddin Aga Khan. Geneva: United Nations, Dec. 1988-. bimonthly.

A bi-monthly publication issued by the Office of the Co-ordinator for Humanitarian and Economic Assistance Programme relating to Afghanistan. It reports on the situation facing Afghan refugees and describes relief measures taken by the Programme. It can be contacted at Villa La Pelouse, Palais des Nations, 1211 Geneva, Switzerland.

Social Conditions

694 **Operation Salam, office of the United Nations co-ordinator for humanitarian and economic assistance programmes relating to Afghanistan: second consolidated report.**
Edited by Sadruddin Aga Khan. Geneva: United Nations, 1989. 166p. maps.
An overview of programme developments, a report on UN field activities, data on population movements, and a run-down of the problems of and current situation in agriculture, food aid, mine clearance, road repair, shelter construction, health, and education is given. Much of the data is presented in chart form for ready reference. As of this report twenty-six different kinds of Soviet mines have been identified and a programme of training Afghans in dealing with mines and unexploded ordnance has been set up.

695 **Operation Salam. United Nations plan of action, 1989: humanitarian and economic assistance programmes relating to Afghanistan.**
Co-ordinator's Office, UN Humanitarian & Economic Assistance. Geneva: United Nations, 1989. 42p. map.
A report which sets out objectives, policy guidelines and implementation strategies as well as giving information on population movements, for example, internally displaced persons, progress of mine clearance programmes, road repairs, and social programmes such as health and education.

696 **Problems of social development in Afghanistan.**
Leon B. Poullada. *Journal of the Royal Central Asian Society.* vol. 49, pt. 1. (1962), p. 33-39.
The author's thesis is that Afghanistan is in the initial stages of transition from a traditional to a modern society. 'The traditional society is characterised by vertical organization, along kinship-ethnic lines, while "modern"society follows horizontal economic lines.'

697 **The social aspects of recovery in the heterogeneous society of Afghanistan.**
Nasim Jawad. *WUFA, Quarterly Journal of the Writers Union of Free Afghanistan.* vol. 5, no. 2. (1990), p. 64-93.
An examination of what the author regards as two fundamental characteristics of the country as 'a nation united against outsider invaders and a nation divided in peacetime'. He analyses the causes of social, religious, economic, and political fragmentation in Afghanistan.

698 **Some aspects of family life in an Afghan village.**
Bodil Hjerrild Carlsen. *Acta Orientalia.* vol. 38. (1977), p. 29-40.
A description of women's rôles in the household with particular reference to the division of labour, and an account of the ways in which women manage pregnancy, delivery, and the raising of children. Also given are examples of local poems obtained from female informants.

# Social Services, Health and Welfare

699  **Afghanistan, a geomedical monograph.**
Ludolph Fischer. Berlin: Springer, 1968. 168p. maps. bibliog. (Geomedical Monograph Series; Regional Studies in Geographical Medicine, no. 2).
This pioneering survey covers the geography, climate, flora and fauna, and population of the country before going on to describe the medical facilities available. The main part of the study then deals with endemic diseases, divided into those transmitted by arthropods, those transmitted by water and food, contagious infections, anthropozoonoses, venereal and dermatological diseases, helminthic diseases, and non-infectious diseases. There are fifteen tables, ten maps and fifteen figures summarizing medical information.

700  **The feminine spirit.**
Elizabeth Naeem. *Afghanistan.* vol. 1, no. 3. (1946), p. 47-48.
A brief account of the setting up of a welfare society for female students by Queen Homaira of Afghanistan in 1945, the nature of its funding, and its aims and objectives.

701  **From mental peace to an impaired mind.**
Mohammed Azam Dadfar. *WUFA, Quarterly Journal of the Writers Union of Free Afghanistan.* vol. 4, no. 2. (1989), p. 1-11.
A report, presented at the 3rd International Seminar on Afghanistan held in Oslo in the autumn of 1989, on the psychological problems encountered among Afghan refugees.

702 **Health services in Afghanistan, Iran and Turkey.**
Neville Goodman. *Journal of the Royal Central Asian Society.* vol. 53, pt. 2. (1966), p. 134-42. bibliog.
A former official in the London Ministry of Health is asked by the Ministry of Overseas Development and the Afghan government to carry out a survey of Afghanistan's medical problems and needs. This is his brief report. See also 'Health services in Afghanistan' in *The Lancet*, 1965, p. 544.

703 **'Hot' and 'cold' in the traditional medicine of Afghanistan.**
Danuta Penkala-Gawęcka. *Ethnomedicine.* vol. 6, no. 1-4. (1980), p. 201-28. bibliog.
This is an examination of traditional medical concepts which still play an important rôle in the folk-medicine of the country. The author considers the possible origins of the 'hot' and 'cold' concept, describes its basic principles and the consequent classification by some of the peoples of Afghanistan of food, plants, people, and illnesses according to their 'hot' and 'cold' qualities in order to determine appropriate treatment.

704 **Operation Salam, committee on assistance to disabled Afghans: guidelines and priorities.**
Edited by Sadruddin Aga Khan. Geneva: United Nations, 1989. 26p.
An overview of the scale of the problem of providing adequate assistance for Afghans disabled in the course of the Soviet war, with specific recommendations regarding health programmes and rehabilitation programmes.

705 **Public health and hygiene in Afghanistan.**
Zuhdi Berke. *Afghanistan.* vol. 1, no. 3. (1946), p. 1-8.
The author cites the reign of Nadir Shah (1929-33) as marking the beginning of modern public health and hygiene projects in the country. He provides a brief history of these developments and then discusses the main infectious diseases encountered by doctors working in the clinics.

706 **Transformations of traditional medicine in Afghanistan.**
Danuta Penkala-Gawęcka. *Ethnologia Polona.* vol. 13. (1987), p. 91-127. bibliog.
Changes in traditional medicine are presented in a context of the changing conditions of medical practice in the country, such as ecological and cultural conditions, and the development of modern medicine. The author attempts to interpret the causes, factors, and nature of these changes as well as account for the persistence of traditional medical beliefs and practices. She concludes that 'traditional medicine turns out to be an exceptionally stable sphere of culture because it is relatively effective and adjusted to social needs'.

**The seminar of Writers Union of Free Afghanistan (WUFA) on current events and reconstruction in Afghanistan.**
*See* item no. 812.

# Politics

707 **Afghanistan: the development of the modern state.**
Asta Olesen. In: *Islam: state and society*. Edited by Klaus Ferdinand, Mehdi Mozaffari. London: Curzon, 1988. 219p. (Scandinavian Institute of Asian Studies, Studies on Asian Topics no. 12).
An analysis of the development of a power structure in the country and the uneasy balance between politics and society. The author identifies various religious and political models which have been employed at different times in the country's history over the past 100 years.

708 **Afghanistan: Amnesty International Report, 1988.**
WUFA Editorial Board. *WUFA, Quarterly Journal of the Writers Union of Free Afghanistan*. vol. 3, no. 3. (1988), p. 88-92.
The editors have extracted information from that part of the *Amnesty International Report* dealing with human rights violations in Afghanistan in 1988.

709 **20th anniversary of the People's Democratic Party of Afghanistan: materials of the jubilee meeting of the PDPA central committee, the DRA revolutionary council, and the council of ministers.**
Kabul: PDPA Central Committee, 1985. 104p.
This is a compilation of numerous speeches made by communist sympathisers many of them from as far afield as Germany, Cuba, Viet-Nam, and Ethiopia. Tributes to Babrak Karmal are woven into self-congratulatory political speeches in what amounts to the proceedings of a mutual-admiration society.

710 **Aerial bombardment of the tribal area by Pakistan Government causing the death of hundreds of our Afghan brothers and concerning a statement made by the Governor-General of Pakistan.**
*Afghanistan*. vol. 4, no. 1. (1949), p. 41-44.
Presents comments on a news report received in Kabul which reflect the border tensions between Afghanistan and the new state of Pakistan.

Politics

711 **Afghanistan.**
John C. Griffiths. London: Pall Mall, 1967. 179p. maps. bibliog.
The first two chapters provide an historical and political background, with emphasis on 'the Great Game', to a discussion of the competition between the United States and the Soviets for the hearts and minds of the peoples of Afghanistan. Five Year Plans are examined in the light of the problems of modernization. The author concludes with an assessment of economic and political prospects for the future.

712 **Afghanistan.**
Michael Gillett. *Journal of the Royal Central Asian Society.* vol. 53, pt. 3. (1966), p. 238-44.
A former Ambassador to the Court of Kabul selects some important geographical and historical factors which have influenced 'the Afghan situation'. His main discussion is political and focuses on the policies of Mohammed Daoud Khan.

713 **Afghanistan: 1966.**
Louis Dupree. New York: American Universities Field Staff Reports Service, 1966. 32p. bibliog. (South Asia Series, vol. 10, no. 4 (Afghanistan)).
A review of the 1964 constitution, the free elections of 1965, the fall of the government of Dr. Mohammad Yousuf, the appointment of Mohammed Hashem Maiwandwal as Prime Minister, and student unrest. Education, the press, and foreign affairs are also examined. Appendices list cabinet members for the period 1963 to 1966 and provide basic information about agriculture and imports and exports.

714 **Afghanistan crisis: implications and options for [the] Muslim world, Iran, and Pakistan.**
Tahir Amin. Islamabad: Centre for Asian Studies, 1982. 144p. map. bibliog. (Institute of Policy Studies).
This traces the rise of communist political influence in Afghanistan and gives an account of Soviet-Afghan relations from 1955 to 1978. It also offers an analysis of the communist coup of 1978 and recounts the circumstances of the Soviet invasion of 1979. Afghan resistance to the puppet regime and the Soviets is examined in chapter four.

715 **Afghanistan: expanding social base of revolution.**
R. B. Gaur. New Delhi: Allied, 1987. 128p.
An enthusiastic account of the great benefits bestowed on the people of Afghanistan by the overthrow of both Western imperialist and Afghan royalist regimes and the new era of peace and prosperity that has been ushered in following the raising of the banner of freedom during the April Revolution - a banner now held aloft by Comrade Najib, assisted by the Soviet Union. The author concludes that 'no attempt to divert Afghanistan from its chosen path can ever succeed'.

716 **Afghanistan in 1919.**
Ikbal Ali Shah. *Journal of the Central Asian Society.* vol. 7, pt. 1. (1920), p. 3-18.
An Afghan examines his country's troubled relations with both Britain and Russia in the light of Afghanistan's internal politics and domestic problems in the early years of the 20th century.

717 **Afghanistan in the 20th century.**
Louis Dupree. *Journal of the Royal Central Asian Society.* vol. 52, pt. 1. (1965), p. 20-30.
An account which briefly covers social, economic, political, and historical factors that lie behind the current scene, characterized by the US-Soviet rivalry which has replaced the Anglo-Russian rivalry of the 19th century. The author concludes: 'If the Russians recognize that they did not gain a friend in Afghanistan, they can also see the Americans did not gain an ally either'.

718 **Afghanistan, Mongolia and USSR.**
Ram Rahul. Delhi: Vikas, 1987. 97p. bibliog.
The part of this study dealing with Afghanistan is concerned with the political position of the country once Britain was no longer in a position to attempt to guide her destiny. Beginning with the Third Afghan War, this provides a political history up to the Soviet occupation. The author concludes that the Soviets are there to stay and any withdrawal of troops will not signal a change of policy, but only show her confidence in a puppet regime.

719 **Afghanistan: political modernization of a mountain-kingdom.**
Balwant Bhaneja. New Delhi: Spectra, 1973. 87p. bibliog.
Using Afghanistan as a model and an example, the author presents a theoretical analysis of political change which examines tradition and modernity, identifies three phases of change, and describes the accompanying political processes. The author concludes with an essay outlining a theory of political modernization.

720 **Afghanistan: politics, economics and society; revolution, resistance, intervention.**
Bhabani Sen Gupta. London: Francis Pinter, 1986. 206p. maps. bibliog. (Marxist Regimes Series).
An analysis of political changes in Afghanistan, examining both internal events and the Soviet invasion of December 1979, and providing an historical sketch of the monarchy. The main account begins with the proclamation by Mohammad Daoud of a Republic of Afghanistan on July 17th, 1973 and it continues through the decade that followed. One of the author's conclusions is that the Saur Revolution will succeed.

Politics

### 721 Afghanistan since the revolution.
Abdul Qadir Khan. *Journal of the Central Asian Society.* vol. 17, pt. 3. (1930), p. 331-33.

A brief look at the political situation in the country following the capture and execution of Bacha Saqao (also known as Habibullah Ghazi), the 'Bandit King' of Kabul.

### 722 The Afghanistan situation.
Richard S. Newell. *WUFA, Quarterly Journal of the Writers Union of Free Afghanistan.* vol. 5, no. 2. (1990), p. 48-63.

An assessment of the military and political situation in the country following the Soviet withdrawal and the political and military stalemate between the *Mujahideen* and the puppet regime in Kabul.

### 723 Afghanistan, the road to reconciliation: a collection of articles commenting on topical problems facing modern Afghanistan.
London: Harney & Jones, 1987. 44p.

A collection of thirteen articles by Afghan Government officials, Russians, Indian, and European writers who extol the blessings of Communism. Lies, torture, the use of chemical weapons, and other human rights violations are the tactics used against them in order to thwart their search for peace. The *Mujahideen* are described as bandits who kill women and children and blow up mosques.

### 724 Afghanistan: the trajectory of internal alignments.
Robert L. Canfield. *Middle East Journal.* vol. 43, no. 4. (1989), p. 635-48. map.

A survey of the religious and political diversity of various groups in the country and the implications of this diversity for future peace in the region.

### 725 Afghanistan's future government: regional federation, Islamic state, or both?
Louis Dupree. *WUFA, Quarterly Journal of the Writers Union of Free Afghanistan.* vol. 3, no. 3. (1988), p. 15-31.

A longtime observer of the Afghan scene, Dupree speculates on the political future of the country. He draws up ten possible scenarios and concludes that the Afghans will decide their own future.

### 726 Afghanistan's two-party communism: Parcham and Khalq.
Anthony Arnold. Stanford, California: Hoover Institution, 1983. 242p. map. bibliog. (Histories of Ruling Communist Parties).

A political account which places Afghan communism in the wider context of international communism and the Soviet Union's long-term interests. The author shows that Soviet political and military aims in the country have been frustrated by the implacable opposition of the Afghan people and by factionalism among Afghan communists. Arnold provides a detailed and authoritative account of politics in the country covering the period from Mohammad Daoud to the Soviet occupation.

727 **Aspects of the national question in Afghanistan.**
Rahmat Zirakyar. *WUFA, Quarterly Journal of the Writers Union of Free Afghanistan.* vol. 5, no. 2. (1990), p. 14-29. bibliog.
A discussion of the problems of achieving political unity and a sense of nationalism in a country so divided by cultural differences.

728 **Biographical review: Muhammad Zahīr Khān, former King of Afghanistan.**
Ralph H. Magnus. *The Middle East Journal.* vol. 30, no. 1. (1976), p. 77-80.
An interview with the King held in Rome on June 20th, 1975 in which the former ruler discusses the 1964 Constitution and the political events in Afghanistan since the *coup* in 1973. Zahir Shah asserts that his cousin, Mohammad Daoud Khan, was not among those who plotted the 1973 takeover, and that he (Daoud) only assumed leadership of the *coup* for the good of the nation.

729 **British plots against Afghanistan: pages from history.**
Naftula Khalfin. Moscow: Novosti, 1981. 100p.
Published one year after the Soviet invasion, this complains that the world is trying to frustrate Afghanistan's 'struggle for a new society'. The author argues that London is displeased with the support that the Soviet Union is giving Afghanistan because England always wanted the country for herself. There follows a version of 19th-century Anglo-Afghan relations which ends with the Third Afghan War and the 'Treaty of Friendship, Goodneighbourliness and Co-operation between the USSR and the Democratic Republic of Afghanistan' which was signed in December 1978 - just one year before the Soviet invasion.

730 **Comrade Najib's address to nation speech at second N. F. congress.**
Kabul: Afghanistan Today, 1987. 37p.
In addition to its regular journal 'Afghanistan Today' the Kabul publisher also turned out a series of English-language booklets of which this is an example. It is the text of a political speech announcing, from the Kabul regime side, a six-month cease-fire, and calling on the *Mujahideen* to do the same so that 'national reconciliation' can be discussed. 'It is our clean and kind hand which has been extended to the other side in a manly manner', Najib tells his audience. Other booklets in this series, all published in June 1987, are: 'Comrade Najib's speech at the plenum of PDPA CC', 'Comrade Najib's press conference for foreign journalists', and 'Documents of the conference of journalists of non-aligned countries'.

731 **The continuity of Pashai society.**
Jan Ovesen. *Folk, Dansk Etnografisk Tidsskrift.* vol. 23. (1981), p. 221-34. maps. bibliog.
A study of local political institutions and the gradual encroachment on 'tribal society' of the State administration.

732 **The decade of Daoud ends: implications of Afghanistan's change of government.**

Louis Dupree. New York: American Universities Field Staff Reports Service, 1963. 29p. (South Asia Series, vol. 7, no. 7 (Afghanistan)).

An account of political change seen against an historical outline of the Afghan royal family and its rôle in government from 1933-1963, this examines Mohammad Daoud's political contributions and considers the start made by his successor, Dr. Mohammad Yousuf. Afghanistan's relations with Pakistan are also reviewed.

733 **The Democratic Republic of Afghanistan, 1979: rhetoric, repression, reforms, and revolts.**

Louis Dupree. Hanover, New Hampshire: American Universities Field Staff Reports, 1979. 11p. (AUFS, 1979, no. 32, Asia).

Here the author describes the rise of *Parcham* and *Khalq* as political forces and the downfall of Daoud in 'the accidental coup' of 27 April, 1978 which followed the murder of the writer and political activist Mir Akbar Khyber. The report goes on to examine the uprisings that took place in the spring of 1979. Written three months before the Soviet invasion (a possibility which the author discusses), he concludes that the Soviets are too clever to make that mistake. Unfortunately they weren't.

734 **Era of democracy in Afghanistan: a saga of mysteries, nightmares.**

Niazi Omidwar. *WUFA, Quarterly Journal of the Writers Union of Free Afghanistan.* vol. 4, no. 3-4. (1989), p. 16-43.

A discussion of political events in the country in the years 1964-73 starts with an assessment of Daoud Khan's career and then examines the rise of communist influence. The author concludes that, compared to Daoud's one-man rule, the period of democracy was glorious; while in comparison to the darkest years of the communist take-over, Daoud's tyranny was paradise.

735 **'From tribe to *Umma*': comments on the dynamics of identity in Muslim Soviet Central Asia.**

M. Nazif Shahrani. *Central Asian Survey.* vol. 3, no. 3. (1984), p. 27-38.

An anthropologist from northern Afghanistan examines the nature of cultural identity in Central Asia on both sides of the Amu Darya. His comments on culture and politics in Soviet Central Asia also have implications for the future success of a Kabul government now that the Soviets have withdrawn from Afghanistan.

736 **Human rights in Afghanistan: myths and reality.**

Edited by H. Khurasani, H. Masroor, H. Abawi, Z. Aziz, Zabihullah, Nasier Ahmad, M. Arizai, Assad Keshtmand. Kabul: Afghanistan Today, 1987. 96p.

The book is devoted to the task of presenting the Communist regime in a favourable light and to destroying the credibility of the opposition. A section entitled 'Peace and progress', contrasts the backward ill-educated Afghanistan of pre-Communist years with all that has been achieved since the Saur Revolution of 1978. Another section, 'Open violation of human rights', catalogues all the horrors perpetuated by the *Mujahideen*, including the use of chemical weapons.

737 **Human rights violations and national reconciliation in Afghanistan.**

Mohammed Asef Ikram. *WUFA, Quarterly Journal of the Writers Union of Free Afghanistan.* vol. 2, no. 4. (1987), p. 53-70.

A series of case studies highlighting the extent to which the basic human rights of members of the civilian population have been violated by the Soviets and the puppet regime in Kabul since the Soviet invasion.

738 **The Imami Sayyed of the Hazarajat: the maintenance of their elite position.**

Lucas-Michael Kopecky. *Folk, Dansk Etnografisk Tidsskrift.* vol. 24. (1982), p. 89-110. bibliog.

A study of political leadership, showing how Imami Shi'ism and the role played by the Sayyed (a direct descendent of the Prophet through his daughter Fatima), provide some mechanisms which 'define, maintain, and integrate the cultural and social universe of the Hazara'.

739 **Inside Afghanistan - a background to recent troubles.**

Andrew Wilson. *Journal of the Royal Central Asian Society.* vol. 47, pts. 3-4. (1960), p. 286-95.

The 'recent troubles' mentioned in the title seem mild in comparison to what was to follow some nineteen years later, when 'Inside Afghanistan' took on a whole new meaning. This describes the build-up of Soviet aid and the Soviet presence in the country, the 'emancipation' of women (when the law requiring women to wear a veil in public was abolished), and tensions with Pakistan over the Pushtunistan issue. The author considers, but does 'not see any immediate possibility of Russia formally taking over Afghanistan'.

740 **Interview with Professor Sabghatullah Mujaddadi, the President of the Afghan Islamic Interim Government.**

A. Rasul Amin. *WUFA, Quarterly Journal of the Writers Union of Free Afghanistan.* vol. 5, no. 2. (1990), p. 1-13.

Excerpts from this interview include views on how to end the political and military stalemate, the holding of elections, a future Islamic government, the possible return of the King, and other political issues.

741 **The Jirgah of Pashtoon free tribes.**

Kabul: State Printing House, 1986. 89p.

No author's or editor's name is given for this Democratic Republic of Afghanistan (DRA) publication, which is an attempt by the Kabul regime to use traditional Afghan institutions, in this case the *jirga* or council, to further its own political aims by trying to show that it fosters and supports the indigenous sociopolitical structure.

742 **Loya Jirgah (Grand Assembly) of the Afghan people: documents.**

Kabul: Ministry of Press and Information, 1989. 80p.

A collection of political speeches and messages from the Communist regime translated into English and distributed under the stamp of the *Loya Jirga* in an attempt to give the messages some veneer of credibility and to show that the traditional Afghan-Muslim institutions have been preserved by Afghan Communists.

743 **National reconciliation of Afghan government: a mere show, or fraud?**

Fazlur Rahman Qureshi. *WUFA, Quarterly Journal of the Writers Union of Free Afghanistan.* vol. 2, no. 4. (1987), p. 31-39.

The author shows that, having failed to win the shooting war in the country, the Soviets, in concert with the Kabul Communist regime, next tried 'a new game' called 'national reconciliation' in an effort to defuse popular opposition.

744 **One year after the Saur-Revolution.**

C. J. Charpentier. *Afghanistan Journal.* vol. 6, no. 4. (1979), p. 117-20.

A concise account of the political events and changes that occurred between the murder of President Daoud and the Soviet invasion of Afghanistan.

745 **The outlook in Afghanistan.**

Abdul Qadir Khan. *Journal of the Royal Central Asian Society.* vol. 19, pt. 3. (1932), p. 459-73.

A geographical, historical, and political look at the country precedes a more detailed account of Amanullah's downfall, the take-over by Bacha-i-Saqao, and the restoration of a more traditional monarchy by Nadir Shah in 1929.

746 **Pakhtunistan - disputed disposition of a tribal land.**

Dorothea Seelye Franck. *The Middle East Journal.* vol. 6, no. 1. (1952), p. 49-68. map.

A discussion of the long-running dispute over the Pushtunistan issue and an evaluation of its political implications for both Afghanistan and Pakistan.

747 **Pakhtunistan: the Khyber Pass as the focus of the new state of Pakhtunistan, an important political development in Central Asia.**

Rahman Pazhwak. Hove, England: Key Press, [n.d.]. 153p. map. bibliog.

Probably written in the late 1950s or early 1960s when the Pushtunistan issue was at its height and relations between Afghanistan and Pakistan were at a low ebb, this well illustrates the legacy of political problems which were left in the wake of the demarcation of the boundary between Afghanistan and India - the Durand Line - and the partition of India.

748 **Political legitimation in contemporary Afghanistan.**
William Maley. *Asian Survey, a Monthly Review of Contemporary Asian Affairs.* vol. 27, no. 6. (1987), p. 705-25.
The author considers that, having no popular support, the Kabul regime's main problem is lack of control over the country. It is one thing for a Soviet military presence to control only the main towns, it is quite another for an Afghan government to survive on that basis. The author concludes that a Soviet troop withdrawal is 'most unlikely to occur unless the military pressure exerted by the *Mujahideen* raises the costs of the Soviet presence to the point where they outweigh the benefits'.

749 **The politics of Afghanistan.**
Richard S. Newell. Ithaca, New York: Cornell University Press, 1972. 236p. maps. bibliog. (South Asian Political Systems).
Following the chapters which provide an introduction to the geographical and cultural background of the country, there is an historical outline which precedes the main sections on government, the economy, and the political developments that took place from 1964 to 1971.

750 **The politics of the resistance.**
Anthony Hyman. In: *Conflict studies 202.* London: Centre for Security and Conflict Studies, 1987. p. 21-33.
This examines the political alignments and political leaders that emerged among Afghans already in exile or who went into exile following the Saur (April) Revolution in 1978. The author discusses the relationships between the anti-Communist political parties, the resistance movement, and the wider relationships between Afghans in exile and the Pakistan Government.

751 **The present situation in the Hazarajat.**
B. M. *Central Asian Survey.* vol. 1, no. 1. (1982), p. 79-91.
A geographical, historical, economic, and cultural survey of the central region of the country which is home to the Hazara peoples. In the second half the anonymous author briefly sketches the political situation in the area following the Soviet invasion.

752 **Problems in the integration of the Afghan nation.**
Vladimir Cervin. *The Middle East Journal.* vol. 6. (1952), p. 400-16.
The author looks at the problems facing the Afghan government in its attempts to integrate the country's diverse cultural groups into a nation state. Writing in the 1950s, he had the view that this was, despite the odds, being accomplished.

753 **The Red Army on Pakistan's border: policy implications for the United States.**
Edited by Theodore L. Eliot, Robert L. Pfaltzgraff. Washington, DC; New York; Oxford: Pergamon, 1986. 88p. (IFPA Foreign Policy Reports, no. 8).
This special report considers reasons for the Soviet invasion of Afghanistan and attempts to assess the dimensions of the threat this poses to the security of Pakistan.

Current US Government policies toward Pakistan and the Soviet Government, shaped by the presence of the Red Army in Afghanistan, are also examined. The authors conclude that a 'steadfast American commitment to Pakistan and to the Afghan resistance is the best means for thwarting Soviet expansionism in that part of the world'.

754 **Red flag over Afghanistan: the communist coup, the Soviet invasion, and the consequences.**

Thomas T. Hammond. Epping, England: Bowker, 1984. 261p. map. bibliog.

A political history of the country from Amanullah to the Soviet occupation which examines in detail Daoud's take-over and downfall, the rise and development of communist groups, successive governments of the post-Daoud period, the murder of Hafizullah Amin, and the Soviet invasion.

755 **Red flag over the Hindu Kush.**

Louis Dupree. Hanover, New Hampshire: American Universities Field Staff Reports, 1979-80. 83p. maps. (AUFS Reports nos. 44, 45 (1979), nos. 23, 27, 28, 29 (1980)).

This report appeared in six parts: 'Leftist movements in Afghanistan'; 'The accidental coup, or Taraki in blunderland'; 'Rhetoric and reforms, or promises! promises!'; 'Foreign policy and the economy'; 'Repressions, or security through terror, purges 1-4'; 'Repressions, or security through terror'. They cover the troubled period that followed the death of President Daoud, the Soviet invasion, and the beginning of the Soviet occupation of Afghanistan.

756 **Revolutionary Afghanistan, a reappraisal.**

Beverley Male. London: Croom Helm, 1982. 229p. bibliog.

A thorough and competent history of political events in Afghanistan in the 1960s and 1970s, with emphasis on the key personalities, their roles, and the political parties they served.

757 **Revolutionary Afghanistan through honest eyes: a collection of views expressed by foreigners about revolutionary transformations in the Democratic Republic of Afghanistan.**

Kabul: Information and publication Department, Ministry of Foreign Affairs of the Democratic Republic of Afghanistan, [n.d.]. 179p.

This is a collection of quotations, mostly brief and largely extracted from any foreign newspaper that expressed views consistent with those of the aims, objectives, and interests of the Communist regime in Kabul. Material has been arranged in several sections, such as: 'Achievements of the Saur Revolution', 'The real situation inside Afghanistan', 'International support for the Saur Revolution', 'The nature of the counter-revolution and its barbarism', 'The undeclared war against Afghanistan', and 'CIA intervention in Afghanistan'.

758 **The right of free access to and from the sea for land-locked states.**
Abdul H. Tabibi. *Afghanistan Journal.* vol. 5, no. 1. (1978), p. 9-10.

A jurist cites international law and numerous other legal rulings to explain the rights of land-locked states. Although Pakistan is not mentioned, it would seem that the origin of the argument, from the Afghan point of view, is the long-running dispute over the Pushtunistan issue which at various times encouraged Pakistan to close her borders and thus disrupt traffic between Afghanistan and the sea.

759 **The Saur revolution?**
A. Rasul Amin. *WUFA, Quarterly Journal of the Writers Union of Free Afghanistan.* vol. 1, no. 2. (1986), p. 3-13.

A critical examination of the nature of the *coup d'état* which took place in Kabul on April 27th, 1978.

760 **Soviet foreign policy: determinants, goals, setbacks.**
Rahmat Djan Zirakyar. *WUFA, Quarterly Journal of the Writers Union of Free Afghanistan.* vol. 1, no. 3. (1986), p. 53-61.

The Soviet invasion of Afghanistan is listed among the political setbacks experienced by the Soviets, as is religion, 'especially Islam', but it is suggested that the varied nationalities within the Soviet Union are potentially her biggest political problem.

761 **Special issue: Afghanistan, the last thirty years.**
*Central Asian Survey.* vol. 7, no. 2- 3. (1988), 221p.

The entire issue is given over to the publication of conference papers (some in English, some in French) presented at the National Assembly in Paris in November, 1986. Subjects include the Soviet invasion, the origins of the Afghan Communist party, and Afghan tribes versus the Kabul Government, among others.

762 **The state, religion, and ethnic politics: Afghanistan, Iran, and Pakistan.**
Edited by Ali Banuazizi, Myron Weiner. Syracuse, New York : Syracuse University, 1986. map. bibliog.

Part one of the book relates to Afghanistan. It consists of four papers dealing with Islam as a unifying force, prospects for 'state building' in Afghanistan, ethnic, regional, and sectarian alignments, and social fragmentation.

763 **Toward representative government in Afghanistan: part one, the first five steps.**
Louis Dupree. Hanover, New Hampshire: American Universities Field Staff Reports, 1978. 12p. (UFS, 1978, no. 1, Asia).

A review of the political changes in Afghanistan which took place following the 1973 coup d'état in which Daoud took over the government when King Mohammed Zahir Shah was out of the country.

Politics

764  **Toward representative government in Afghanistan: steps six through nine - and beyond?**
Louis Dupree.  Hanover, New Hampshire:  American Universities Field Staff, 1978. 10p. (AUFS, 1978, no. 14, Asia).
This describes the elections of 1977, the new constitution, legal changes, new personalities in government, and new administrative structures created in the move towards a more democratic government in Afghanistan.

765  **Traditional leadership in Afghan society and the issue of national unity.**
Nabi Misdaq. *WUFA, Quarterly Journal of the Writers Union of Free Afghanistan.* vol. 5, no. 2. (1990), p. 42-47.
A sketch of the nature of traditional leadership in the country and an account of the kinds of leaders who have emerged during a decade of war.

**The geography and politics of Afghanistan.**
*See* item no. 55.

**The great game: on secret service in high Asia.**
*See* item no. 106.

**Afghanistan: puppets without props.**
*See* item no. 437.

**Afghanistan: seven years against a superpower.**
*See* item no. 438.

**On the diplomatic and political front:  Afghanistan from April, 1978 through February, 1989.**
*See* item no. 471.

**Islam reawakening in Central Asia.**
*See* item no. 678.

**Soviet Islam since the invasion of Afghanistan.**
*See* item no. 683.

**Buzkashy game in Afghanistan.**
*See* item no. 964.

# Foreign Relations

## 19th Century

**766 Afghanistan and British India, 1793-1907, a study in foreign relations.**
Asghar H. Bilgrami. New Delhi: Sterling, 1972. 360p. bibliog.
This traces the political and geographical factors that led to British-Russian rivalries in Central Asia and the consequent growing importance of Afghanistan in the policies of these two 19th-century superpowers.

**767 A collection of treaties, engagements and sanads relating to India and neighbouring countries. Vol. XIII, containing the treaties, &c., relating to Persia and Afghanistan.**
C. U. Aitchison. Calcutta: Government of India, 1933. 534p. (A Collection of Treaties, Engagements and Sanads relating to India and Neighbouring Countries).
Part two of this volume (p. 203-305) contains the treaties and engagements relating to Afghanistan and includes a narrative history of Anglo-Afghan relations from the first decade of the 19th century to 1930. In addition to giving the full text of each treaty and listing them in chronological order, it also provides copies of some of the relevant official correspondence from both sides.

**768 The Durand Line.**
Mohammed Ali. *Afghanistan.* vol. 10, no. 4. (1955), p. 5-12.
An Afghan professor of history examines the political events that led to the setting up of the country's Eastern boundary with India toward the close of the 19th century. He argues that, as this boundary excluded 'over a third of the Afghan people from their national kingdom' it is the root cause of all the frontier troubles down to the present day.

769 **The eastern question from the treaty of Paris 1856 to the treaty of Berlin 1878, and to the second Afghan war.**

The Duke of Argyll [George Douglas Campbell]. London: Strahan, 1879. 2 vols.

The author held, among many other distinguished appointments, that of Secretary of State for India (1868-74). The material on Afghanistan is contained in volume two from chapter fourteen on to the end. He deals with British relations with Afghanistan from the First Afghan War to the Agreement with Russia in 1873, the Frere Note of January 1875, the Viceroyalty of Lord Lytton, the Peshawar Conference of 1877 and the beginning of the Second Afghan War. He is scathingly critical of British policy and actions, both military and otherwise.

770 **England and Russia in Central Asia.**

Demetrius Charles Boulger. London: W. H. Allen, 1879. 2 vols.. maps.

Surveys the history, geography, and politics of Central Asia, showing how the imperialist policies of both Russia and Britain caused the two contries to converge and finally meet in the Hindu Kush. Unlike the Duke of Argyll, George Douglas Campbell (q.v.), the author is an advocate of the Forward Policy, convinced that Russia's aim is the invasion of India. Afghanistan is therefore seen as the key to the security of British interests in India.

771 **The problem of the North-West Frontier, 1890-1908, with a survey of policy since 1849.**

C. Collin Davies. Cambridge, England: Cambridge University Press, 1932. 220p. map. bibliog.

An excellent study of the political, geographical, and cultural problems caused by colonial Britain's need to demarcate a boundary between her Indian empire and the ever-expanding Russian empire in Central Asia. Afghanistan - 'a grain of wheat between two millstones' - was caught in the middle. Chapter nine looks at 'The Afghan problem, 1890-1908'.

772 **Russia in Central Asia in 1889 and the Anglo-Russian Question.**

George Nathaniel Curzon. London: Longmans Green, 1889. 477p. maps. bibliog.

A well-written and well-informed history of Russian expansion in Asia which serves to place British attitudes and British policies in perspective. Afghanistan, as usual, is caught in the middle.

773 **Russo-Afghan relations.**

Mohammed Asef Ikram. *WUFA, Quarterly Journal of the Writers Union of Free Afghanistan.* vol. 1, no. 1. (1985), p. 51-60. bibliog.

An historical look at Russian expansion in Central Asia and the political and territorial interests of both Britain and Russia which came to a focus in Afghanistan. Afghan-Russian relations from the time of Amir Abdur Rahman onwards are summarized.

# 20th Century

### 774 Afghanistan and Pakistan.
S. K. *Afghanistan.* vol. 4, no. 2. (1949), p. 25-27.
The problem of the tribal areas along the North-West Frontier and whether the people living there should belong to Pakistan, Afghanistan, or be independent is restated and discussed. The impracticalities of the Durand Line, created and unresolved by the British, lives on.

### 775 Afghanistan in world affairs.
K. P. Ghosh. *Afghanistan.* vol. 9, no. 4. (1954), p. 51-55.
An optimistic view of the country's political, economic, and social well-being and its future prospects, with stress on the country's past, present, and future independence.

### 776 Afghanistan: the present position.
Percy Sykes. *Journal of the Royal Central Asian Society.* vol. 27, pt. 2. (1940), p. 141-71. map.
The author begins his largely historical presentation with the Second Afghan War and then moves forward to look at Anglo-Russian relations, German intrigues in World War I (the Niedermayer expedition), Habibullah's policies, the Third Afghan War, the reign of Amanullah, the 1928-29 rebellion, Nadir Shah's reign and assassination, and, finally, the reign of Zahir Shah.

### 777 Afghanistan's desire for friendly relations with Pakistan: Najibullah Khan explains cause of Pukhtoonistan.
Indian News Chronicle. *Afghanistan.* vol. 5, no. 1. (1950), p. 40-45.
An explanation of the Pushtunistan issues by the Afghan Ambassador to India, as reported in a New Delhi newspaper. Najibullah argues for a free independent Pushtunistan comprising all Pathans living between the Durand Line and the Indus. See also 'Pakhtoons determined to achieve independence' on p. 46-47 and 'Afghan minority in Pakistan', p. 48-49 in that same issue.

### 778 Basic postulates of Afghan foreign policy.
Mohammad Khalid Ma'aroof. *WUFA, Quarterly Journal of the Writers Union of Free Afghanistan.* vol. 4, no. 3-4. (1989), p. 44-75.
A political scientist examines the nature of Afghanistan's foreign policy in the light of a range of political criteria.

779 **The death of a soldier-statesman.**
WUFA Editorial Board. *WUFA, Quarterly Journal of the Writers Union of Free Afghanistan.* vol. 3, no. 3. (1988), p. 1-5.
Eulogy in honour of President Zia ul Haq who was killed on August 17th, 1988 in a plane crash. The editors summarize the steadfast support which he gave to the Afghan cause.

780 **Dr. Najib-Ullah's press conference on the 19th June, 1952.**
Najibullah Khan. *Afghanistan.* vol. 7, no. 3. (1952), p. 45-50.
Another episode in the war of words between Afghanistan and Pakistan over the Pushtunistan issue, this time sparked off by Pakistan's disruption of air links between Kabul and India in 1952.

781 **The federation of the Central Asian States under the Kabul Government.**
Ikbal Ali Shah. *Journal of the Central Asian Society.* vol. 8, pt. 1. (1921), p. 29-48.
A discussion of the idea that Central Asian states can save themselves from Russia only by creating a common federation. The author concludes that '...our common enemy is Bolshevism, and to defend ourselves we must have a Central Asian Alliance'.

782 **Friendly visit of His Majesty Mohammad Zahir Shah, King of Afghanistan, to USSR.**
Ministry of Press and Information. *Afghanistan.* vol. 12, no. 3. (1957), p. 25-35.
Presents the texts of speeches exchanged in the Soviet Union between the King and his hosts during an official visit in July-August, 1957.

783 **Frontier discord between Afghanistan and Pakistan.**
Ahmad Ali Kohzad. *Afghanistan.* vol. 6, no. 1. (1951), p. 54-67.
A sharply critical and well presented look at an article on the subject of frontier discord by Sir George Cunningham, ex-Governor of the N.W.F.P., which appeared in the *Manchester Guardian* on February 2nd, 1951. Among other things, Kohzad examines the causes of the discord and finds them to be of British origin.

784 **A glimpse of the Afghan-Soviet relations.**
A. K. Moheb. *WUFA, Quarterly Journal of the Writers Union of Free Afghanistan.* vol. 3, no. 1. (1988), p. 67-82.
An historical survey of political and economic relations between the two countries. The author considers that Mohammed Daoud Khan's rise to political power marked the real beginning of Soviet influence in Afghanistan.

785 **The mountains go to Mohammad Zahir: observations on Afghanistan's reactions to visits from Nixon, Bulganin-Khrushchev, Eisenhower and Khrushchev.**
Louis Dupree. New York: American Universities Field Staff Reports Service, 1960. 40p. map. (South Asia Series, vol. 4, no. 6 (Afghanistan)).
This consists of descriptive accounts of the state visits to Afghanistan, together with a political analysis of what the hosts and visitors hoped to gain. The text of the Treaty Protocol between Afghanistan and the USSR (1955), and the Joint Statement and Economic Agreement is given, as are the texts of other official documents.

786 **Mr. Suhrawardy, Prime Minister of the Islamic Republic of Pakistan in Kabul.**
Ministry of Press and Information. *Afghanistan.* vol. 12, no. 2. (1957), p. 29-38.
This gives the full texts of an exchange of speeches between the Prime Minister of Pakistan and Sardar Mohammad Daoud, Prime Minister of Afghanistan, during an official visit of the former to Kabul. Nothing much of real substance is said, though references are made to the political differences between them, i.e. the Pashtunistan issue.

787 **A new state - Pakhtunistan - emerges in Asia.**
*Afghanistan.* vol. 6, no. 4. (1950), p. 17-30.
This discusses, as if describing a political reality, the 'rise of an independent buffer state' which stretches 'almost 600 miles from Chitral in the north to Baluchistan in the south', and which has an area of some 60,000 square miles and a population of 'nearly six million Pakhtuns'. The political history of the area is outlined and friendly relations between Pakistan, Kashmir, Afghanistan, Pushtunistan, and 'even Iran' is urged as a bulwark against the advance of the Soviets and Communism.

788 **On Sir Zaferullah Khan's statement.**
*Afghanistan.* vol. 4, no. 2. (1949), p. 28-31.
The argument concerning the 'independent tribes' on the North-West Frontier of India (Pakistan) continues. The author argues with some logic that as the 'tribal areas' were not part of British India, so they should not be part of Pakistan.

789 **Pashtoonistan.**
Bcnava. *Afghanistan.* vol. 5, no. 1. (1950), p. 10-23.
A description of Pushtunistan which treats it as an independent state, part of which is 'captured', occupied first by the British and later by the Pakistanis. The author has a vision of a greater Pushtunistan which includes Swat, Chitral, Dir, Peshawar, and Baluchistan. This appeal to the United Nations combines rage, political ambition, and frustration in roughly equal measures.

790 **The Pathan borderlands.**
James W. Spain. *The Middle East Journal.* vol. 15, no. 2. (1961), p. 165-77.

This article draws upon some of the material published later in 1961 in the author's book with a similar title. An historical summary of the problems of the North-West Frontier and a discussion of possible ways of resolving them.

791 **Permanent people's tribunal: Afghanistan, 16-20 December, 1982.**
Paris: Permanent People's Tribunal, 1982. 26p.

The tribunal convened to consider a long list of charges against the Soviet Union, to receive and to consider the evidence, and to reach a verdict. Subsequently the tribunal condemned the Soviet Union for violations of the laws and customs of war and for violations of the inalienable rights of the Afghan people.

792 **Prospects for federation in the northern tier.**
Donald N. Wilber. *The Middle East Journal.* vol. 12, no. 4. (1958), p. 385-94.

The 'northern tier' refers to Turkey, Iran, Afghanistan, and Pakistan. The author discusses historical and political events and examines the factors which favour regional cohesion.

793 **Pukhtoonistan question: a survey.**
Najibullah Khan. *Afghanistan.* vol. 6, no. 3. (1950), p. 52-57.

The desire for friendly relations with Pakistan is reaffirmed, as is the desire for the political independence of 'all the Pathans living between the so-called Durand Line and river Indus'. Other short statements regarding the Pushtunistan issue are to be found in vol. 6, no. 4 (p. 35-36).

794 **Radio broadcast by H. E. Najibullah Khan, extraordinary envoy of His Majesty Mohammed Zahir Shah of Afghanistan to Mohammed Ali Jinnah, Governor-General of Pakistan.**
Najibullah Khan. *Afghanistan.* vol. 3, no. 2. (1948), p. 1-38.

This is the text of a radio broadcast made over Radio Kabul in January, 1948 following an official visit to Pakistan by Mohammed Zahir Shah. It begins with a summary of Afghan-British relations and describes negotiations between the Afghan Government and the British Government regarding 'the future destiny of the Afghans living between the Durand Line and the River Indus'.

795 **Regarding the views of Sir George Cunningham.**
Saidal Yusufzai. *Afghanistan.* vol. 6, no. 1. (1951), p. 68-74.

In commenting on Sir George's views of the dispute with Pakistan over the Pushtunistan issue this writer begins by summarizing the former Governor's Indian Empire career and then examines his *Manchester Guardian* article in critical detail, ending with some personal advice for Sir George's future conduct (see also the article by Ahmad Ali Kohzad).

796 **Some problems of the Indian frontier.**
Evelyn Howell. *Journal of the Royal Central Asian Society.* vol. 21,
pt. 2. (1934), p. 181-98.
Historical, geographical, and political considerations with an interesting glimpse of
Nadir Shah, later to be King of Afghanistan, as he was when the author met him in
Peshawar in 1924.

797 **Statement given by His Excellency Dr. Najib-Ullah, Ambassador for
Afghanistan in India, on the 11th of August, 1951.**
Najibullah Khan. *Afghanistan.* vol. 6, no. 3. (1951), P. 38-42.
Another plea from the Afghan side that the 'Pukhtoon Movement of Independence'
is a nationalist movement like any other and should be so regarded. The policy
of Pakistan is, according to the author, one of 'annihilating the [Pukhtoon] nation
by all repressive measures' and the Pakistan government appears to consider that
they have inherited 'these 7 to 8 million people like a herd of sheep...from a former
Colonial power'.

798 **A suggested Pakistan-Afghanistan-Iran federation: the empty triangle.**
Louis Dupree. *The Middle East Journal.* vol. 17, no. 4. (1963), p.
383-99.
A consideration of historical, geographical, political, religious, and cultural factors
bearing on a possible federation between Pakistan, Afghanistan and Iran, and the
difficulties of achieving even a token agreement among these politically independent
units.

799 **The UN shuttle diplomacy on Afghanistan: an appraisal.**
M. Hakim Aryubi. *WUFA, Quarterly Journal of the Writers Union of
Free Afghanistan.* vol. 1, no. 4. (1986), p. 1-12.
The Soviet policy of pursuing a military offensive in Afghanistan while at the same
time trying to give the impression that they are seeking an early political solution is
examined, as are the actions taken by the United Nations.

800 **White book: the implementation of the Geneva accords is in the interests of all mankind.**
Kabul: Ministry of Foreign Affairs, 1988. 71p. maps.
This contains the text of the Geneva Agreements of April 14th, 1988, the text of
the Joint Soviet-Afghan statement of April 7th, 1988, the text of a resolution of
a session of Afghanistan's national council, and the texts of three speeches made
by Najibullah in May, June, and July, 1988. Following this are four chapters of
propaganda and four appendices detailing crimes against the people committed by
counter-revolutionaries with the backing of imperialists in pursuit of their undeclared
war on the freedom-loving peoples of Afghanistan. It is illustrated.

**Pakhtunistan - disputed disposition of a tribal land.**
*See* item no. 746.

# Constitution, Legal System

801 **The Constitution of Afghanistan.**
  Karimi. *Afghanistan.* vol. 1, no. 1. (1946), p. 3-8.
A summary of the 1931 Constitution drawn up during the reign of Nadir Shah (1929-33) in which the nature of parliament and other government bodies is laid down, as are the rights and duties of the King, citizens' rights, and other legal matters.

802 **Document: Constitution of Afghanistan.**
  Donald N. Wilber. *The Middle East Journal.* vol. 19, no. 2. (1965), p. 215-29.
A copy of a translation of the Constitution, dated 1 October, 1964, with comments by Donald N. Wilber.


**The Afghan syndrome: how to live with Soviet power.**
*See* item no. 424.

**A new try for Afghanistan.**
*See* item no. 810.

# Administration and Government

803 **Afghan progress in the fourth year of the plan.**
London: Afghan Information Bureau, 1959. 88p.
A progress report on the 1955-60 Five Year Plan with an outline of the aims of
the plan, an overview of the work of the Ministry of Planning, and a description
of improvements in primary and secondary education, museums, Kabul University,
agriculture, community development, mines and industries, public works, communications, commerce, and public health. There are also short sections on the geography,
history, people, languages, and cultures of the country. A copy of the constitution
is included, as is an essay on the government.

804 **Afghanistan and Nadir Shah.**
A.S. *Journal of the Central Asian Society.* vol. 17, pt. 3. (1930), p.
340-43.
A brief biographical sketch of the man who, together with his brother Shah Wali
Khan, took the throne of Kabul from the Brigand King, Bacha Saqao in 1929. There
is a genealogy of the Mohammadzai and Sadozai families, a list of members of Nadir
Shah's Cabinet, and a summary of political reforms drafted and implemented by the
new ruler.

805 **Afghanistan in 1934.**
Abdul Qadir Khan. *Journal of the Royal Central Asian Society.* vol.
22, pt. 2. (1935), p. 211-20.
A tribute to the progressive statesmanship of King Nadir Shah, the smooth transition
of power following his assassination, and the economic and political reforms which
he set in motion.

806 **The Afghans' right to self-determination.**
M. Hakim Aryubi. *WUFA, Quarterly Journal of the Writers Union of Free Afghanistan.* vol. 4, no. 3-4. (1989), p. 1-5.
A summary of UN General Assembly resolutions and the substance of the Geneva Accords are set against a background discussion of the rights of the peoples of Afghanistan to self-determination.

807 **Authority patterns and the Afghan coup of 1973.**
Christine F. Ridout. *The Middle East Journal.* vol. 29, no. 2. (1975), p. 165-78.
The writer considers that the *coup d'etat* of 17 July, 1973 '...was the natural outcome of a political situation in which the government had little or no authority...'. This state of affairs, according to the writer, may be attributed to traditional Afghan authority patterns which prevented the extension of legitimacy, authority, and power to the central government. The general conclusion is that political stability is elusive in Afghanistan.

808 **Historical and political who's who of Afghanistan.**
Edited by Ludwig W. Adamec. Graz, Austria: Akademische Druck-u. Verlagsanstalt, 1975. 385p.
Divided into two main parts, this provides biographical sketches of prominent citizens who figured in the country's history from 1747-1945. It then does the same for the more recent period from 1945-1974. It also contains lists of members of successive Afghan governments, the royal family and royal households. Appended are 118 pages of genealogies of prominent families throughout the country.

809 **Local organs of Soviet pattern in Afghanistan.**
A. Rasul Amin. *WUFA, Quarterly Journal of the Writers Union of Free Afghanistan.* vol. 1, no. 4. (1986), p. 53-68.
A look at the 'Soviet' or 'worker's councils' which emerged in Russia in 1905 and which have served as the building blocks of Communist organization ever since. The administration structure which was established in Afghanistan by Amir Abdur Rahman and later modified by Mohammad Zahir Shah was still that used by government up until the Soviet invasion. It was then replaced by a structure modelled after the Soviet system.

810 **A new try for Afghanistan.**
Theodore S. Gochenour. *The Middle East Journal.* vol. 19, no. 1. (1965), p. 1-19.
The 'new try' refers to political developments following the resignation of Mohammed Daoud Khan, who had held the job of Prime Minister from 1953 to 1963. The author examines constitutional changes, legal reforms, and improvements in education and communications.

811 **A preliminary investigation of contemporary Afghan councils.**
Lynn Carter, Kerry M. Connor. Peshawar, Pakistan: [no publisher],
1989. 52p.
This identifies, describes, and explains the local councils (*shura*) in Afghan society
which need to be known and understood if humanitarian aid resources are to be
allocated equitably throughout the local population. The alternative, often adopted,
is to distribute aid through local *Mujahideen* commanders, which unintentionally
serves to strengthen their political position, and at the same time, may exclude those
members of the community not in the commander's faction.

812 **The seminar of Writers Union of Free Afghanistan (WUFA) on current events and reconstruction in Afghanistan.**
A. Rasul Amin. *WUFA, Quarterly Journal of the Writers Union of Free
Afghanistan.* vol. 4, no. 3-4. (1989), p. 103-12.
An account of a seminar, organized by Afghans in exile, on the rehabilitation of
Afghanistan. It was held in Peshawar in 1989 and was attended by leading Afghan
scholars, academics, former members of government, military experts, and medical doctors. Main conference topics were: political/military problems, education,
agriculture, and health.

**H.M. King Nadir Shah-i-Ghazi, of Afghanistan: Naji-i-Millat (Saviour of
the Nation).**
*See* item no. 413.

**The administrative and social structure of Afghan life.**
*See* item no. 685.

**The modernization of Afghanistan.**
*See* item no. 690.

# Economy

813  **Current economic development and policies in the developing countries of the ECAFE region: Afghanistan.**

In: *United Nations Department of Economic and Social Affairs, economic survey of Asia and the Far East, 1969.* Bangkok: United Nations, 1969. p. 101-09.

A development report on the country covering agriculture, livestock, industry and mining, money, prices, and banking, public revenue and expenditure, and external trade and balance of payments.

814  **Afghanistan.**

In: *United Nations Department of Economic and Social Affairs, economic survey of Asia and the Far East, 1956.* Bangkok: United Nations, 1957. p. 59-62.

This report summarizes basic economic information about the country and its Five Year Plan.

815  **The Afghan economy: money, finance, and the critical constraints to economic development.**

Maxwell J. Fry. Leiden, The Netherlands: E. J. Brill, 1974. 332p. maps. bibliog. (Social, Economic & Political Studies of the Middle East, vol. XV).

A detailed study examining the factors which have hindered economic growth in Afghanistan. Five main determinants of the country's development potential are identified and the economic history of Afghanistan between 1929 and 1973 is examined critically. The author concludes that the main constraints have been government policies rather than lack of capital and in the final chapter he makes recommendations which he hopes will be useful to those who plan Afghanistan's development in the future.

816  **Die afghanischen Entwicklungspläne vom ersten bis zum dritten Plan.**
(Afghan development plans from the first to the third plan.)
Werner Jensch. Meisenheim am Glan: Anton Hain, 1973. 377p.
maps. bibliog. (Afghanische Studien, Band 8).
Afghanistan's first three development plans covered the years 1956-1962, 1962-1967, and 1967-1972. This study examines each of these from the point of view of the Afghan economy, finance, government priorities, and foreign aid. There is a good bibliography with many references to English-language publications.

817  **Afghanistan.**
In: *United Nations Department of Economic and Social Affairs, economic survey of Asia and the Far East.* Bangkok: United Nations, 1955. p. 57-64.
Chapter six of this volume comprises a survey of the country's natural resources, the economy, development planning, trade and payments, and finance. The report concludes that the government is trying to deal with '...the immense difficulties which confront a country trying to develop its resources with inadequate power, transportation and trained personnel'.

818  **Afghanistan 1977: does trade plus aid guarantee development?**
Louis Dupree. New York: American Universities Field Staff Reports Service, 1977. 13p. (South Asia Series, vol. 21, no. 3 (Afghanistan)).
An overview of various countries which had trade agreements with Afghanistan, the nature and extent of the trade involved, and the Seven Year Plan which was soon to be interrupted by the Soviet invasion.

819  **Afghanistan and the USSR.**
R. K. Ramazani. *Middle East Journal.* vol. 12, no. 2. (1958), p. 144-52. map.
The author considers that Afghanistan has become '...one of the major targets of the recent Soviet economic offensive in the underdeveloped countries of the world...' and warns that 'the complete economic and political domination of that country by the Soviet Union, if established, may well jeopardize the position of the West in the area between the Mediterranean and South China Seas'.

820  **Afghanistan between east and west, the economics of competitive co-existence.**
Peter G. Franck. Washington, DC: National Planning Association, 1960. 86p. (The Economics of Competitive Coexistence).
This examines the political and economic environment which existed in Afghanistan in the 1950s. Economic plans, trade, and economic aid programmes are surveyed. An overview of financial and technical assistance from the Soviet Union and the West is provided. Numerous tables show imports and exports for the 1950s.

821 **Afghanistan: past and present.**
Social Sciences Editorial Board. Moscow: USSR Academy of Sciences, 1981. 268p. bibliog. (Oriental Studies in the USSR, no. 3.).
A collection of papers by Soviet scholars on the history and contemporary development of Afghanistan. The general emphasis is on agricultural production and economic development, but topics covered include archaeological research, the Anglo-Afghan Wars, agricultural problems, and the revolutionary struggle.

822 **Afghanistan: the dangers of cold war generosity.**
Richard S. Newell. *The Middle East Journal.* vol. 23, no. 2. (1969), p. 168-76.
The author surveys the bewildering array of foreign aid projects in the country supported by West Germany, the Soviet Union, the United States, and the United Nations, and concludes that 'Afghan development to date has been dominated, if not overrun, by foreign money and foreign ideas'. He suggests that less glamorous (and less expensive) projects might have a more positive effect on the host country.

823 **Economic progress in an encircled land.**
Peter G. Franck. *The Middle East Journal.* vol. 10, no. 1. (1956), p. 43-59. map.
A concise survey of economic developments in Afghanistan since the Second World War.

824 **The economic reforms of Amir Abdul Rahman Khan.**
R. D. McChesney. *Afghanistan.* vol. 21, no. 3. (1968), p. 11-34.
An interesting study which throws light on the Amir's plans and policies during a crucial period of the country's history, when the administration was overhauled, industry was developed by calling in European experts, and attempts were made to discover the extent and value of the nation's natural resources.

825 **Economic review: Afghanistan's foreign trade.**
Zabioullah A. Eltezam. *Middle East Journal.* vol. 20, no. 1. (1966), p. 95-103. bibliog.
A descriptive analysis of the country's foreign trade and an evaluation of the potential contributions of agriculture and industry to the trade sector.

826 **Economic review: marketing and business practices in Afghanistan.**
Hakim A. Hamid. *The Middle East Journal.* vol. 14, no. 1. (1960), p. 87-93.
An economist looks at business facilities, trade practices, marketing structure, wholesalers, brokers, and retailers in the country in order to set out some recommendations on buying, turnover, pricing, advertising, and selling.

827 **The first Afghan seven year plan, 1976/77 - 1982/83: a review and some comparisons of the objectives and means.**
M. S. Noorzoy. *Afghanistan Journal.* vol. 6, no. 1. (1978), p. 15-23.
The plan, which called for an increase in the Gross National Product (GNP) by an average of six per cent per annum over the planning period, is outlined, its objectives set out, and its financing discussed. The success of this plan required, among other things, an annual investment of Afs 25 billion. The most costly project of the plan was to be the construction of a railroad between Kabul and Herat. Two main political events disrupted the plan: the Saur (April) Revolution of 1978 and the Soviet invasion of the country in December, 1979.

828 **Government revenues and economic development of Afghanistan: a summary.**
K. Glaubitt, F. Saadeddin, B. Schäfer. *Afghanistan Journal.* vol. 4, no. 1. (1977), p. 20-25.
This deals with tax income and government expenditures, deficit finance, customs earnings (duties), monopolies and internal indirect taxes, road tolls, and administration. The section on taxes is broken down into corporation tax and land tax. The authors prepared a book-length study on the subject published by Anton-Hain in 1975 under the title *Das System der Staatseinnahmen und seine Bedeutung für die Wirtschaftsentwicklung Afghanistans* (The state revenue system and its significance for the economic development of Afghanistan).

829 **Issues on and problems of social and economic reconstruction and recovery in Afghanistan.**
M. Siddieq Noorzoy. *WUFA, Quarterly Journal of the Writers Union of Free Afghanistan.* vol. 4, no. 2. (1989), p. 34-61.
The author examines a range of problems facing Afghanistan after the withdrawal of Soviet troops: refugees, war-disabled persons, irrigation and water resources, transportation, manufacturing, mining, international assistance, and planning.

830 **The Kabul, Kunduz, and Helmand Valleys and the national economy of Afghanistan: a study of regional resources and the comparative advantages of development.**
Aloys Arthur Michel. Washington, DC: National Academy of Sciences, National Research Council, 1959. 441p. maps. bibliog. (Foreign Field Research Program, Office of Naval Research, Report no. 5).
A geographic and economic study of the three main valley systems of the country, with a survey of arable land in the various regions and an overview of agricultural production. Also included is a study of regional development potential in terms of natural resources, power, and transportation.

831 **The problem of Afghanistan.**
*Journal of the Central Asian Society.* vol. 13, pt. 3. (1926), p. 187-204.
A geographical discussion of Russian influence, improved communications in Central Asia, and the economic and political consequences for Afghanistan. The anony-

# Economy

mous author concludes that it is '...only by getting a sound commercial footing in the country [that Britain can] hope to contest Russian progress towards India'.

832 **Problems of economic development in Afghanistan: I, the impact of world conditions; II, planning and finance.**
Peter G. Franck. *The Middle East Journal.* vol. 3, no. 3; no. 4. (1949), p. 293-314; p. 421-40. map.
A concise description and analysis of the Afghan economy and a discussion of development planning for the postwar years.

833 **The third five year economic and social plan of Afghanistan, 1967-1971.**
Ministry of Planning. Kabul: The Author, 1967. 306p. map. (Five Year Economic and Social Plans of Afghanistan).
A detailed statement of the plan, covering objectives, strategies, and policies across a wide range of fields including agriculture and irrigation in Ningrahar, Helmand, and Paktia, mines and industries, transportation and communications, social services, education, health, rural and urban development, and information and culture.

**Afghan Financial Statistics, a monthly publication.**
*See* item no. 850.

178

# Industry

834 **An account of the production of bricks in the Kabul region during the late 1970's and early 1980's.**
P. W. M. Wright. *Afghanistan Journal.* vol. 8, no. 4. (1981), p. 132-37.
Illustrated with drawings and photographs, this describes traditional methods of handmade brick production from raw material preparation to the firing of the kilns.

835 **Afghan carpet industry.**
M. Aref Ghaussi. *Afghanistan.* vol. 8, no. 4. (1953), p. 42-45.
A brief description of carpet-making techniques and the dyes, designs, and types produced.

836 **Afghan government views the Kabul River Valley development.**
K. L., Civil Engineer. *Afghanistan.* vol. 3, no. 4. (1948), p. 44-49.
An examination of various proposals set out for the development of the Kabul River Valley in the light of key priorities: making the best use of water resources, developing irrigation potential, and anticipating and providing for hydro-electric needs (domestic and industrial).

837 **Afghan marble.**
L. F. Rosset. *Afghanistan.* vol. 1, no. 2. (1946), p. 4-11.
This identifies the principal quarries which produce the finest marble and alabaster for the Kabul marble works in Karta Char and also provides a description of the factory where the stone is cut, polished, and turned into finished products for the domestic market.

838 **The bow-drill and the drilling of beads, Kabul, 1981.**
P. W. M. Wright. *Afghan Studies.* vol. 3-4. (1982), p. 95-101.
bibliog.
An illustrated account of the use of the bow-drill by itinerant specialists in piercing
stone beads for the jewellery trade in the bazaars of Afghanistan.

839 **Karakul as the most important article of Afghan trade.**
Ali Mohammed. *Afghanistan.* vol. 6, no. 4. (1949), p. 48-53.
An historical account of the karakul (Persian lamb) trade, giving export figures,
prices, and a description of the organizations set up to manage and control quality
and marketing.

840 **The *naddaf.***
Peter W. M. Wright. *Afghanistan Journal.* vol. 9, no. 1. (1982), p.
21-23.
A description and account of the use of the *gholak, kamaun,*, and *kobah,* the tools
used by the *naddaf* (fluffer), whose work it is to rejuvenate the contents of quilts,
pillows, and mattresses. The self-employed *naddaf* walks the streets carrying the
tools of his trade and calling out to advertise his services to householders. The
article is illustrated with ten line drawings.

841 **Some facts about three important handicrafts of Afghanistan.**
M. Aref Ghaussi. *Afghanistan.* vol. 9, no. 2. (1954), p. 22-26.
An illustrated report on cotton weaving, silk weaving, and carpet making, with
information about the techniques used and the products made.


**Into northern Afghanistan.**
*See* item no. 82.

**The horizontal windmills of Western Afghânistân.**
*See* item no. 844.

# Agriculture

**842 The agricultural survey of Afghanistan.**
Azam Gul. Peshawar, Pakistan: Swedish Committee for Afghanistan,
1988. 68p. map.
Summary results of a 1987 survey which involved interviews with farmers and villagers in *Mujahideen*-controlled areas in each of the country's twenty-nine provinces.
It is said that members of about 20,000 farm family households, both in Afghanistan
and in the refugee camps, were interviewed and, after screening for reliability 11,000
were entered into a database. One set of findings was that cereal crop yields have
declined sharply by thirty-three per cent for irrigated wheat and fifty per cent for
dryland wheat. At the same time the amount of land under cultivation has declined
by thirty per cent.

**843 Economic geography of Afghanistan.**
G. Omar Saleh. *Afghanistan.* vol. 18, no. 3; vol. 19, no. 1; no. 2.
(1963), p. 37-43; p. 15-22; p. 37-41.
A survey of the resources, mainly agricultural, of the country, with information
about crops grown, animal breeding and animal products, and finally considering
industry, communications, and transportation.

**844 The horizontal windmills of Western Afghânistân.**
Klaus Ferdinand. *Folk, Dansk Etnografisk Tidsskrift.* vol. 5. (1963), p.
71-88. bibliog.
An illustrated description of the 'horizontal' windmills found on the plains between
Herat and the Iranian frontier, which is thought to be the region where they were
first made, possibly as early as the 7th century AD. Used to grind grain, they consist
of a grinding room on top of which is built a tower, open to the prevailing wind
and containing a vertical shaft or axle, to which the vanes are attached. In the
same journal (vol. 8-9, 1966-67, p. 83-88) the author publishes further information
on them under the title 'The Horizontal Windmills of Western Afghânistân: an
additional note'.

181

845  **The Musallis - the graincleaners of east Afghanistan.**
Asta Olesen. *Afghanistan Journal.* vol. 9, no. 1. (1982), p. 13-19. bibliog.

The author describes a tradition of agricultural specialization with particular emphasis on the *musallis* who are threshers. An account of the annual cycle of work and its associated seasonal migrations is given, as well as an outline of the changes that were taking place in the mid-1970s.

846  **Survey of land and water resources: Afghanistan, general report.**
N. D. Tkachev, (et al). Rome: Food and Agriculture Organization of the United Nations, 1965. 191p. maps. (FAO Reports).

This volume deals with the soils, hydrology, and irrigation potential of the country on a regional basis: the Hari Rud basin, the Farah Rud basin, the Kabul River basin, the basins of Ghazni and Nahar, and the Adraskand River basin. Having presented a survey of national water resources, the conclusions focus on the development of irrigation. An appendix deals with the management of land and water use. Twenty-eight folding maps and plans accompany the report.

847  **The threat of famine in Afghanistan: a report on current economic and nutritional conditions.**
Frances D'Souza. London: Afghan Aid, 1984. 57p. maps. bibliog.

This examines food supplies and distribution in the country under wartime conditions and looks at consequent nutritional problems. Ten provinces and thirty-nine districts were sampled. Prices, transportation, and the problems caused by displaced persons are also considered.

848  **War impacts on Afghan agriculture.**
Abdul Qahar Samin. *WUFA, Quarterly Journal of the Writers Union of Free Afghanistan.* vol. 4, no. 2. (1989), p. 22-33. bibliog.

A study of the effects of the war on agriculture by the former Dean of the Faculty of Agriculture at Kabul University. The author presents useful comparative data on crops, crop yields, use of fertilizers, land under cultivation, and prices.

849  **Zemledl'cheskiy Afganistan.**
(Agricultural Afghanistan.)
N. I. Vavilov, D. D. Bukinich. Leningrad: Bulletin of Applied Botany, Genetics and Plant Breeding, 1929. 610p. maps.

A comprehensive survey of the geography, soils, climate, agricultural products, and agricultural systems of the country by an internationally famous plant geneticist. Detailed information on all cereals, root crops, soft fruits, nuts, legumes, and other agricultural products, region by region, with data on varieties, yields, seasons, and altitudes. This is a unique mine of valuable information.

**The Kabul Times Annual.**
*See* item no. 33.

Fossils of north-east Afghanistan.
*See* item no. 79.

Travels in the Himalayan provinces of Hindustan and the Panjab; in Ladakh and Kashmir; in Peshawar, Kabul, Kunduz, and Bokhara [in the years] 1819-1825.
*See* item no. 131.

Botanical literature of Afghanistan.
*See* item no. 179.

English East India Company and the Afghans, 1757-1800.
*See* item no. 317.

Afghanistan, 1980: the world turned upside down.
*See* item no. 428.

USAID and social scientists discuss Afghanistan's development prospects.
*See* item no. 606.

The Democratic Republic of Afghanistan, 1979: rhetoric, repression, reforms, and revolts.
*See* item no. 733.

The seminar of Writers Union of Free Afghanistan (WUFA) on current events and reconstruction in Afghanistan.
*See* item no. 812.

Afghanistan 1977: does trade plus aid guarantee development?
*See* item no. 818.

Afghanistan between east and west, the economics of competitive coexistence.
*See* item no. 820.

Afghanistan: past and present.
*See* item no. 821.

An account of the production of bricks in the Kabul region during the late 1970's and early 1980's.
*See* item no. 834.

# Statistics

850   **Afghan Financial Statistics, a monthly publication.**
Kabul: Bank of Afghanistan Research Department, 1964- . monthly.
*Afghan Financial Statistics* (AFS) was an English-language monthly devoted to providing data on banking, public finance, foreign trade, foreign exchange transactions, and prices, with summary tables of statistics from 1962 (1341 AH). The institutions and categories from which the data were gathered include the Central Bank, deposit banks, investment banks, public finance, foreign trade, and includes retail price indexes for basic commodities from wheat to electricity and from unbleached calico to eggs. These monthly publications continued at least until 1968 and probably beyond, but later issues were not found by the bibliographer.

# Environment

851 **Herat, the Islamic city; a study in urban conservation.**
Abdul Wasay Najimi. London: Curzon, 1988. 175p. maps. bibliog.
(Scandinavian Institute of Asian Studies, Occasional Papers, no. 2.).
An excellent study by an architect and town planner who carried out a survey of
Herat prior to the Soviet invasion of Afghanistan. The geographical setting and
historical background is given and the city described in detail. The author then
goes on to set out planning proposals for both the development of the city and the
conservation of its general character, with special emphasis on the preservation of
traditional architectural styles and the protection of historic buildings. Numerous
maps, plans, drawings, and photographs illustrate the book.

852 **National parks and wildlife of Afghanistan.**
Ahmad Shah Jalal. *WUFA, Quarterly Journal of the Writers Union of
Free Afghanistan.* vol. 4, no. 3-4. (1989), p. 6-15.
An appeal for the establishment of a series of National Parks in the country in the
planning priorities for reconstruction after the Afghan-Soviet war in an effort to
preserve the landscape and wildlife for future generations.

853 **Programme on man and the biosphere (MAB): regional meeting on integrated ecological research and training needs in the southern Asian
mountain systems, particularly the Hindu Kush-Himalayas. Final Report.**
Lanham, Maryland: UNESCO, 1977. 76p. (MAB Report, series no.
34).
This identifies what are described as major problems for study: population pressure, erosion and other severe consequences of the over-use of mountain slopes,
migration, and resettlement projects. It then goes on to look at an overall design
for integrated ecological research, the development of guidelines for mountain-area
projects, and proposals for increasing problem awareness through environmental education projects. This report is a result of meetings held in Kathmandu in September-
October, 1975.

854 **Recurrent patterns in traditional Afghan settlements.**
Donald J. Watts. *Afghanistan Journal.* vol. 8, no. 2. (1981), p. 66-72. bibliog.
An examination of traditional urban and rural architecture in Afghanistan and its relevance for the ongoing urbanization of the capital.

855 **The regions of dry belts in Afghanistan.**
Mohammad Zaman. *Afghanistan.* vol. 6, no. 2. (1951), p. 63-68.
A geographical description and discussion of the arid regions of the country and recommendations for protecting the natural vegetation of these areas in order to prevent erosion and an expansion of the dry zones.

856 **The role of squatter housing in the urbanization of Kabul.**
William B. Bechhoefer. *Afghanistan Journal.* vol. 4, no. 1. (1977), p. 3-8.
Illustrated with drawings and photographs, this describes the rapid growth of the capital in the 1960s and shows the kinds of self-built housing which appeared on the rocky slopes of Koh-i-Asmai and Koh-i-Sher Darwaza. In this case the term 'squatter' means that the single-family residential development has been owner-built on city land without permission. The dwellings themselves are substantial structures and compare favourably with other residential developments in the city.

857 **Serai Lahori: traditional housing in the old city of Kabul.**
William B. Bechhoefer. *Afghanistan Journal.* vol. 3, no. 1. (1976), p. 3-15. map. bibliog.
An architect's fully illustrated study of 19th century urban housing in the old city of Kabul in which he argues that future redevelopment should seek to retain its best features and to draw inspiration from this source.

858 **To build a village.**
Syed N. Sibtain. *Afghanistan Journal.* vol. 8, no. 3. (1981), p. 79-89.
An architect's account of the rebuilding of the village of Saighanchi in northern Afghanistan eight months after it was destroyed by an earthquake. Specially designed earthquake-resistant dwellings which could be made by the villagers themselves were used and the project took sixteen months to complete. A book by the same author and with the same title containing a full acount of the project was published in Sydney in 1982 (q.v.).

859 **To build a village; earthquake-resistant rural architecture - a technical handbook.**
Syed N. Sibtain. Sydney: Australian Council of Churches, 1982. 107p. bibliog.
This sets out the planning, design, and construction of an earthquake-resistant village in Afghanistan. On 21 March, 1976 the village of Saighanchi was destroyed by an earthquake. By November that year the Afghan government had approved plans for reconstruction and the villagers themselves began the work, building units based on the design of the Central Asian *yurt* . The village was completed and occupied in

1979. The following eighteen months saw more than 100 earthquakes in the region, the strongest reading 5.9 on the Richter scale. Not a single building in the new village was damaged. Numerous photographs, plans, and drawings are included.


**Afghanistan.**
*See* item no. 7.

**War impacts on Afghan agriculture.**
*See* item no. 848.

**Architectural education in Afghanistan.**
*See* item no. 918.

# Education

860 **Education in Afghanistan.**
Sayed Qasim Reshtia. *Afghanistan.* vol. 1, no. 1. (1946), p. 20-25.
Modern education systems in the country date from the reign of Habibullah (1901-19) during which the famous Habibia College was founded in the capital (1904). The author traces the development of education from that date forward.

861 **Education in Afghanistan: a speech delivered by Najibullah Khan, Afghan Ambassador to India.**
Najibullah Khan. *Afghanistan.* vol. 5, no. 2. (1950), p. 47-62.
An account of the history and development of modern education facilities and practices in the country.

862 **Educational development projects under Second Five Year Plan and future long-term plan.**
Hakim Ziyaee. *Afghanistan.* vol. 18, no. 4. (1963), p. 1-22.
The plans include the development of secondary, vocational, and higher education facilities and the construction of a large number of new schools and other buildings throughout the country with assistance from UNESCO. The funds required and the agencies involved are given.

863 **Foreign assistance to Afghan higher education.**
M. G. Weinbaum. *Afghanistan Journal.* vol. 3, no. 2. (1976), p. 83-86.
Examines the nature and extent of foreign assistance from 1932 to the 1970s, with special reference to USAID programmes involving 727 individuals between 1952 and 1972.

864  **General development of Afghanistan up to 1957.**

A. Hakim Ziai. *Afghanistan.* vol. 16, no. 3. (1961), p. 38-55.

A survey of political changes and economic development in the country with particular focus on the development of the educational system.

865  **Islamic studies review:  Sharia and Islamic education in modern Afghanistan.**

Abdul Satar Sirat. *The Middle East Journal.* vol. 23, no. 2. (1969), p. 217-19.

A discussion of Islamic education, thought, and practice in Afghanistan by the Dean of the Faculty of Islamic Law, Kabul University.

866  **Mahmud Tarzi and Saraj-ol-Akbar: ideology of nationalism and modernization in Afghanistan.**

Vartan Gregorian. *The Middle East Journal.* vol. 21, no. 3. (1967), p. 345-68.

A sketch of the life and times of one of the country's most progressive and influential figures of the 20th century - the first 'modern' Afghan - writer, thinker, educator, publisher, and ardent nationalist.

867  **Report of the mission to Afghanistan.**

William Abbot, Harold Benjamin, Jean Debiesse. Paris: UNESCO, 1952. 87p. map. (Educational Missions).

A report on the problems of developing educational standards and facilities in Afghanistan which was drawn up following a two-month visit to the country by three consultants in 1949. The report considers adult education, teacher training, technical education, the education of girls and women, elementary and secondary education.

868  **The role of education in securing human rights.**

A. Hakim Ziai. *Afghanistan.* vol. 19, no. 2. (1964), p. 1-19.

A discussion presented at a seminar on human rights in developing countries organized by the United Nations in cooperation with the government of Afghanistan. The rights of all citizens of the country to free education is spelled out in quotes from the Constitution.

869  **Ten years of war and civil war in Afghanistan: an educational catastrophy for an entire generation.**

Inger W. Boesen. *WUFA, Quarterly Journal of the Writers Union of Free Afghanistan.* vol. 3, No. 3. (1988), p. 32-44. bibliog.

A description of the political and physical destruction of educational facilities, both formal and informal, in Afghanistan, and the problems of providing an adequate educational environment in exile.

**Education**

The seminar of Writers Union of Free Afghanistan (WUFA) on current
events and reconstruction in Afghanistan.
*See* item no. 812.

# Science and Technology

870  **Science, technology and development in Afghanistan.**
    D. Gopal, M. A. Qureshi. New Delhi: Navrang, 1987. 123p.
This examines the socioeconomic and cultural features of the country and then surveys development policy and planning against a background of industrial objectives and strategy. Education is dealt with briefly while agriculture is examined in some detail, as are mineral resources, transportation and communications, foreign trade, and science and technology.


**To build a village; earthquake-resistant rural architecture - a technical handbook.**
*See* item no. 859.

# Literature

**871 Abouraihan Al-Beiruni and his time.**
Najibullah Khan. *Afghanistan.* vol. 6, no. 1. (1951), p. 17-27.
An article about Abu'l-Rayhan Muhammad Biruni Ahmad, usually known as al-Biruni or al-Khwarizmi, one of the greatest scholars of mediaeval Islam. He was a Persian who, in the spring of 1017 AD, was taken to the Court of Sultan Mahmud of Ghazni as a prisoner. He later travelled to northwest India where he taught Greek sciences and learned Sanskrit. One of his greatest works is the *Description of India*, completed in 1030. He is thought to have died in Ghazni in 1050.

**872 Afghan folk literature after Soviet invasion.**
M. I. Negargar. *WUFA, Quarterly Journal of the Writers Union of Free Afghanistan.* vol. 2, no. 2. (1987), p. 78-91.
A selection of folk poems and songs reflecting Afghanistan's turbulent military history from the Anglo-Afghan Wars to the Soviet invasion.

**873 Afghan poetry of the seventeenth century, being selections from the poems of Khush Hal Khan Khatak, with translations and grammatical introduction.**
Edited by C. E. Biddulph. London: Kegan Paul, Trench, Trübner, 1890. 196p.
A tribute to one of Afghanistan's most famous Pushtun writers, Khushhal Khan Khatak (1613-90 AD) and his work. Following a seventeen-page introduction, the editor provides a forty-page section on Pashto grammar and vocabulary. The poems, some 150 pages in all, are given in English translation and in the original Pashto. Not everything that appears in Pashto has been translated into English, however.

874 **Alexander in Afghanistan: a play in four acts.**
Ahmad Ali Kohzad. *Afghanistan.* vol. 1, no. 3; no. 4. (1946), p. 9-23; p. 1-17.

This unusual literary work is made rather more so by the fact that the first two acts (published in vol. 1, no. 3) are written in English and the last two (vol. 1, no. 4) are rendered in French.

875 **Amir Kror.**
Manohar Singh Batra. *Afghanistan.* vol. 19, no. 1. (1964), p. 9-14.

An account of the life of a chief of Ghor (which occupied what is now central Afghanistan) in the 8th century AD, who was both warrior and poet, taken from *The history of Pushto literature* by Abdul Hai Habibi (q.v.). Batra considers that Pushto was a pure literary form without Arabic or Persian influence only up to the 8th or 9th centuries AD, after which it began to acquire loan words.

876 **A foreign approach to Khushhal: a critique of Caroe and Howell.**
Dost Mohammad Khan Kamil Mohmand. Peshawar, Pakistan: Maktabah-i-Shaheen, 1968. 157p. bibliog.

A detailed and scholarly appraisal of Olaf Caroe's *The Pathans, 550 B.C. - A.D. 1957* (q.v.) and Sir Evelyn Howell and Olaf Caroe's *The poems of Khushhal Khan Khatak*, constituting an important contribution to English language sources on the famous Afghan poet.

877 **The Ghulshan-i-Roh: being selections, prose and poetical, in the Pushto, or Afghān language.**
Edited by Henry George Raverty. London; Calcutta: Williams & Norgate, 1867. 412p.

Raverty has selected texts from 'the most standard authors, together with extracts from several rare works' with a view to providing a textbook for students in the hope that it would 'facilitate and encourage the acquirement of the Pushto language.' This forms a companion volume to his grammar and dictionary (q.v.). All the text is in Arabic script.

878 **Hashim - the son of Zaid Sarwani (223-297 A.H.).**
Manohar Singh Batra. *Afghanistan.* vol. 19, no. 3. (1964), p. 24-27.

An account of some of the earliest known literary works from the 9th century AD in the Pashto language derived from *The history of Pushto literature* by Abdul Hai Habibi (q.v.).

879 **The History of Pushto literature.**
A. H. Habibi. Kabul: [Ministry of Education], 1325 A.H. (1946). 137p.

Professor Habibi was Professor of Pashto in the Faculty of Literature at Kabul University. This history, written in Pashto, was prepared as a textbook for his students.

# Literature

880 **Jami - the great mystic poet.**
Mohammed Ali. *Afghanistan.* vol. 19, no. 1. (1964), p. 1-8.
A sketch of the life and works of a Sufi poet, Nur-ud-din Abdur Rahman Jami, who lived in Herat in the 15th century AD (1414-92) during the late Timurid period. Of his prose and poetic works, forty-six examples survive, including his *Lawaih*, a prose treatise with quatrains which was completed in ca. 1480.

881 **The *Kalid-i-Afghani*, being selections of Pushto prose and poetry for the use of students.**
Edited by T. P. Hughes. Peshawar, Pakistan: Afghan Mission, 1872. 417p.
This work (written mainly in Pashto) contains both prose selections and poetry. In a brief introduction, in English, the editor talks about the writers selected and their works. An English translation of this volume, edited by T. C. Plowden (q.v.), was published in 1875.

882 **Khushhal Khan Khattak, the soldier poet.**
Mohammed Ali. *Afghanistan.* vol. 17, no. 3. (1962), p. 1-6.
An introduction to the life and times of a famous 17th century Afghan writer whose career was bound up with those of the Mogul Emperors Shah Jehan and Aurangzeb.

883 **Khushhal Khan - the national poet of the Afghans.**
Georg Morgenstierne. *Journal of the Royal Central Asian Society.* vol. 47, pt. 1. (1960), p. 49-57.
An essay on the life, times, and works of the Afghan poet Khushhal Khan (1613-90). by the Norwegian linguist and expert on the languages of Afghanistan.

884 **Maulana Jalal-ud-din Balkhi, the great Sufi poet and profound philosopher.**
Mohammed Ali. *Afghanistan.* vol. 18, no. 1. (1963), p. 1-12.
An article about one of the country's famous sons who was born in Balkh in 1207 AD. He travelled widely in Khorasan, Iran and Iraq, later moving to eastern Turkey where he lived for much of the remainder of his life. He is renowned as a great teacher, as well as a philosopher, interpreter of laws and a poet. His greatest work was a poetical rendering of the Holy Khoran into Pahlawi (Persian), completed during the last decade of his life. He died in 1273.

885 **The oldest poems in Pashto, or the oldest Pashto poet, Amir Krore Jahan Pahlawan.**
A. H. Habibi. *Afghanistan.* vol. 1, no. 1. (1946), p. 9-15.
A brief historical account of the 8th century poet Amir Krore Jahan Pahlawan, and his work, together with an example of his verse rendered into English.

886  **Paxto [Pashto] folklore and the *landey*.**
Saduddin Shpoon. *Afghanistan.* vol. 20, no. 4. (1968), p. 40-50.
A discussion of one particular form of Pashto oral tradition, the *landey*. These are anonymous couplets, usually thought to have been composed by women, and are distinguished from other verse forms by having nine syllables in the first line and thirteen in the second. They are sometimes incorporated into songs where they serve to make some topical point. The subjects dealt with by *landey* are love and beauty, parting, social tragedies, and nature. Examples of each are given in Pashto and in translation.

887  **Paxto [Pashto] literature at a glance.**
A. H. Habibi. *Afghanistan.* vol. 20, no. 3; no. 4; vol. 21, no. 1. (1967-68), p. 45-54; p. 51-64; p. 53-57.
A brief historical/linguistic sketch of the language is followed by examples of Pashto prose and poetry, with notes regarding the authors, down through the centuries. The 1950s and 1960s saw a spate of publications by Afghan authors on Pashto writers and their works, all anxious for political reasons to demonstrate that there was an ancient tradition here which not only compared with but rivalled the literary traditions of the Persian language.

888  **Plain tales of the Afghan border.**
John Charles Edward Bowen. London: Springwood, 1982. 95p.
A collection of stories told to a serving British officer by Mohammad Zarif Khan, an Afghan of the Kuki Khel Afridis, during the last days of the British Raj.

889  **Popular poetry of the Baloches.**
M. Longworth Dames. London: Royal Asiatic Society, 1907. 2 vols.
The Introduction is devoted to a discussion of the sources, the character, and a classification of the poems. The forms of the verse, methods of singing, and their historical nature are explained. The first volume is in English, while the second presents the same material in Baluchi, rendered in Latin script. There is a general index.

890  **Selections from the poetry of the Afghans from the sixteenth to the nineteenth century, literally translated from the original Pushto, with notices of the different authors and remarks on the mystic doctrine and poetry of the Sufis.**
Henry George Raverty. London: William & Norgate, 1867. 348p.
This is a translation of the *Gulshan-i-Roh* (q.v.), edited and published by Raverty in 1860.

891  **A short history of Pashto prose.**
Siddiqullah Rishtin. *Afghanistan.* vol. 19, no. 1. (1964), p. 23-29.
This is an attempt to trace the origins of the written language, and to determine its place among other Asian languages. The author offers a classification of its written form into 'old', 'middle', and 'present' periods. Various writers and their works are discussed, as are the styles associated with the different periods.

892 **Translation of the** *Kalid-i-Afghani,* **the text book for the Pakkhto examination, with notes, historical, geographical, grammatical, and explanatory.**
Trevor Chichele Plowden. Lahore, Pakistan: Central Jail Press, 1875. 406p. map.
English translation of the Pashto prose and poetry selections contained in T. P. Hughes' *Kalid-i-Afghani* (q.v.).

893 **Young Afghan prose in Dari.**
Jiří Bečka. *Afghanistan Journal.* vol. 5, no. 3. (1978), p. 102-04.
A survey of literary styles and writers which, after a brief historical review, begins with Mahmud Tarzi (1868-1935), whom the author singles out as the founding spirit of a new literary era characterized by 'realistic prose'. The writer Asadullah Habib (born in 1942) is mentioned as having achieved a significant place among today's authors. His novel *Sapidandam* is discussed in some depth.

**Sifat-Nāma-Yi Darvīs Muhammad Hān-i Ġāzī: Cronaca di una crociata musulmana contro i Kafiri di Laġmān nell'anno 1582. Manoscritto persiana-kābulī edito e tradotto, con introduzione e indici ...** A tribute to darvish Muhammad Khan-e Ghazi: chronicle of a Muslim crusade against the Kafirs of Laghman in the year 1582; a Kabuli-Persian manuscript published in translation with an introduction and an index of [personal, tribal, and ...
*See* item no. 312.

**Through the looking glass: a look at the official Soviet version of the war in Afghanistan.**
*See* item no. 497.

# Children's Books

### 894  Afghanistan.
Christine Weston. New York: Charles Scribner, 1962. 162p. maps. (World Background Books).

A general introduction for young readers with numerous illustrations, this describes the capital, the country, the nomads, the eastern borderlands and then goes on to provide chapters on 'Women', 'Social customs', 'Village life', 'The Afghan personality', 'The past and the conquerors', 'Religion', 'Modern rulers', 'Education', and 'Sports and pastimes'. It is written as a personal travel narrative.

### 895  Afghanistan in pictures.
Camille Mirepoix. New York: Sterling, 1974. 64p. map. (Visual Geography Series).

A general introduction to the country, written for young readers, with a large number of black-and-white illustrations, and accompanying text on the land, history, government, the people, and the economy.

### 896  Clevely Sahib: a tale of the Khyber Pass.
Herbert Hayens. London: Thomas Nelson, 1929. 413p.

A stirring tale of adventures during the First Afghan War in which the hero, Paul Clevely, manages against great odds to keep the Union Jack flying, saves one outpost after another by his quick actions, and, weak from loss of blood, hears the Commander say, 'Moreton, take this brave lad to my tent, and do what you can for him', just before sinking into unconsciousness. This is great stuff in true G. A. Henty style, the recurring theme of which is 'in England they will know that we did our duty'.

### 897  Flight to Afghanistan.
Dean Finley Herbst. Austin, Texas: Steck-Vaughn, 1969. 269p.

A novel for young readers described by the publisher as 'a tale of international intrigue'.

898 **The land and people of Afghanistan.**
   Mary Louise Clifford. Philadelphia; New York: J. B. Lippincott, 1973. 159p. map. (Portraits of the Nations).
Written for young readers, this provides 'an introduction to the history, geography, people, and culture of [the country]...with special sections on recent political, economic, educational, and social reforms'.

899 **The story of Afghanistan.**
   Harold L. Amoss. Wichita, Kansas: McCormick-Mathers, 1965. 164p. maps. (Global Culture Series).
A general account for young readers of the land and its peoples, written as the story of a young boy and girl who visit the cities and travel around the country with their parents. It is intended as a reader for school children.

900 **To Herat and Cabul, a story of the First Afghan War.**
   G. A. Henty. London: Blackie, 1902. 352p. map.
A novel for young readers which closely follows the historical events of the First Afghan War. This is an exciting tale of adventure by one of the 19th century's most able historical novelists.

901 **With Lord Roberts through the Khyber Pass.**
   David Ensor. London: Frederick Muller, 1963. 143p. map. bibliog. (Adventures in Geography Series).
An account of Frederick Roberts' life and career which includes his military adventures on the North-West Frontier, in the Khyber, and in Afghanistan.

# Fiction

### 902 Afghan Adventure.

John Fox, as told to Roland Goodchild. London: Adventurers Club, 1958. 190p.

An adventure story based on a supposed minor military operation on the North-West Frontier and in Kabul carried out at the end of the Second World War to catch smugglers.

### 903 Among the Dervishes.

O. M. Burke. London: Octagon, 1973. 203p.

Chapter eighteen purports to be a factual account of the author's travels in 'Kafiristan' but nothing he describes actually exists there. He tells of 'market days' and 'markets' where none exist, relates stories of imaginary Persian-speaking 'Christian communities' which 'joined the Sufis', tells of the 'rarified atmosphere' and the difficulties of adjusting to high-altitude village life (at 2,000 metres above sea level!), and finally meets an eighty-year-old Scot who lives in a stone castle, complete with library, where he had (apparently) been at home since the 1920s.

### 904 Caravans.

James A. Michener. New York: Random House, 1963. 370p.

A work of fiction in which the author has an American girl disappear in Afghanistan and then sends a US Embassy official out to search for her. The chase covers much of the country and numerous obstacles are placed in the path of the hero.

### 905 The far pavilions.

M. M. Kaye. New York: St. Martin's, 1978. 1191p. map.

The last one hundred pages of this novel take the reader across the North-West Frontier into Afghanistan in 1879 where the hero, in G. A. Henty style, takes part in the actual historical events which marked the beginning of the Second Afghan War - Sir Pierre Louis Napoleon Cavagnari's Mission to Kabul, the Afghan uprising, and the destruction of the British force at the Bala Hissar.

# Fiction

**906  Lie down with lions.**
Ken Follett. London: Corgi, 1986. 364p.
A novel in which a 'young Englishwoman, a French doctor, and a roving American each has private reasons for arriving in Afghanistan where mountain-bred natives fight a fierce guerilla war against the Russian invaders'.

**907  The man who would be king.**
Rudyard Kipling. In: *Wee Willie Winkie, Under the Deodars, The Phantom Rickshaw, and other stories.* London: Macmillan, 1895. p. 193-242.
In fashioning this short story, Kipling was apparently inspired by rumours in India of the exploits of a Colonel Alexander Gardner - an adventurer who claimed to have lived for some years in Afghanistan. Among Gardner's supposed exploits were extensive travels in Kafiristan. No convincing evidence that he was ever closer to Afghanistan than Peshawar has yet come to light. Although not named in it, Gardner's most enduring memorial is doubtless Kipling's story, which in 1975 was made into a feature film starring Sean Connery and Michael Caine.

**908  Salang.**
Sandy Gall. London: Bodley Head, 1989. 247p. map.
A novel based on the struggle between the Afghan *Mujahideen* and the occupying Soviet forces which puts a former SAS officer and a Soviet defector inside Afghanistan on a secret mission to blow up the Salang tunnel - the key link in the overland route from the USSR to Kabul. The author's personal experiences in Afghanistan with the *Mujahideen* give the story an authentic ring.

# The Arts

## General

909  **The arts and crafts of Turkestan.**
Johannes Kalter. London; New York: Thames & Hudson, 1984. 167p.
map. bibliog.
A richly illustrated survey of the material culture of the nomadic peoples of northern
Afghanistan and the southern Soviet Union. Old archive photographs and modern
colour studio pictures, combined with drawings, make this a valuable and visually
interesting handbook to the subject. Jewellery, carpets, clothing, household objects,
wood carvings, and textiles are all shown, described, and identified.

910  **Muslim art in western eyes.**
Richard Ellinghausen. *Afghanistan.* vol. 6, no. 3. (1951), p. 43-46.
An appreciation of the great influence which Islamic art has had in Europe since
the Middle Ages. The author looks at paintings, calligraphy, coins, architecture,
bookbinding, and ivory carving, among others.

# Ancient Period

**911 Ancient arts of Central Asia.**
Tamara Talbot Rice. London: Thames & Hudson, 1965. 288p. maps.
bibliog.
Much of this excellent book deals with a wider geographical region than that occupied by present-day Afghanistan, but it serves to put in perspective the main cultural forces that shaped the country's early history. Chapter four is of particular interest.

**912 The art of Afghanistan.**
Jeannine Auboyer. Feltham, England: Hamlyn, 1968. 140p. map.
bibliog.
Essentially a book of photographs, the author follows a thirty-five-page historical introduction with a twenty-two-page description of the plates. The remainder of the book consists of a bibliography and 140 plates, forty-two of them in colour. The objects depicted range from historic buildings and monuments to coins, and from the archaeological to the ethnographic.

**913 The art of Gandhara.**
Sami Said Ahmed. *Afghanistan.* vol. 21, no. 1. (1968), p. 8-16.
A survey of the religious art of eastern Afghanistan which was dedicated to the expression of Buddhist ideals and which flourished from the first century BC to the third century AD.

**914 Art of the Bronze Age: southeastern Iran, western Central Asia, and the Indus Valley.**
Holly Pittman. New York: Metropolitan Museum of Art, 1984. 99p.
maps. bibliog.
An illustrated account of the art of the Bronze Age, drawing upon objects in the collection of the Metropolitan Museum of Art, New York, as well as items on loan to the museum. Some sites in Afghanistan are included in the study.

**915 Buddhism in Afghanistan and Central Asia.**
Robert Jera-Bezard, Monique Maillard. Leiden, The Netherlands: E.
J. Brill, 1976. 30p. bibliog. (Iconography of Religions, Section XIII:
Indian Religions).
This well-illustrated volume containing seventy-five plates has an interesting introduction and a useful bibliography. The main text consists of scholarly essays and descriptions of Buddha and Bodhisattva images with historical and archaeological notes.

**916 The Graeco-Buddhist art of Gandhara.**
Mohammed Ali. *Afghanistan.* vol. 19, no. 2. (1964), p. 20-25.
An explanation of the term Gandhara, a satrapy of the Achaemenid Empire which extended from Kabul to Peshawar. The author provides a brief history, and an account of the art forms associated with it.

# Architecture

**917 The Afghan empire in India.**
Joël de Croze. *Afghanistan.* vol. 2, no. 1. (1947), p. 6-12.
The author's interests are architectural as well as historical and he discusses Mogul buildings in both Afghanistan and in India.

**918 Architectural education in Afghanistan.**
William B. Bechhoefer. *Afghanistan Journal.* vol. 4, no. 4. (1977), p. 147-49.
A discussion of the role of the architect in a developing nation and the achievements of the Department of Architecture at Kabul University in educating architects so that they may contribute to Afghanistan's development.

**919 The Baluchistan barrel-vaulted tent and its affinities.**
Klaus Ferdinand, Lennart Edelberg. *Folk, Dansk Etnografisk Tidsskrift.* vol. 1. (1959), p. 27-50. bibliog.
An illustrated descriptive and comparative study of certain tent types found in Baluchistan and in Afghanistan. The conclusion is that the Durrani tent-form 'gradually merges into a Baluch tent type' and that the primitive form of this tent type is represented by the barrel-vaulted mat-covered hut. Additional material on the subject was later provided by Klaus Ferdinand in the same journal (vol. 2, 1960, p. 33-50).

**920 A building by the name of Gowharshad in Kohsan Herat.**
Shahibye Mustamandi. *Afghanistan.* vol. 20, no. 4. (1968), p. 65-66.
A brief illustrated description of what is said to be a previously unrecorded building containing three unidentified graves about 120 kilometres west of Herat in the village of Kohsan in Herat Province. The local villagers call it the 'tomb of Gauhar Shad' because of its impressive size and style. Adjacent to the tomb is a mosque, both structures having an internal plan in hexagonal shape. A detailed discussion in French of this building can be found in *Afghanistan,* vol. 21, no. 1, (1968) on p. 27-41.

**921 The cistern of Char-Suq, a Safavid building in Herat, built after 1634 A.D.**
Abdul Wasay Najimi. *Afghanistan Journal.* vol. 9, no. 2. (1982), p. 38-41.
Illustrated with drawings and photographs, this describes the largest cistern (measuring some 400 square metres) in Herat - that of the 'Four Bazaars' which was built in the first half of the 17th century. The author, an architect and town planner, also provides an account of the construction methods used for the great dome.

### 922 From Herat to Kabul.
Robert Byron. *Journal of the Royal Central Asian Society.* vol. 22, pt. 2. (1935), p. 204-10. map.

On a journey from Herat to Kabul via the northern route, the author describes the roads, the weather, and, above all, the history and architecture of the region.

### 923 The general mosque of Herat.
Guya Itemadi. *Afghanistan.* vol. 8, no. 2. (1953), p. 40-50.

An historical and architectural description of the great Friday Mosque, originally built at the end of the 15th century, but later burned and rebuilt.

### 924 The green dome, or the mausoleum of the Timurid princes.
Sarwar Goya. *Afghanistan.* vol. 1, no. 1. (1946), p. 16-19.

A brief history and description of the famous 15th century buildings in Herat designed by the architect Qwamuddin Shirazi on the instructions of Gauhar Shad and built as a centre of art and learning that made Herat famous.

### 925 Nuristani buildings.
Lennart Edelberg. Moesgaard, Aarhus, Denmark: Jutland Archaeological Society, 1984. 223p. map. bibliog.

This book, lavishly illustrated with photographs and drawings, provides a comprehensive description of the dwellings and other buildings of Nuristan, showing how they are built, decorated, and furnished. So numerous are the illustrations that this volume also stands as an historical record, region by region, of these remote mountain communities as they were prior to the Soviet invasion of Afghanistan.

### 926 Nuristan's cliff-hangers.
Stanley Ira Hallet, Rafi Samizay. *Afghanistan Journal.* vol. 2, no. 2.. (1975), p. 65-72.

Illustrated with photographs and drawings depicting traditional Nuristani architecture this, at first sight, gives an authoritative impression, but the author spent only a short time in the field and subsequently had to rely on his notes and sketches. His lack of understanding of some of the solutions devised by Nuristani craftsmen to solve construction problems shows in his own drawings. Those interested in traditional Nuristani architecture and building techniques should see Lennart Edelberg's *Nuristani buildings* (q.v.).

### 927 Traditional architecture of Afghanistan.
Stanley I. Hallet, Rafi Samizay. New York; London: Garland, 1980. 202p. maps. bibliog.

This is an ambitious attempt to present a representative selection of the country's dwelling types in order to 'illustrate the inventive ways in which Afghans traditionally solved the problems of climate and terrain'. The illustrations show tents, houses, and, in one or two cases, other building types such as mosques. The presentation makes full use of both drawings and photographs. As time was short and investigators few the work displays inaccuracies and in some instances it is clear that the authors do not understand some of the construction principles involved, but this is, nevertheless, a useful contribution.

# Music

928 **Afghan music.**
J. Delor. *Afghanistan.* vol. 1, no. 3. (1946), p. 24-29.
A brief illustrated account of music, musical instruments, and musical traditions in the country.

929 **Afghan musical instruments: chang.**
Lorraine Sakata. *Afghanistan Journal.* vol. 7, no. 4. (1980), p. 144-45.
The *chang*, a plucked idiophone known to most of us as the jew's harp, is not regarded as a serious musical instrument in Afghanistan, but rather as a toy for girls and women. The author begins by using the terms 'jaw's harp' or 'jew's harp', and goes on to use 'jaw's harp' in preference, though it has no logical or acceptable historical meaning in ethnomusicology.

930 **Afghan musical instruments: drums.**
Lorraine Sakata. *Afghanistan Journal.* vol. 7, no. 1. (1980), p. 30-32.
An illustrated description of the four basic drum types in use in Afghanistan: 'a single-headed frame drum, a single-headed, goblet-shaped drum,...kettle drums, and a large double-headed drum,' each having its own regional distribution and contexts of use.

931 **Afghan musical instruments: Dutar and Tanbur.**
Lorraine Sakata. *Afghanistan Journal.* vol. 5, no. 4. (1978), p. 150-52.
An illustrated description and comparison of two types of long-necked string instruments commonly found in Afghanistan. The two main types of *dutar* are the Turkoman and Uzbek *dutar* and the Herat *dutar*, both with two strings. The *tanbur* is similar to the *dutar*, except that the neck is thicker, the body shape more rounded and it usually has six strings.

932 **Afghan musical instruments: Ghichak and Saroz.**
Lorraine Sakata. *Afghanistan Journal.* vol. 6, no. 3. (1979), p. 84-86.
An illustrated description of the 'two most common forms of bowed instruments' to be found in Afghanistan. The *ghichak* is described as a two-stringed 'spike fiddle with a tin can body'. The *saroz* has two or three main playing strings and a number of sympathetic strings. It has a carved wooden body with an open resonating cavity.

933  **Afghan musical instruments: sorna and dohl.**
Lorraine Sakata. *Afghanistan Journal.* vol. 7, no. 3. (1980), p. 93-96.
Two instruments widely played in combination on festive occasions, especially those connected with *rites de passage* such as weddings and circumcisions, as well as being used for publicizing theatrical performances and other public events, are the *sorna* (oboe) and *dohl* (drum). This illustrated article describes both instruments and the contexts in which they are used.

934  **Afghan musical instruments: the dambura.**
Lorraine Sakata. *Afghanistan Journal.* vol. 5, no. 2. (1978), p. 70-73.
An illustrated description of the two-stringed lute known as the *dambura*, of which there are two types in northern Afghanistan: 'the larger Aibak or Turkestani dambura...and the smaller, Sheghni or Badakhshi...type'.

935  **Afghan musical instruments: the Nai.**
Lorraine Sakata. *Afghanistan Journal.* vol. 6, no. 4. (1979), p. 144-46.
An illustrated description of various types of traditional flutes (including the *nai* and the *tula*), commonly found in the country. These shepherd's flutes are solo instruments and may be made of reed cane, wood, or metal. They may be end-blown, side-blown, or block flutes. They are, however, generally 'not considered musical instruments, but...toys for young boys and soldiers' as well as being the traditional shepherd's instrument.

936  **Afghan musical instruments: the Rabab.**
Lorraine Sakata. *Afghanistan Journal.* vol. 4, no. 4. (1977), p. 144-46.
An illustrated description of what 'is indisputably the best known of all the Afghan musical instruments'. The rabab is a plucked lute which originated in eastern Afghanistan, but which is today also found in Pakistan, Kashmir, and India.

937  **The Kafir harp.**
Thomas Alvad. *Man, A Monthly Record of Anthropological Science.* vol. 54. (Oct. 1954), p. 151-54. map.
An account of the discovery by Lennart Edelberg of a previously unknown type of harp in central Nuristan in 1948. The author provides a description of the instrument, and discusses its possible relations to ancient south Asian harps.

938  **Music in the culture of northern Afghanistan.**
Mark Slobin. Tucson, Arizona: University of Arizona, 1976. 297p. maps. bibliog. (Viking Fund Publications in Anthropology, 54).
A fully illustrated and detailed description and analysis of the music of the Tadjiks, Uzbeks, Turkmens, and Pashto-speaking peoples of northern Afghanistan. The author provides discussions on music 'subcultures', an analysis of selected musical styles, and descriptions and illustrations of the instruments commonly used.

939  Two Pashai popular songs.
Georg Morgenstierne. *Acta Orientalia.* vol. 10. (1932), p. 31-42.
Presents Pashai texts with translations, but no music. The Pashai peoples live in
scattered villages north of the Kabul River from Kunar and Laghman in the east up
to Gulbahar and Panjshir in the West.

940  Volksmusik in Afghanistan.
(Folk music in Afghanistan.)
Felix Hoerburger. Regensburg, Germany: Gustav Bosse, 1969. 153p.
(Regensburger Beiträge zur musikalischen Volks und Völkerkunde).
A well-illustrated account of Afghan music and musical instruments based on three
months' fieldwork in various parts of the country during which nearly 400 sound
recordings were made.

941  Women and music in Herat.
Veronica Doubleday. *Afghanistan Journal.* vol. 9, no. 1. (1982), p.
3-12. bibliog.
An account by a British musicologist who lived in Herat for twenty-six months
between 1973 and 1977 carrying out anthropological research with her husband,
John Baily. As a woman she had the advantage (denied to male investigators) of
being able to carry out research among women musicians. She provides information
on musical instruments and musical traditions in the context of weddings, birth
celebrations, circumcisions, and engagement parties.

# Calligraphy

942  Afghan calligraphy, illumination, and miniature work in the 9th century A.H.
Ali Ahmad N'aimi. *Afghanistan.* vol. 1, no. 1. (1946), P. 33-38.
An illustrated account of the arts of calligraphy, book-binding, and illumination as
practised in Herat, together with examples of some of the finest works and most
famous artists known from this period (15th century).

# Costume

943  **Afghan sheepskin coats.**
Vicki L. Beyer. *Afghanistan Journal.* vol. 9, no. 2. (1982), p. 42-47.
A description of the design, manufacture, and decoration of the traditional Afghan *posteen*, with drawings and photographs showing details of the embroidery patterns used.

944  **The 'Chitrali', a Macedonian import to the West.**
Bonnie M. Kingsley. *Afghanistan Journal.* vol. 8, no. 3. (1981), p. 90-93.
The author suggests that the hat worn by men in Chitral and in Nuristan (later adopted as standard headgear by the *Mujahideen*) was found by Alexander's men in what is now Afghanistan and taken back to Greece in the 4th century BC, where it was called *kausia* and came to be regarded as Macedonian.

945  **Ikat in Afghanistan.**
Alfred Janata. *Afghanistan Journal.* vol. 5, no. 4. (1978), p. 130-39. bibliog.
An account in German of various types of *ikat* textiles found in Afghanistan, together with colour illustrations of the designs and older archive photographs showing *ikat* costumes being worn by both men and women.

946  **Schmuck in Afghanistan.**
(Jewellery in Afghanistan.)
Alfred Janata. Graz, Austria: Akademische Druck-u. Verlagsanstalt, 1981. 212p. map. bibliog.
A useful and well-illustrated survey of jewellery collected in Afghanistan by the curator of the Museum für Völkerkunde in Vienna. In addition to seventy-two pages of photographs (many of them in colour) and detailed picture captions, there is a forty-three-page introduction to the history and society of the country, a valuable bibliography, and a glossary of relevant ethnic terms.

# Crafts

947  **Arms of the Arian heroes in Avesta period.**
Ahmad Ali Kohzad. *Afghanistan.* vol. 8, no. 3. (1953), p. 27-33.
A description of the arms and armour of the 3rd to 1st centuries BC derived from historical manuscripts and archaeological research.

948 **Bazaar-e Tashqurghan; ethnographical studies in an Afghan traditional bazaar.**
C. J. Charpentier. Uppsala, Sweden: Almqvist & Wiksell, 1972. 193p. maps. bibliog. (Studia Ethnographica Upsaliensia, XXXVI).

A detailed ethnographical and geographical survey of the bazaar in Tashkurgan, carried out in 1970-72, in which each individual shop and craftsman in each street is located, identified and described. The book thus provides an account of the main arts and crafts of Afghan Turkestan. Considering the paucity of such research in Afghanistan, it is remarkable that two major studies of this same bazaar should have appeared in print in the same year. See also the study in French by P. Centlivres (q.v.).

949 **Un bazar d'Asie Centrale; forme et organisation du bazar de Tashqurghan (Afghanistan).**
(A Central Asian bazaar; the nature and organisation of the bazaar in Tashqurghan.)
Pierre Centlivres. Wiesbaden, Germany: Ludwig Reichert, 1972. 278p. map. bibliog. (Beiträge zur Iranistik).

A major study of an ancient market town, manufacturing centre, and caravan staging post in northern Afghanistan, as it was before the Soviet invasion. The author examines the history and geographical position of the town as part of the wider network of Central Asian trade routes and then describes the bazaar, its architecture, its specialist sectors, and its administrative organization. A detailed survey of the professions represented and craft specializations found is given. The study was carried out in 1966-68 and contains numerous maps, plans, drawings, and photographs.

950 **The Saltiq Ersari carpet.**
G. O'Bannon. *Afghanistan Journal.* vol. 4, no. 3. (1977), p. 111-21. bibliog.

A description of the carpets woven by the Ersari Turkomans with specific information on those aspects of design, colour, and weaving technique that serve to identify the type.

# Folk Art

951 **Afghan trucks.**
Jean-Charles Blanc. London: Mathews Miller Dunbar, 1976. 106p.

A collection of 106 colour photographs showing the art work lavished on lorries by artists who specialize in the genre. The tradition was carried over from decorating horse-drawn carriages and today the painted lorry is a remarkable feature of the highways of Afghanistan and Pakistan. This book is a tribute to that Pushtun tradition and the wide variety of subjects from which the artists draw their inspiration.

952  **An overview of Herat folk literature.**

Hafizullah Baghban. *Afghanistan.* vol. 21, no. 1. (1968), 81-90.

The author, a specialist in the subject, includes within the field of folk literature 'plays performed by rural theatre groups, and stories, proverbs, riddles, and quatrains recited on different occasions in the villages'. He goes on to describe the folk plays, the actors, theatre, costumes, audience, and the form and function of performances, following this with a similar analysis of the folk story tradition. This two part article is concluded in vol. 21, no. 2.

953  **Popular art in Afghanistan: paintings on trucks, mosques and tea-houses.**

Micheline Centlivres-Demont. Graz, Austria: Akademische Druck- u. Verlagsanstalt, 1976. 64p. map.

This work documents the bright, lavishly painted lorries of Afghanistan, the wall paintings found in tea houses, and the related artistic styles which decorate some village mosques. The text, illustrated with thirty-six colour plates, describes the traditions behind such paintings, the artistic themes of the genre, and the sources from which they are derived.

# Ethnographic Art

954  **Die Afghanistan-Sammlungen des Museums für Völkerkunde in Wien.**

(The Afghanistan collection in the Anthropological Museum in Vienna.)

Alfred Janata. *Afghanistan Journal.* vol. 1, no. 1. (1974), p. 5-12.

An illustrated article describing the collections (musical instruments, looms, household utensils, jewellery, textiles, etc.) to be found in the museum. Starting in 1958 museum staff began to make systematic field collections in Afghanistan. Fifteen years later the museum had more than 1,700 artefacts, mostly from the Tadjik, Char Aimaq, and the nomad peoples.

955  **A collection of Kafir art from Nuristan: a donation by the Federal Republic of Germany to the National Museum of Afghanistan.**

Max Klimburg. *Tribus, Veröffentlichung des Linden-Museums.* no. 10. (1981), p. 155-202. bibliog.

This is an illustrated catalogue, with extensive notes, of a collection of furniture, carved wooden household utensils, wrought iron stands for food and lighting, weapons, ornaments, musical instruments, and other objects obtained in Kabul and in Nuristan by the author. He subsequently arranged for the collection to be presented to the Kabul Museum.

956  **Die Firuzkuhi-jurte des Museums für Völkerkunde in Wien.**
(The Firozkohi *yurt* in the Anthropological Museum in Vienna.)
Werner Herberg, Alfred Janata. *Afghanistan Journal.* vol. 9, no. 4.
(1982), p. 95-103. bibliog.
A detailed description of a yurt purchased for the museum near the town of
Chaghcharan in the province of Ghor in 1977. Twenty-two photographs and five
drawings illustrate the article.

957  **A Kafir goddess.**
Ahmad Ali Motamedi, Lennart Edelberg. *Arts Asiatiques.* tome 18.
(1968), p. 3-21. map. bibliog. (Annales du Musée Guimet et du
Musée Cernuschi).
A description of the circumstances surrounding the discovery in 1963 of a wooden
statue of the Kafir goddess Disni in the Parun Valley, Nuristan.

958  **A *kuna urei* in the Victoria and Albert Museum.**
Schuyler Jones. *Afghanistan Journal.* vol. 8, no. 4. (1981), p. 138-39.
Illustrated description of a rare pre-Islamic silver wine bowl (*kuna urei*) from Kafiris-
tan (Nuristan) held in the Victoria and Albert Museum collections in London.

959  **Male-female polarity symbolism in Kafir art and religion: new aspects
in the study of the Kafirs of the Hindu-Kush.**
Max Klimburg. *East and West.* vol. 26, nos. 3-4 (new series). (1976),
p. 479-88.
The author, an art historian, shows himself to be unaware of much that has been
published about the Nuristan region and not to have read very carefully the remainder. He does deserve credit, however, for bringing to the attention of scholars a
few surviving examples of pre-Islamic art from Parun Valley which are illustrated
in this paper.

960  **On the function of KK32: an ethnographic specimen from Nuristan
in the Kabul Museum.**
Schuyler Jones. *Folk: Dansk Etnografisk Tidsskrift.* vol. 26. (1984),
p. 179-89.
Description, analysis, and discussion of the pre-Islamic carved wooden post. An
article which includes a discussion of this ethnographic specimen entitled 'Statue
de bois rapportées du Kafiristan à Kabul après la conquête de cette province par
l'Émir Abdul Rahman en 1895-96', published by Lennart Edelberg (q.v.), is also
considered.

961 **Die Sammlungen des Linden-Museums aus Afghanistan und den Nachbargebieten.**
(The Linden Museum's collections from Afghanistan and neighbouring areas.)
Johannes Kalter. *Afghanistan Journal.* vol. 9, no. 3. (1982), p. 76-85. bibliog.
An illustrated overview of the jewellery, clothing, tools, household objects, and textiles contained in the museum.

962 **Statues de bois rapportées du Kafiristan à Kabul après la conquête de cette province par l'Émir Abdul Rahman en 1895-96.**
(Wooden statues taken to Kabul from Kafiristan after the conquest of that province by Amir Abdur Rahman in 1895-96.)
Lennart Edelberg. *Arts Asiatiques.* tome 7, fasc. 4. (1960), p. 243-86. map. bibliog. (Annales du Musée Guimet et du Musée Cernuschi).
A fully illustrated article which describes the wooden anthropomorphic statues, many of them life-sized, which were carved in some areas of Kafiristan (present-day Nuristan), and discusses the role they played in the pre-Muslim cultures of the region.

**Die materielle Kultur des Kabulgebietes.** The material culture of the Kabul region.
*See* item no. 35.

**The road to Oxiana.**
*See* item no. 168.

**Three women of Herat.**
*See* item no. 171.

**Beyond the Oxus: archaeology, art and architecture of Central Asia.**
*See* item no. 199.

**The first horsemen.**
*See* item no. 289.

**Légendes et coutumes Afghanes.** Afghan legends and customs.
*See* item no. 569.

**Pashai; Landschaft, Menschen, Architektur.** Pashai; landscape, people, architecture.
*See* item no. 589.

**Afghan carpet industry.**
*See* item no. 835.

**Some facts about three important handicrafts of Afghanistan.**
*See* item no. 841.

**Herat, the Islamic city; a study in urban conservation.**
*See* item no. 851.

**Recurrent patterns in traditional Afghan settlements.**
*See* item no. 854.

**The role of squatter housing in the urbanization of Kabul.**
*See* item no. 856.

**Serai Lahori: traditional housing in the old city of Kabul.**
*See* item no. 857.

**To build a village.**
*See* item no. 858.

# Sports and Recreation

**963 Buzkashi: game and power in Afghanistan.**
G. Whitney Azoy. Philadelphia, Pennsylvania: University of Pennsylvania, 1982. 147p.
A very readable and informative work on the Afghan national game which resembles polo only in that it is played on horseback, and the rôle it plays in the larger political arena. It is a violent game in which the riders try to get hold of the headless body of a goat or calf and complete a circuit of the playing area while everyone else tries to stop them. It is a game within a game and the author produces a convincing analysis which reveals its underlying political characteristics, associations, and functions.

**964 Buzkashy game in Afghanistan.**
Ahmad Ali Motamedi. *Afghanistan.* vol. 12, no. 2. (1957), p. 1-6.
An account of the game, both in its traditional form and the modern 'cleaned-up' version which used to be played near Kabul on the King's birthday. For a more detailed analysis see *Buzkashi: game and power in Afghanistan* (q.v.), by G. Whitney Azoy.

**965 Common Afghan street games.**
Nico J. van Oudenhoven. Lisse, Netherlands: Swets & Zeitlinger, 1979. 78p.
This describes 146 games commonly played by children in Afghanistan. The rules for each game are given (including whether played by boys or girls or both) and the age-group for each game is identified. The text is illustrated with diagrams and photographs.

966  Common Afghan 'street' games and child development.
     Nico J. van Oudenhoven. *Afghanistan Journal.* vol. 7, no. 4. (1980),
     p. 126-38. bibliog.
Written by a Dutch child psychologist who spent three years in Afghanistan, this
regards games as a natural resource with potential low-cost applications in the field
of education, as games have an important role to play in stimulating intellectual and
emotional development. Several popular games are described and discussed.

967  Falknerei in Afghanistan.
     (Falconry in Afghanistan.)
     Gerd Kühnert. Bonn: Rudolf Habelt, 1980. 102p. map. (Homo
     Venator, Schriften zur Geschichte und Soziologie der Jagd, Nr. 3).
A study of falconry in Afghanistan with a sketch of its history, a description of the
equipment used by falconers (illustrated with line drawings), and information on the
localities in the country where it is still practised.

968  Horsemen of Afghanistan.
     Roland Michaud, Sabrina Michaud. London: Thames & Hudson,
     1988. [n.p.].
A celebration, in colour photographs taken betw~ n 1964 and 1978, of Afghanistan
and *buzkashi* - the national game. There is ver  little text, but those unfamiliar with
the sport may consult Whitney Azoy's book (q.v.).

969  Village buzkashi.
     Asen Balikci. *Afghanistan Journal.* vol. 5, no. 1. (1978), p. 11-21.
*Buzkashi*, sometimes described as the country's national game, is a violent sport
played on horseback. This illustrated article begins with a cultural survey of northern
Afghanistan, an account of the rôle of horses in these societies, and the relationships
between *buzkashi* and local political leadership.

# Libraries, Galleries, Museums and Archives

970 **Ancient art from Afghanistan: treasures of the Kabul Museum, catalogue of the exhibition presented under the patronage of His Majesty King Mohammed Zaher Shah.**
Benjamin Rowland, Jr. New York: Asia Society, 1966. 144p. map. bibliog.
An illustrated catalogue of the major finds from Mundigak, Begram, Hadda, Bamiyan, Kabul, Fondukistan, Bactria, and the Ghaznavid and Gandharan periods to be found in the Museum. This provides a useful guide to the artefacts and styles of the earlier periods, as well as a partial record of the museum's holdings.

971 **Art in Afghanistan: objects from the Kabul Museum.**
Francis Mortimer Rice, Benjamin Rowland. London: Allen Lane for the Penguin Press, 1971. 93p.
A lavishly illustrated catalogue, mainly of archaeological materials, but including some ethnographic artefacts. The archaeological emphasis is on the sites at Mundigak, Begram, Hadda, Bamiyan, and Fondukistan and the Bactrian, Kushan and Ghaznavid periods. The ethnographic artefacts shown are from the pre-Muslim cultures of Nuristan.

972 **The Historical Society of Afghanistan.**
Syed Ikbal Ali Shah. *Afghanistan.* vol. 10, no. 1. (1955), p. 44-50.
This describes the founding of the Society, its aims, its rules and regulations, and provides a list of publications issued by the Society.

973   **Manuscrits d'Afghanistan.**
      (Manuscripts of Afghanistan.)
      S. de Laugier de Beaurecueil. Cairo: Institut Français d'Archéologie
      Orientale, 1964. 420p. (Recherches d'Archéologie, de Philologie et
      d'Histoire, tome XXVI).
A catalogue of 1,596 manuscripts located in six libraries in Afghanistan, including
the private library of King Mohammad Zahir Shah. The annotated entries include
manuscripts in Arabic, Persian, Pashto, Turkish, and Urdu. There is an index of
authors, scribes and calligraphers, place names, and other works mentioned in the
manuscripts. In an earlier work the compiler catalogued 551 manuscripts contained
in three other libraries in Afghanistan. This was published in *Mélanges de l'Institut
dominicain d'Etudes orientales* (MIDEO, vol. 3, [1956], p. 75-206).

# Media

974 **Afghanistan at the beginning of the twentieth century: nationalism and journalism in Afghanistan, a study of** *Serâj ul-akhbâr* **(1911-1918).**

May Schinasi. Naples, Italy: Istituto Universitario Orientale, 1979. 302p. map. bibliog. (Seminario di Studi Asiatici, Series Minor III).

A study of the Kabul newspaper *Seràj ul-akhbâr afghâniya* and its founder-editor Mahmud Tarzi. The newspaper, written in Persian by Afghans and for Afghans, was published from 1911 to 1918.

975 **Afghanistan's newspapers, magazines and journals.**

Ibrahim V. Pourhadi. *Afghanistan Journal.* vol. 3, no. 2. (1976), p. 75-77.

A list of publications arranged alphabeticaly by name, with year founded, frequency of publication, and language (Dari, Pashto, French, Arabic, English), together with a brief descriptive statement about each.

976 **Afghanistan's press and its literary influence, 1897-1969.**

Ibrahim V. Pourhadi. *Afghanistan Journal.* vol. 3, no. 1. (1976), p. 28-35.

A survey of the press and the contributions made by key writers and editors from the early days of newspaper publishing in the country.

977 **The background and beginning of the Afghan press system.**

Mohammad Kazem Ahang. *Afghanistan.* vol. 21, no. 1. (1968), p. 70-76.

An account of the publishing history of *Shums-u-Nahar* (The Morning Sun), a newspaper which first appeared in Kabul in 1873. The author also provides an analysis of the newspaper's style and content.

978  Journalism in Afghanistan, a brief historical sketch.
Sayed Qasim Reshtia. *Afghanistan.* vol. 3, no. 2. (1948), p. 72-77.
This describes the country's first newspaper, *Kabul*, published in 1867 by Said Jamaludin al-Afghani during the reign of Amir Mohammed Azam Khan. Afghanistan's second newspaper, which was a revival of the first, started in 1875 in the reign of Amir Sher Ali Khan and was called *Shamsun-Nahar*. This was more successful, but it was in the reign of Amir Habibullah that modern journalism can be said to have begun with the publication of *Saraj-ul Akbar Afghania* in 1912.

979  Kabul calling.
Sayed Qasim Reshtia. *Afghanistan.* vol. 1, no. 2. (1946), p. 1-3.
A brief account of Radio Kabul, which had its beginnings in the setting up of a 100 watt transmitter in the capital in 1925, and later expanded to a 20 kilowatt Telefunken transmitter at the outbreak of the Second World War. In the years immediately following the War, the station was on the air for two hours each day.

# Periodicals

980  **Afghan Information Centre: Monthly Bulletin.**
Edited by Sayed Naim Majrooh. Peshawar, Pakistan: Afghan Information Centre, 1980-.
Founded by Professor Sayed B. Majrooh as an English-language monthly and designed to inform a wider international audience of what was going on inside the country, this has now produced more than 110 issues which contain a great deal of military, social, economc, medical and other information, including news about refugees and humanitarian aid.

981  **Afghan Jehad, quarterly magazine of the Cultural Council of Afghanistan Resistance.**
Edited by Sabahuddin Kushkaki. Islamabad, Pakistan: Cultural Council of Afghanistan Resistance, 1987-. maps. bibliog.
The editorial in the first issue is entitled 'A Magazine Devoted to Objectivity' and the editor states that the journal's policy would be to 'devote itself to a factual presentation of events related to the Afghan-Soviet war'. The first issue, 179 pages long, contains an annotated bibliography of 'Books for the Mujaheddin by the Mujaheddin' which lists nearly thirty recent publication in either Dari or Pashto - everthing from war to poetry. But this is primarily a news magazine reporting events in the country and quoting relevant reports from newspapers and magazines abroad.

982  **The Afghan Mujahid.**
London: Hizb-i-Islami Afghanistan, 1981- . monthly.
An English-language monthly news and propaganda magazine published in London. It is pro-Hikmatyar and anti-Russian, anti-American, anti-Afghan Royal Family, and anti-Najibullah. In 1990 it celebrated its ninth year of publication.

983 **Afghanica, the Afghanistan studies newsletter.**
Edited by Jadwiga Pstrusinska, Anna Krasnowolska. Krakow, Poland: Universitas, Jagellonian University, 1987-.
Founded in 1987 in Oxford, this newsletter is now edited and published in Krakow, Poland. It provides information on conferences, publications, exhibitions, courses, projects, even individual lectures, on any subject related to the history, art, politics, religion, anthropology, archaeology, linguistics and geography of Afghanistan wherever they may occur. Material for inclusion or enquiries should be directed to The Editor, *Afghanica*, Institute of Oriental Philology, Jagellonian University, Al. Mickiewicza 9/11, 31-120 KRAKOW, Poland.

984 **Afghanistan Journal.**
Graz, Austria: Akademische Druck und Verlaganstalt, 1974-1982. maps. bibliog..
The *Afghanistan Journal*, edited by Karl Gratzl, appeared quarterly from 1974 to 1982 with a wide variety of illustrated articles in English, French, and German on a range of subjects: natural history, anthropology, archaeology, history, arts and crafts, material culture and technology, musicology, and, after the Soviet invasion, refugees.

985 **Afghanistan Report.**
Edited by Ijaz S. Gilani, Fazal-ur-Rahman. Islamabad, Pakistan: Ross Masood Husain, quarterly. (Afghanistan War Reports).
A quarterly publication put together by the Crisis and Conflict Analysis Team of the Institute of Strategic Studies in Islamabad for the purpose of providing 'an objective analysis of the Afghan resistance, the Soviet-Kabul military and psychological warfare, and socio-political and economic developments'. Intelligence for the reports is gathered from a wide variety of sources, both within and outside Afghanistan. A useful resource for anyone studying the Soviet occupation of the country and Afghan resistance to that occupation.

986 **Afghanistan Report: A monthly monitor of Afghan resistance.**
Edited by Hasan Akhtar Gardezi, Mohammad Ashraf Poswal. Islamabad, Pakistan: Centre for Asian Studies, monthly.
This is one of a series of reports on political and military events during the Soviet occupation. They offer a summary of information regarding the course of the war. As they were compiled on a monthly basis, they were relatively up-to-date - a modern, though public, version of the secret 19th century British Intelligence series known as *Kabul Diaries, Peshawar Diaries,* and *Trans-Frontier Memoranda.*

987 **Afghanistan Today: a bi-monthly magazine of peace, solidarity, and friendship organization of the Democratic Republic of Afghanistan.**
Edited by Anahita Ratebzad, Mohammad Qabool, Ghulam Eqbal, Zarina Majid. Kabul: Ministry of Press and Information, [1980].
An illustrated journal intended to show an international audience that the country is flourishing under Communism. Articles on the arts, education, industrial development, cultural advances, and religion are contrasted with a background of violence against the people caused by 'mercenaries', 'bandits', 'spies', and 'counter-revolutionaries', meaning the *Mujahideen*.

988 **Central Asia File: newsletter of the Central Asian Studies Association.**
Edited by Shirin Akiner. London: Central Asian Studies, 1987-. three times a year.
This lively and informative publication appears three times each year and regularly provides information about Afghanistan and current research on or in that country, as well as giving advance notice of conferences, seminars, and exhibitions. Particularly useful is the section on 'Recent Books and Publications'. For details contact Dr. Shirin Akiner, School of Oriental and African Studies, University of London, Malet Street, London WC1E 7HP.

989 **The Mujahideen Monthly.**
Edited by Abdul Qadeer Karyab, Sur Gul Speen. Peshawar, Pakistan: Press and Information Department, Political Committee, 1986-. monthly.
An illustrated English language magazine giving news of the war, political messages, interviews with key military and political figures, and general information. Available from *Mujahideen Monthly*, G.P.O. 255, Peshawar, N.W.F.P., Pakistan.

990 **WUFA, Writers Union of Free Afghanistan.**
A. Rasul Amin. Peshawar, Pakistan: Writers Union of Free Afghanistan, 1986- . quarterly.
An English-language journal written and edited mainly by Afghan educators and members of the pre-Communist government who went into exile following the Soviet invasion. Founded in 1985, the organization (WUFA) promotes understanding of Afghan literature, history, current events, and culture by publishing a wide range of articles on everything from *Mujahideen* offensives against the Soviets to Pashto poetry.

**Afghan Financial Statistics, a monthly publication.**
*See* item no. 850.

# Reference Works

### 991 Afghanistan.
In: *The Imperial Gazetteer of India*. Edited by W. W. Hunter. London: Trübner, 1881. 9 vols.

The first edition of this gazetteer, consisting of nine volumes, appeared in 1881 after ten years of preparation. It remains a valuable source of information, containing authoritative articles on 'Afghánistán' (vol. 1, p. 20-42) and a range of other geographical, economic, and historical topics relating to the country. The second edition of the *Gazetteer*, in 14 volumes, appeared in 1886-87. The final volume in each edition is an index to the entire set.

### 992 Afghān.
Georg Morgenstierne. In: *The Encyclopaedia of Islam*. Edited by H. A. R. Gibb, J. H. Kramers, E. Lévi-Provençal, J. Schacht. London: Luzac, 1960. vol. 1, p. 216-21. bibliog.

Concise and learned, this discusses 'The people', 'Geographical distribution of the Afghān tribes', 'The Pashto language', and 'Pashto literature'.

### 993 Afghanistan.
In: *The Europa World Year Book*. London: Europa Publications, annual.

Volume one, part two (Afghanistan-Jordan) provides basic but detailed information on some eighty countries. The information on Afghanistan is concise, useful, and much of it is not readily available elsewhere. Several pages are devoted to recent history, government, defence, economic affairs, social welfare, and education. This is followed by a statistical survey dealing with tables of figures on area and population, agricultural production, livestock, forestry, mining, fishing, industry, finance, external trade, transport, tourism, and education. Information on the government includes sections on the Constitution, the office of the President, the National Assembly, and the Judiciary. Senior Government office holders are named and the addresses of the various ministries are given. Political organizations are listed and described, as are the main daily newspapers, periodicals, and publishers. A valuable source of information which is revised annually.

994 **Dictionary of Indian biography.**
C. E. Buckland. London: Swan Sonnenschein, 1906. 494p. bibliog.
A valuable reference work for anyone reading or writing about the history of Afghanistan, the North-West Frontier, the Punjab, and India, as it contains brief biographical accounts of the lives of the key figures, mainly European in this selection, who played an important part in that history.

995 **A gazetteer of the countries adjacent to India on the north-west; including Sinde, Afghanistan, Beloochistan, the Punjab, and the neighbouring states.**
Edward Thornton. London: W. H. Allen, 1844. 2 vols. map. bibliog.
A major and most valuable compilation of geographical, cultural, and historical information. All entries are listed alphabetically and the sources from which they are derived are given in the margin beside each entry.

996 **A guide to the archives of the central record office, N.-W. F. Province.**
S. M. Jaffar. Peshawar, Pakistan: Government Printing & Stationery, 1948. 50p.
A handbook which lists and describes 'the nature, scope and importance of the North-West Frontier Province Government records ranging over half a century (1849-1899)'. In addition there is an account of the records of the political branch of the Province for the years 1849-1900. A large number of the records relate to Afghanistan and the Afghans.

997 **Historical & cultural dictionary of Afghanistan.**
M. Jamil Hanifi. Metuchen, New Jersey: Scarecrow, 1976. 141p. bibliog. (Historical and Cultural Dictionaries of Asia, no. 5).
A handy reference work with, as the term 'dictionary' implies, entries arranged alphabetically; place names, personal names (especially of rulers and political leaders), geographical features, and subjects such as history, agriculture and musical instruments. Persian and Pushtu terms are also included.

**Archaeological gazetteer of Afghanistan.**
*See* item no. 188.

# Bibliographies

998 **Annotated bibliography of Afghanistan.**
Donald N. Wilber. New Haven, Connecticut: Human Relations Area
Files, 1968. 252p. bibliog. (Behavior Science Bibliography).
This is the third edition of the bibliography which first appeared in 1956, and
then was brought up to date for the second edition in 1962. The third edition was
'extensively revised and re-edited' and contains 1,600 entries, making it a very useful
supplement to Mohammad Akram's *Bibliographie analytique de l'Afghanistan* (q.v.)
of 1947.

999 **An annotated bibliography of Nuristan (Kafiristan) and the Kalash
Kafirs of Chitral, part I.**
Schuyler Jones. Copenhagen: Royal Danish Academy of Sciences
and Letters, 1966. 110p. maps. (Historisk-filosofiske Meddelelser,
vol. 41, no. 3).
This bibliography offers an overview of materials mainly published in the 19th
century on the 'Kafirs' (literally 'pagans') and Kafiristan (as the region was then
known), as well as information on more recent books and articles in English, French,
German, and Danish.

1000 **Archival resources for Afghan history in Afghanistan and Pakistan.**
Lesley A. Hall. *Afghan Studies.* vol. 2. (1979), p. 75-77.
An archivist from the India Office Library and Records in London summarizes the
research materials to be found in the National Archives of Afghanistan and other
institutions in Kabul as well as relevant institutions in Peshawar, Lahore and Quetta.

1001 **Bibliografiya Afganistana: literatura na russkom yazyka.**
(A bibliography of Afghanistan: literature in Russian.)
Tatiyana I. Kukhtina. Moscow: Nauka, 1965. 272p. bibliog.
Despite the title, this contains a section listing works in European languages other
than Russian. There are 5,680 entries altogether, covering all fields of study.

Bibliographies

1002 **Bibliographie de l'Afghanistan, I, ouvrages parus hors de l'Afghanistan.**
(Bibliography of Afghanistan, I, works published outside Afghanistan.)
Mohammed Akram. Paris: Centre de Documentation Universitaire, 1947. 507p. bibliog.
The first book-length annotated bibliography on Afghanistan to be published, this appeared nine years before Donald Wilber's 1956 bibliography and contains nearly 2,000 entries describing books and articles in English, French, German, and other European languages. It is arranged in the following sections: Bibliographies, General Works, Geology, Geography and Travels, The Afghan Frontier, The Hindu Kush, Turkestan, Badakhshan and the Pamirs, Nuristan, Eastern Afghanistan, Southern Afghanistan, Western Afghanistan and Seistan, Climate, Maps, History, The Pre-Islamic Period, Islam, The Turco-Mongols, The Lodis, The Durranis, 19th Century Anglo-Russian Rivalry in Central Asia, The First Afghan War, The Second Afghan War, Amir Abdur Rahman, The 20th Century, Archaeology and the Arts, Numismatics, Ethnography and Religion, Language and Literature, Manuscripts.

1003 **Bibliographie der Afghanistan-Literatur, 1945-1967. Teil I: Literatur in europäischen Sprachen; Teil II: Literatur in Orientalischen Sprachen und Ergänzungen in europäischen Sprachen.**
(Bibliography of publications on Afghanistan, 1945-1967. Part I: Publications in European languages; Part II: Publications in Oriental Languages and a supplement in European languages.)
Edited by Willy Kraus, E. A. Messerschmidt. Hamburg, Germany: Arbeitsgemeinschaft Afghanistan und Deutsches Orient-Institut, 1968-69. 2 vols. bibliog.
A useful reference work which draws on several earlier published bibliographies as well as individual research collections made by various scholars. Unfortunately the publishers, presumably to cut costs, decided to glue rather than stitch the volumes and consequently they shed pages like autumn leaves.

1004 **A bibliography of Afghanistan: a working bibliography of materials on Afghanistan with special reference to economic and social change in the twentieth century.**
Keith McLachlan, William Whittaker. Cambridge, England: Middle East & North African Studies, 1983. 671p.
A bibliography of ambitious proportions, listing some 7,500 published and unpublished books and articles across a wide range of subject areas, with large sections devoted to 'Agriculture and Forestry', 'History and Politics', 'Economy and Infrastructure', and 'Flora and Fauna', to mention only a few. The entries are not annotated and the work suffers from careless editing and/or proof-reading, but is nevertheless a useful guide to a large number of publications.

**1005 Bibliography of American periodical literature on Afghanistan, 1890-1946.**
Leila B. Poullada. New York: Afghanistan Council, the Asia Society, 1979. p. 21. (Occasional Paper, no. 18).
A very useful checklist which serves to guide the researcher straight to relevant material. Although not annotated, this is a great time-saver and indispensable aid for the serious scholar. We look forward to the compiler's annotated bibliography, covering a greater time span, which is promised in the Introduction.

**1006 Bibliography of Russian works on Afghanistan.**
London: Central Asian Research Centre, 1956. 12p.
This bibliography lists 160 works, both books and articles, written by various Soviet authors on a wide range of economic, political, ethnological, linguistic, literary, and historical subjects. Although there are no annotations, most of the titles are given in English.

**1007 Bibliotheca Afghanica.**
Paul Bucherer-Dietschi. Liestal, Switzerland: Schweizerisches Afghanistan-Archiv, 1979-.
This is a bibliography with a difference. The founder-editor conceived the idea of collecting books, articles, reports - anything relating to Afghanistan - and eventually presenting the entire collection to whichever institution in Switzerland had, in the meantime, done the most for Afghan studies. Out of this grew the idea of publishing a continually updated bibliographic card index to which libraries could subscribe. The first cards were sent out in 1979. Printed on international standard library cards, the records are sent to subscribers in batches of 200 cards, with an average annual delivery of between 1,000 and 2,000 entries, making what may well be the largest and most complete bibliography of the country available. For further information write to Afghanistan-Archiv, Benzburgweg 5, 4410 Liestal, Switzerland.

**1008 A brief guide to sources for the study of Afghanistan in the India Office records.**
Lesley A. Hall. London: India Office Library and Records, 1981. 60p.
Part I of the guide provides a chronological survey of sources and a brief historical sketch with notes on the records available for the period, the type of information they contain, and references to publications which rank as primary sources. Part II deals with the files of the British Legation in Kabul from 1923 to 1948 and includes correspondence with the Foreign Office and India Office, the Government of India, the Government of the North-West Frontier Province, and the Government of Afghanistan.

1009 **Deutsche Veröffentlichungen über Afghanistan.**
(German publications on Afghanistan.)
Ludolph Fischer. *Institut für Auslandsbeziehungen.* no. 9/10. (Sept.-
Oct. 1954), p. 222-25. bibliog.
A useful bibliography listing 141 German-language books and articles on geography,
anthropology, botany, geology, linguistics, medicine, archaeology, travel, politics,
economics, and other fields.

1010 **Deutschen Afghanistan-Archivs.**
(German Afghanistan Archive.)
Bochum, Germany: Institute for Development Research and Development Policy, Ruhr University, Bochum, 1987- . quarterly.
A quarterly publication which lists books, articles, and reports in English, French,
and German covering all subjects relating to Afghanistan. An indication of the scale
of the project is shown by the fact that between 1987 and 1990 they published some
200 pages of unannotated bibliographic references.

1011 **International bibliography of the social sciences.**
Edited by Nathalie Fauriaut, John B. Black. London: Tavistock, 1951-
. annual. bibliog. (International bibliography of the social sciences).
These bibliographies are published annually in four parts: 'The international bibliography of sociology', 'The international bibliography of political science', 'The
international bibliography of economics', and 'The international bibliography of social and cultural anthropology'. Anyone carrying out research on Afghanistan in any
of these areas would find a search of these volumes profitable. The series originated
in 1951-55.

1012 **An inventory of Afghanistan research materials.**
Nake M. Kamrany, Lois H. Godiksen, Eden Naby, Richard N. Frye.
*Afghanistan Journal.* vol. 4, no. 2. (1977), p. 79-82.
Presents a proposal to undertake 'the first comprehensive bibliographic reference
work' on Afghanistan and, at the same time, an invitation to interested scholars
to comment and collaborate. The purpose of the project is to inform and promote
scholarly activity, 'historical, cultural, social, political, geographical, and economic'.

1013 **A partially annotated bibliography on Afghan linguistics.**
Don L. F. Nilsen, Fazel Nur, Sajida Kamal. *Afghanistan.* vol. 23, no.
1. (1970), p. 43-56.
A bibliography of linguistic studies which lists books and articles by both Afghan
and European scholars. A brief practical introductory guide for anyone interested in
this field.

1014 **Les problemes d'une bibliographie exhaustive de l'Afghanistan.**
(Problems of compiling a comprehensive bibliography of Afghanistan.)
Charles M. Kieffer. *Afghanistan.* vol. 13, no. 2 and no. 3. (1958), p.
1-15 and p. 12-40.
A well-organized and thorough examination of the problems of constructing a comprehensive bibliography of published works on the country, together with a critical survey of existing bibliographies.

**Nouveaux ouvrages sur les langues et civilisations de l'Hindou-Kouch (1980-1982).** New works on the languages and cultures of the Hindu Kush [1980-1982].
*See* item no. 582.

**Quelques ouvrages récents sur les langues et civilisations de l'Hindou-Kouch (1976-1979).** Some recent works on the languages and cultures of the Hindu Kush [1976-79].
*See* item no. 595.

# Indexes

There follow three separate indexes: authors (personal and corporate); titles; and subjects. Title entries are italicized and refer either to the main titles, or to other works cited in the annotations. Subject entries refer to topics covered by the book and articles, but which are not necessarily mentioned explicitly in the annotations. The numbers refer to bibliographic entry rather than page numbers. Individual index entries are arranged in alphabetical sequence.

## Index of Authors

232

235

237

# Index of Titles

241

242

250

254

# Y

# Index of Subjects

267

271

278

# Map of Afghanistan

This map shows the more important towns and other features.

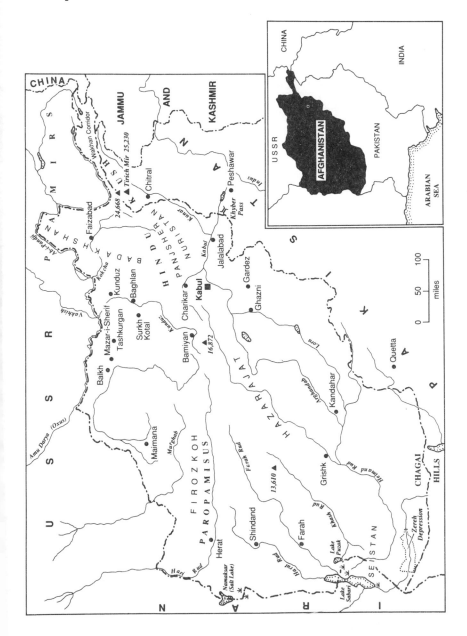